Garden Madness

The Unpruned Truth About a Blooming Passion

Susan M. Watkins

Fulcrum Publishing
Golden, Colorado

With deeply rooted thanks to Susan Benedict McCann and Mary Geo Tomion, editors past and present of the Dundee, New York, Observer. Portions of this book originally blossomed in the open-pollinated pages of that newspaper, in somewhat hybridized form.

Copyright 1995 © Susan M. Watkins

Cover design by Alyssa Pumphrey

Library of Congress Cataloging-in-Publication Data

Watkins, Susan M.
    Garden madness : the unpruned truth about a blooming passion / Susan Watkins.
       p.   cm.
    Includes bibliographical references (p.   ) and index.
    ISBN 1-55591-222-2 (pbk.)
    1. Gardening—Miscellanea. 2. Gardening—Humor. I. Title.
SB455.W295   1995
635—dc20   95-21507
                                           CIP

Printed in the United States of America

0 9 8 7 6 5 4 3 2 1

Fulcrum Publishing
350 Indiana Street, Suite 350
Golden, Colorado 80401-5093
800/992-2908

This book is dedicated to the memory of
Daniel Lynn Stimmerman
1947–1992

Danny:
In the Lower Garden,
walk with me,
footsteps falling in the snow.
In the brittle air
with time to spare,
let us tell eachother all we know.

Contents

The Nine Muses of Garden Madness

(1) Compostope—epic mulching, rapture. Symbol: pitchfork
(2) Florio—biospheric history, aroma. Symbol: ovary
(3) Vegeto—roughage, stir-fry. Symbol: molar
(4) Mammalpomene—disasters, manure. Symbol: incisor
(5) Insectichore—disasters, pollen. Symbol: stinger
(6) Catalognia—seeds, plants, bankruptcy. Symbol: credit card
(7) Gizmodipe—silliness, weirdness, lust. Symbol: 8-Ball
(8) Harvestia—picking, canning, insanity. Symbol: zucchini
(9) Frosterpe—death, winter, respite. Symbol: ice cube tray

INTRODUCTION
from Gaia

*I*N THE BEGINNING, there was bare dirt and rocks.

And the Plot was without form, or mulch; and no sweat *was* upon the face of the Gardener: and the Spirit of Growing Things moved across the land.

And the Gardener said, "Let there be leaf mold": and there was leaf mold.

And the Gardener saw the leaf mold that *it was* filled with worms and aerobic bacteria; and the Gardener divided the chicken bones from the vegetable leavings.

And the Gardener threw the chicken bones out *into* the woods and the vegetable leavings *into* the leaf mold, and that was the first composting.

And the Gardener said, "Let there be moisture sprinkled in the midst of the compost: and let it not divide the nitrogen-rich ingredients from the fibrous."

And the Gardener sprinkled the water, and really started the compost cooking.

And the Gardener mulched the firmament, and covered the rocks which *were* under the bare dirt from the compost, and it was fertile.

And the Gardener called the composted firmament Heaven: and the evening and the morning *were* filled with plans drawn up on graph paper.

And the Gardener said, "Let the rain and the snow be not gathered together but spread out through the seasons of the land," and it was so, more or less unpredictably.

And the Gardener called the rest of the firmament Lawn; and the not-gathering together of the waters the Weather;

And the Gardener said, "Let the catalogs bring forth seeds of vegetables and flowers, *and* the fruit-yielding trees each after its four-color glossy photo," and it was so, plus shipping and handling.

And the lawn brought forth grass *and* the weather brought forth hailstorms *and* the catalogs brought forth plants;

And the Gardener saw that the seeds of the grass and the weather of the Stations *and* the seeds of the weeds were everywhere upon the land but most *especially* upon the Plot.

And the weeding and the hoeing *were* most of the rest of the season: and the Gardener saw that it was hard work.

And the Gardener said, "Let there be twelve to fourteen hours a day of sunlight to bring forth the vegetables and the flowers; and let there be planting by the moon for crops of root and corm, and let it be warm enough but *not* too warm," and it was so, until the invention of fossil fuels;

And the Gardener said, "Let not too many woodchucks or possums or raccoons come forth and multiply abundantly within the Plot or especially underneath it, that I may not bless them *with* a Forty-ought-Twelve," and the creatures *merely* laughed;

And the Gardener said, "Let there not be substances of chemical persuasion upon the firmament *nor* upon the waters *nor* upon the grass *nor* the seeds of the weeds *nor* the beasts or the fowl *including* the flying crawling sucking things even should they yearn to desiccate all of mine tomatoes *before* I may pick but a few of their number," and the firmament heard this, and knew *that* it was possible;

And the Gardener said, "Let us make sure that we do *not* imagine in our most *speciest* of dreams that any one of us *hath* dominion over the fish of the sea, or the fowl of the air, or whatever creeping thing that creepeth upon the Earth, or we shalt mess things up but good," and the firmament listened indulgently, and knew *that* it was naive;

And the Gardener said, "Behold, for my Plot is growing every seed-bearing herb which *is* upon the pages of the catalogs, and every flower, every vegetable, and many trees and shrubs in which there *are* fruit-bearing seeds, and I shall use it for sustenance of flesh *and* spirit," and the firmament heard this, and understood completely;

And the Gardener saw every thing that had been grown, and behold, *it was joyous*. And that evening and the morning *and* the next, and the next, and the next, and the *next*, were spent in the Harvest; and a river of tomato paste went out of the kitchen; and from thence it was parted, and became unto all of the *friends* of the Gardener, and the friends saw this, and knew that it was desperation;

And the Gardener rounded up the experts in the field, and called them all sorts of names, but for the Gardener there was not found any help meet among them;

And the Gardener pulled several muscles *of* the shoulders and *in* the lower back, and fell *upon* the upturned rake; and the ribs, which *were* bruised, caused the Significant Other to *take* pity, and *help* with the Mulching and the Harvest; and the Gardener saw this, and thought that it was about time;

And the Gardener said, "Let me not again order from the Tree of the Fruits of the Catalogs, or I think I *shall* surely die."

And the Gardener and the Significant Other, they were naked and *in* the hot tub for a long time, and were not ashamed; and the firmament saw this, and knew that it was good: and then it snowed.

And the Gardener said, "Let there be another Season Ever Lasting," and there was.

CHAPTER ONE
The Roots of Garden Madness

*T*he desire to till the soil, fertilize the flowers, reap the harvest, and have someone else do the canning and preserving has been a part of the human psyche for as long as anybody can figure, or at least as far back as when the first meat-eating caveman mother started nagging her children to eat their vegetables or else. Since there weren't any such things as vegetables yet, everybody just sidled away from the table while muttering remarks about unpredictable mood swings, thus beginning a centuries-long underestimation of "mood swings" in all their hormonal glory. Undaunted, the caveman mother took down her knapsack, gathered her few crude tools—a trowel, an oscillating hoe, a sixteen-horsepower Troy-Bilt tiller with two sets of revolving tines—and left home on an eternal Quest for Roughage that would change the passage, and not incidentally the urgency, of our collective march through time and tide.

But this is not Garden Madness, O My Best Beloved. This is merely survival. Garden Madness is something else, something more. Garden Madness is something beyond vegetables and flowers, which are its glorious by-products. It is something even beyond dirt and manure, which are its essentials, its cookies and ice cream, its coffee and doughnuts, its Hostess Ho-Hos and cream-filled Whoopie Pies, its Be-All and End-All Here.

If you see what I mean. Which you will, if you have the Madness. In fact, if you really have it, you are not reading this at all. You are right this minute outside in the humidity, digging yet another dahlia border. Oh, yes you are! You can't fool me! For Garden Madness is my

Shepherd, and though I walk through the Valley of the Shadow of Everyday Life, I will fear no Expanse of Weeds, for my Spade and my Claw, they are with me, and I shall dwell out in my Perennials forever. Or at least until First Frost.

Gardening, as anyone bitten by the Madness can tell you, is not so much a pastime of choice as it is an urge that cannot be denied. In that way it is much like writing, only worse. While you are writing you are very seldom attacked by tormenting hordes of stinging, biting insects that zoom down relentlessly into your hair and scalp, unless you want to count your editors and/or agent, who all live in faraway cities where the closest thing to gardening involves scraping the mold off the shower curtain. Also, you hardly ever do your writing chores all slathered up with sunscreen products that for reasons known only to Hem-H'ep-Sut, Lord of the Pharmacists, are made from liquefied magazine perfume ads mixed with gnat sex pheromones, though human beings don't usually have the olfactory capabilities to detect this last, unless you want to talk about agents again, which you probably don't. But I digress.

As with writing, the typical Mad Gardener will never get rich in this our chosen passion, but that isn't the reason for doing either one anyway. The reason has nothing to do with reason. It has to do with deeper, darker urges of the soul. It has to do with immortality and the intangibles of beauty and, yes I will say it, Goodness and Truth. It has to do with the sublime love of puttering around and avoiding the inevitable, such as the actual physical, sometimes dangerous, labor required in both writing and gardening—though granted, the writer never courts explosion and fire by pouring gasoline into a hot mechanical device, unless you are speaking metaphorically of the sort of inspiration that only happens when you are in the midst of something else that you cannot gracefully jump up from so you can rush to your computer, such as making foo-foo with your not very understanding partner, or driving on the thruway, or whatever. On the other hand, in gardening you never risk the hazards that accrue from years of sitting motionless in front of a blinking gray screen that will eventually burn a hole through your eyeballs and incinerate the more troublesome portions of your frontal lobe.

And if you are a Writer and Mad Gardener both, you are Doomed.

Once it is in your blood, gardening will form your basic character for the rest of your life and probably beyond. It will lead you to insist upon growing things under circumstances that would utterly defeat less tenacious creatures. It will sprout many side addictions and strange behaviors, such as the need to discuss over lunch the relative bulk and heat value of various animal manures with your soon-to-be-former friends, or the inexplicable urge to compete in flower shows for the dubious honor of winning big ugly blossom-shaped blue ribbons, or the truly bizarre notion that by gardening, one might even be doing something in some small way to save the planet from the results of all other forms of human activity, including writing.

There are three basic levels of gardening: Beginner, Professional, and Amateur. For innumerable reasons both psychological and financial, the Mad Gardener exists solely within the Amateur category. Beginners haven't yet caught the Fever and Professionals, such as farmers, are way beyond it, up in the rarefied air of combines and Ag-Cat spray-em-dead services. Also, Beginners are people who actually believe that those lush and gorgeous gardens pictured in magazines were accomplished by those such as themselves, simple souls wielding trowel and hoe alone in the hours between May and September.

Nothing could be further from the gritty truth. All of those magazine gardens were created by Professionals using hired help who work the kinds of hours unknown in this country since the building of the Erie Canal with picks and shovels. Furthermore, most of those knockout glossy flower photos are enhanced by the clever spot-placing of potted plants from the neighborhood florist, an editorial secret smuggled out of the Garden Magazine Board of Trustees Room at a cost of many lives. You know the sort of magazine I'm talking about here—the one supposedly devoted to you and your own plot of dirt? The kind with the Question and Answer column written by the Person Who Knows Everything?

Q: My rhododendrons didn't blossom at all this year. Am I doing something wrong? I follow all the directions given in this magazine.

A: Obviously, you are of coarse breeding and suspect lineage, unlike myself. Your rhododendrons are merely reflecting this fact. You will have to send for my newest book, entitled, *Gardening for the Very, Very Inferior,* now on sale for only $54.95. Gold Card only, if you please.

All of which is plotted out in editorial meetings where the Madness for beautiful gardens is evaluated with a cynicism one might expect of the Coke-Pepsi wars:

FIRST EDITOR: Let's run a story this month showing how people can throw away their lawn mowers and without any effort at all turn their dull yards into a wildflower garden of Unearthly Delight.

SECOND EDITOR: Great idea! We can put a photo of the Wilmingtonshire-BedfordHampton Wildflower Conservatory on the cover.

THIRD EDITOR: You mean that place that's maintained twenty-four hours a day by prisoners? The six-hundred-year old garden once owned by Henry VIII? The one the peasants had to keep in perfect shape or they'd be killed?

SECOND EDITOR: That's the one.

FIRST EDITOR: Great! Then we can run ads all over the inside pages listing places where people can send for thousands of dollars worth of wildflower seeds, tillers, sowers, edgers, sprinklers, grommers, blathers, and phoofers.

THIRD EDITOR: And then we can run a story three months later on how to grow a beautiful new lawn out of the ruins of over-grown, weed-infested garden disasters!

ALL TOGETHER: Ha! Ha! Ha!

So you see, my friends, we have lots to talk about here. I'm just slogging through like everybody else who Madly Gardens Alone. In this book, we will look upon Garden Madness and uncover it for what it is. We will scrutinize its symptoms, uproot its causes, classify its characteristics, and divine its cures, if any. We will dig deep within the groundwork of this, America's most popular pastime, and tell the truth about everything, including the catalogs, for there is much to tell and miles to go before we reap.

And by the way, all those fancy magazines make great mulch after they've been sent through a $299 mail-order shredder.

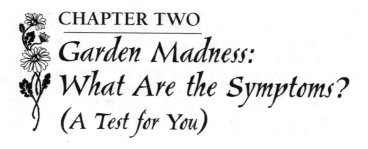

CHAPTER TWO

Garden Madness: What Are the Symptoms? (A Test for You)

SO HOW CAN ONE FIND OUT, before one gets all worked up and sweaty for no reason, if one is truly a Mad Gardener or merely an ordinary human being? After all, we can't have you reading all the way through this book, expecting to discover the secrets of the universe or at least the best way to prevent hornworm infestations, unless we know for sure that you are really and truly affected by the Madness in all its Beatific Glory.

Therefore, I have devised the following test, one specially designed to get down to the roots of your gardening habits and determine if you have just wasted your money on a nonetheless perfectly fine piece of literature, or if you are indeed holding in your soil-encrusted hands the ultimate voice of your *hortulanus insanus mente.*

Answer each question as honestly as possible. You may be tempted to cheat and sneak a look at the answers of the person sitting next to you. But just remember, that person could very well be taking a test to find out if he or she is capable of working in a nuclear submarine far beneath the Arctic ice for years at a time in rooms resembling heated road culvert pipes except that they (the rooms) are also radioactive. This would throw your test results into a cocked hat and could possibly get you drafted.

AND NOW THE TEST. CHECK OFF THE APPROPRIATE ANSWER AND KEEP SCORE. NO, WE DID NOT SAY "CHEKHOV," WE SAID "CHECK OFF." "CHEKHOV" IS EITHER A FAMOUS RUSSIAN

PLAYWRIGHT OR AN EVEN MORE FAMOUS CHARACTER FROM A CERTAIN TELEVISION SERIES THAT SHALL REMAIN NAMELESS EVEN IF EVERY AGING TREKKO-MANIAC IN THE COUNTRY DOES WRITE THREATENING LETTERS TO MY PUBLISHER. I MEAN, GET A LIFE, PEOPLE. BESIDES, I WANT TO KNOW WHERE CAPTAIN PICARD BUYS HIS OFF-DUTY CLOTHES, DON'T YOU? AND SHALL WE EVEN DARE TO MENTION NUMBER ONE? THOUGH WHY ANYONE WOULD NAME A FIRST OFFICER AFTER A BODY FUNCTION IS BEYOND ME. IN THE MEANTIME, HOWEVER, I SEEM TO HAVE FORGOTTEN WHAT WE WERE TALKING ABOUT. OH, YES, THE GARDEN MADNESS TEST. WELL, HERE GOES. ARE YOU READY? TO CHECK OFF? WARY FUNNY, NO? HVA! HVA!

1. Your ideal garden is:

(a) The carefully tended rose garden at Bennington-Barrington von Hereford-Hampshire Estates, Shropespume, England.

(b) A neat planting of wax begonias surrounded by sterilized white gravel encircling the base of the central air-conditioning unit.

(c) A single-file strip of marigolds and petunias mixed with red-hot poker plants bordering your sidewalk along with Porky Pig and Minnie Mouse holding plastic whirling sunflowers with Day-Glo yellow petals and a hilarious wooden bent-over buttboard suggesting that the resident female is both meaty and immodest.

(d) All over the place in every available nook and cranny of your yard, sometimes with vegetables and flowers in the same plot, or in pots all over your porch, or anywhere else you can possibly put some dirt.

(e) Somewhere else.

2. Your favorite gardening activity is:

(a) Assigning the week's pruning and lawning duties to your impeccably attired Gardening Staff.

(b) Getting the driveway hosed off before cocktail hour arrives.

(c) Picking the discarded cigarette butts off the backs of your velcro Yard Sheep.

(d) Side-dressing the bok choy with wheelbarrow loads full of homemade compost and observing the healthy millipede population within.

(e) Huh?

3. You budget your gardening expenses by:

(a) Allowing your accountant to depreciate the value of your Tasmanian soil technician's social security payments, thus gaining annuities on the plus side of your fiscal deductions.

(b) Purchasing the same two kinds of flowers year after year, so you know exactly what to expect.

(c) Buying your geraniums at garage sales and keeping the Dixie Cup container pots for refrigerator leftover dishes.

(d) Adding your monthly income to the "unused credit" portion of your MasterCard account and subtracting the total cost of purchases from all order forms that you filled out last year and hope to fill out this year, vowing that whatever is left over will be specifically earmarked for rent, food, taxes, and insurance.

(e) What?

4. You attend your town's annual Fourth of July parade. To you, the piles left behind in the street by the horses are:

(a) A damned fine argument for animal diapers.

(b) A substance completely foreign to your everyday existence.

(c) A good time for the street crew to start earning its overburdened-taxpayer-sonofa-funded-goddamned-bitching-minimum-wage hourly pay scale.

(d) The reason you brought along a shovel and bushel basket, and you hope nobody else has the same idea, because it looks to be exactly the right consistency to mix in with the load of chicken feathers and sawdust you had delivered last week from the organic egg factory.

(e) Poop.

5. You go out to a nice restaurant for a pleasant dinner with friends. Suddenly, you notice that you forgot to clean your filthy fingernails. You:

(a) Hastily exit to the loo, where you spend at least fifteen minutes scrubbing with the nail brush that you always carry on your person just in case of accidental digital contamination.

(b) Are on your third martini along with everybody else, so nobody notices and you have forgotten what the question was.

(c) Put your hands in your lap and dig at the dirt with your fork and dinner napkin, which you then use to blow your nose and wipe off your forehead.

(d) Draw attention to the condition of your nails by explaining that you prefer to turn your compost heap by hand every three weeks without fail and that this afternoon's turn was especially fruity with baby red wiggler maggots.

(e) Have got to be kidding!

6. Worms are:

(a) Mildly disgusting though probably necessary invertebrates that exist somewhere near the bottom of the Evolutionary Ladder of Social Progress and Civilized Deportment.

(b) The things responsible for creating those swirly patterns that highlight the veneer of your triumphantly expensive *faux* antique coffee table.

(c) Bait, or more to the point, your Ex. Hopefully both.

(d) Saviors of the soil and among your favorite creatures. You are careful not to hurt them with shovels and you always pick them off hot sidewalks and return them to the nearest dirt patch.

(e) Catching.

7. Woodchucks are:

(a) Mammals of the order *Rodentia*, characterized by an insufferable propensity to undermine the flooring beneath the wine-tasting gazebo, thus scaring the wits out of poor Muffy.

(b) Those little scorekeeping pins you use on cribbage boards, probably.

(c) Your uncle Gomer's favorite moving targets, not to mention dinner and hat material.

(d) Harmlessly repelled using the latest mail-order catalog electrical fencing devices now on sale for only $379.95 plus $32 shipping and handling.

(e) Oh, I don't know, sort of cute. Aren't they?

8. Catalogs are:

(a) Delivered to you periodically from Sotheby's to keep you apprised of items upon which you might wish to offer sealed bids, if they are not imposing upon your time too awfully much.

(b) Easier than driving all the way up to Mr. Bean's nice little store in that quaint little town in, where is it? New Hampshire?

(c) Stuck in the Sunday newspaper with all those coupons that Grandma likes to cut out and save.

(d) Probably the most wonderful invention of the twentieth century, aside from, maybe, birth control and the microwave oven.

(e) A real pain in the neck. You can get fined for throwing them out in the trash, for the luvva gawd.

9. A true test of your boyfriend's commitment to your relationship is:

(a) Showing up when promised to unplug your toilet and/or septic tank.

(b) Willingness to run to the store and buy tampons for you in emergency situations.

(c) Not commenting out loud about inevitable male-mind connection between (a) and (b).

(d) Not jumping up to put on pants and run downstairs to for crying out loud *fix* something five seconds after finished with *another* of those typically insensitive male-oriented afternoon quicWE INTERRUPT THIS RESPONSE TO BRING YOU A SPECIAL BULLETIN. THIS QUESTION RECENTLY ESCAPED FROM *NEW WOMAN* MAGAZINE AND WAS APPREHENDED WHILE SEEKING REFUGE IN THE PAGES OF THIS BOOK. WE APOLOGIZE FOR ANY INCONVENIENCE THIS MAY HAVE CAUSED. THANK YOU AND HAVE A NICE DAY.

10. In winter, you pass the time waiting for gardening season by:

(a) Enjoying the view off the terrace overlooking the Queen's Royal Arboretum of Cairo.

(b) Playing bridge with the Dysons and sewing skirts for the dried flower baskets you are making for the country club's spring charity luncheon event.

(c) Driving the camper-trailer to Disney World so you can stand in line for six hundred hours for the privilege of floating through the Future Moon City FlowerScape display on a plastic boat piloted by Goofy.

(d) Reading, and ordering out of, more catalogs than there are trees on the entire planet and for that matter ever *were* on the entire planet and certainly ever will be again.

(e) Z-Z-Z-Z-Z-Z-Z-Z-Z-zzzzzzzzzzflbbbfflbbbabblllllzzzzz

11. Your garage does not contain any garden tools. This is because:

(a) You do not have a "garage." You have a "carriage house."

(b) Your Neighborhood Beautification Committee voted against allowing anything in garages except hose-holders and clean, late-model cars.

(c) There is no room in the garage, what with the RV and the gas grill and the busted washing machine and the leftovers from Ma's rummage sale last year.

(d) They are all kept out in the gardening shed, next to the garden.

(e) Garden *what?*

12. Besides grass, your front yard contains:

(a) The electronically-controlled wrought iron gate and guardhouse.

(b) Nothing.

(c) A collection of colorful plastic flamingos and gnomes, one of which holds a sign declaring that your family, along with a grammatically incorrect apostrophe, lives here.

(d) An ecologically friendly mailbox and sixteen flowering trees.

(e) You don't know.

13. Your compost pile is:

(a) Located somewhere out behind the riding stables. You'll have to ask Mr. Yoto when he comes in from the rose hedge.

(b) Not allowed in your neighborhood, thank God.

(c) Kind of all over the yard. Maybe some on the porch and down between the stove and the sink. Does the spot under the TV tray-table count?

(d) Your life's pride and joy. You cheer it on when it heats up in the spring. You turn it over just for the thrill of sniffing its earthy odors. You write notes about its progress on Christmas cards. You carry pictures of it in your wallet.

(d) My *what*???

14. Your grass clippings are:

(a) Taken up in bundles and shipped to the poor people in India, who are jolly well grateful to have them.

(b) Carefully placed on the curbside each Monday in clear plastic bags alongside the three Rubbermaid snap-top trash cans on wheels and the blue recycling box, which this week contained one copy of *National Geographic* and a #2 plastic milk jug that you rinsed out and flattened according to the rules.

(c) Since you haven't gotten around to mowing the lawn in five or six weeks, you don't have any grass clippings. In fact, you can't even find the lawn mower. Last time you looked, it was out behind the doghouse.

(d) Left on the lawn or layered in the compost pile, where they belong.

(e) Oh, criminy, what now, another citation?

15. A severe storm sends damaging wind, rain, and hailstones across the land. Afterward, you:

(a) Instruct Jeeves to send condolences to old Grimes, the Yard Man who sees to the raking. What with the poor codger's arthritis and all, it certainly was a spot of bloody rotten luck, wasn't it?

(b) Speak to your insurance representative when you meet at the club for your Thursday morning foursome at nine.

(c) Spend a couple of days propping the Holy Mother's blue-painted bathtub back up where it belongs in the coleus shrine.

(d) Realize that the forces of Nature are part of the cycle of life, and that broken-off blossoms and branches will make fine additions to the compost heap, at least.

(e) Complain to the cable company about power outages during *Wide World of Sports*.

16. Hordes of insect pests are attacking your vegetables and flowers. You:

(a) Have already left for the Opening Day Races at Ascot Downs, so you are not available to answer this question.

(b) Happen to run into the town supervisor's wife at the church bazaar, where you have a chat about upcoming aerial spraying schedules, during which you will of course stay indoors and make canapés.

(c) Douse your whole yard with that stuff that What's-His-Name, you know, that grizzly old actor on TV, said you could hook up to your watering hose and blast the bejeezus out of the little bastard bugs and you wind up with seventy-five-pound radishes at the County Fair.

(d) Do nothing, other than hand-pick a few of the more obvious offenders off your tomato leaves, leaving your well-mulched and carefully weeded darlings to defend themselves with their own glowing organic fitness and health.

(e) Could not possibly care less, except maybe if you were dead.

17. To dress for gardening, you put on your:

(a) Best face, to properly encourage the help.

(b) Green and pink striped culottes and green polo shirt with the alligator pocket and topsiders with bunny-tail socks. This is the way you dress for everything, including gardening, golfing, and sex.

(c) Old jeans that occasionally cover up almost all of the crack in your butt.

(d) Nikki's khaki garden pants, W. Atlee Burpee's cotton garden tee shirt, Smith & Hawken's plastic garden clogs, Garden Supply's padded garden knee pads, Gardens Alive!'s gripper-ripper fitted garden gloves, Whiteflower Farm's imported Colombian liana-brimmed garden hat, J.I. Rodale Book Club's organic gardening sunscreen, and Your Friendly Credit Card Collection Protection Service's fake nose and mustache gardening disguise.

(e) To dress for *what?*

18. **Your utility vehicle looks like:**

(a) A mirror.

(b) Everyone else's Chrysler mini-van.

(c) A four-by-four Dodge Rammit Badboy with eighty-eight DualDexter mag wheels, a six-sixty Souper Charger under the hood, and a rack for the ole double-barrel. No piece a'crap Jap-an pickup in *this* driveway you better believe.

(d) A piece of crap Toyota pickup with a bungee cord holding up the tailgate.

(e) A beer cooler.

19. **You inherited your gardening consciousness from:**

(a) Sir Aston Piticott Courteney Abernathy IV, the Earl of Glouchestershire, Knight of the Royal Argyle, and nineteenth in line for ascension to the Throne.

(b) Permitted Landscaping Model Number Three.

(c) The old lady's great-grampa Derndorf, who left her the blue looker ball when he croaked.

(d) Your mother, who took you on walks through the woods when you were a child so you could look at the wildflowers and listen to the birds and later talk about what you saw while you helped her weed the beautiful annual and perennials beds that she created by sprouting inexpensive seeds on bricks placed in pans of water on the windowsills, a feat that in its simplicity seems almost mystical to you now.

(e) Television.

20. **You would describe your gardening life as:**

(a) Noblessedly obligeable.

(b) Pleasantly predictable.

(c) More fun than a fart in a mitten.

(d) More than the Ethereal sum of its Heavenly parts.

(e)

Scoring

For every "a" you selected, give yourself five points; for every "b," ten points; for every "c," fifteen points; for every "d," twenty points; and for every "e," twenty-five points.

Add up your score and rate yourself as follows:

5–100: BRITISH DEVOLVED. You fancy enormous hedges trimmed, by others, to resemble mythological beasts, and typically reside in domiciles larger than the entire downtown section of Albany, N.Y. Your garden is characterized by ramrod-straight hedgerows and geometrically precise pathways paralleled by rosebushes that are trimmed daily with tweezers, nose hair scissors, and whisk brooms. You employ squadrons of garden help and thus often wear wool clothing in the middle of July without discomfort. In fact, you do everything without discomfort, such as inspecting the arborvitae from the tinted window of your chauffeured limousine. In your leisure time you are the editor of a prestigious gardening magazine that would vomit, collectively speaking, if it saw what was crawling around inside the food-scraps pail currently residing in my kitchen sink.

You do not even know that the people in these other categories exist.

100–200: AMERICAN SUBURBAN. Gardening is not so much a pastime for you as it is an exterior decorating skill. You enjoy neatness and uniformity in all things, including your flowers, which are carefully lined up around flagpoles and patio edges and never vary in color or kind from year to year. Your backyard vegetables consist of two neatly-staked hybrid tomato plants, whose yield you dutifully put by every fall in the form of relishes, chutneys, and jellies, which you give as Christmas presents in Williams-Sonoma catalog jars with preprinted "Specially Grown By" labels embossed on the tops. While one might see an occasional white iron bench reposing alongside your azaleas, you would never stick inspiring statuettes or wooden anatomical effigies in your yard, mainly because your Neighborhood Landscaping Committee would have your real anatomicals on a platter if you even joked about doing such a thing.

You adore, and are in fact required to have, a bright green, uniformly weedless, totally chemicalized front lawn.

200–300: AMERICAN GOTHIC. You enjoy colorful landscaping featuring old toilets and blue tractor tires with petunias growing out of them, and other interesting lawn decorations made from recycled materials such as bus seats and/or plumbing. Your vegetable garden consists of tomatoes stuck in black plastic kettles, runner beans crawling up the rainspouts, and blistering hot little peppers hilariously destined to incinerate everyone's digestive tract at the annual firehouse Chili Wars this summer. You own enormous overfinanced pickup trucks that have flame decals and chrome hood-locks affixed upon them to express your patriotic attitude, although you rarely use these vehicles to transport anything but deceased wildlife and the weapons needed to dispatch them. You are the mainstay and the backbone of America, particularly that portion of this Great Land that makes a living from stick-in-the-ground cartoon characters whose legs spin around with every passing breeze.

You are very likely the happiest people alive on the planet today.

300–400: THE GARDENING MAD. Ah, yes. You are the ones who send away for worms and stinging insects advertised in mail-order catalogs. You are the ones who devote yourselves to the love and lore of composting and its materials; of hoeing and deadheading and digging and planting, and of thinking deeply about it and planning to do and buy and gather even more of everything, winter and summer, including, or especially, large quantities of steaming pig manure, which you consider an extremely fascinating topic of conversation. You may also believe in such things as gardening by the moon, holistic blackberry enemas for curing headaches, and the possibility of a balanced federal budget in your personal lifetime. You are, let us say, idealistic. But then, you are also a purchaser of this book, and you will recommend it to all of your friends and you will buy them copies for their birthdays and you will … What? Oh. Sorry about that. Anyway, you are smitten, and that's all there is to it.

You may request to be buried with trowel and claw crossed over your bosom and an onion on each of your eyes.

400+ NEVER MIND. I don't know who you people are at all. I don't even know what you are doing here. Possibly you thought this was one of those licentious romance novels with Fabio rippling his muscles over the clinging tumescent beauty who has just fainted while digging up the potatoes. Come to think of it, that sounds pretty interesting. I will suggest it to my editor immediately. In the meanwhile, those of you who scored in this category can go back to whatever it was that you were doing before this test came along. I'm sure it was every bit as worthwhile as gardening, such as figuring out how to buy the air space over Wal-Mart, or planning the industrial development of Tierra del Fuego, or whatever.

But you, fellow MADNESS folk—read on!

CHAPTER THREE
Getting Started

GARDEN MADNESS always starts out small. An old hoe, a trowel, your great-grandmother's sunhat. One little plot of marigolds out by the back door. One fall day, you realize how sorry you are to see them frosted out. You think, "Maybe next year I'll plant some more." Then you think, "Maybe I'll rip out the grass along the fence and put in some zinnias, too." Then, seamlessly, almost without noticing, you think, "Maybe I'll start some tomato seeds on the windowsill this winter."

The next day—not by coincidence, for Gaia has Her giant grassy ear upon the rails of the Earth, make no mistake—the very next day, a W. Atlee Burpee catalog appears in your mailbox, with—and here is the key—*your name and Customer Service Number preprinted on the order form within.*

Even then, at the last moment, you could save yourself. But do you? No, you do not. Blithely, with no consideration of what your life will be like from then on, you open the catalog and start paging through. Your eyeball latches like a heat-seeking missile upon a photo of Chinese eggplants. They are so purple. They are so oval. They are so … eggplanty. Undaunted, your other eye careens around the corner and smashes headlong into a full-color page packed with gossamer photos of a magical herb garden bordered with sweet William and baby's breath. Nearby, at the bottom of the page, is a list of all the plants displayed above and how much each seed and root will cost. Not that you pay a moment's attention to this. In the face of price, you are as a sugarholic stumbling through open-air markets filled with Ben & Jerry's Cookie Dough ice cream topped with chocolate Cool Whip and Necco Wafer Yummy Sprinkles. The gardens, they are so lush. They are so green. They are so gorgeous. They are so well-tended by employees of the W. Atlee Burpee catalog department.

And you are so lost. The Madness is upon you.

The fact is that every year in this country, about five thousand people start gardening for the first time in their lives.[*] Most of those innocents think they can just grab a spoon out of the silverware drawer, rush outside, and start hacking away at the ground without any preparation whatsoever! Of course, your complete ignorance is exactly what the garden catalogs bank on. They know the statistics, too. What do you think all those glossy flower photos are in there are for?

FIRST CATALOG EDITOR: Here's the latest scoop on new gardeners. According to the statistics, four thousand nine hundred and ninety-eight couch potatoes and two old hippies have just sent in requests for their very first seed catalogs.

SECOND CATALOG EDITOR: Great! Now let's run some pictures of that ninety-eight-year-old fat man standing in front of the five-acre perennial bed that he supposedly takes care of all by himself, in his spare time!

FIRST CATALOG EDITOR: Good idea! We should be getting him back from taxidermy repairs any day now.

SECOND CATALOG EDITOR: Yeah, you know, the stuffing coming out of his eyes in last year's photo story was a little embarrassing.

FIRST CATALOG EDITOR: Also we have to keep his seams away from the camera.

SECOND CATALOG EDITOR: And the hired help out in the barn.

ALL TOGETHER: Chortle! Chortle! Chortle!

Therefore, in the face of this onslaught, the Mad Gardener should have some rational notion of what You Really Need to Survive and Prevail. In the midst of your initial wild enthusiasm, it is important to understand that there are certain essentials that you must acquire in order to do the job of turning pieces of the outdoors into your

---

[*] Statistic from the U.S. Bureau of Lots of Numbers.

heart's desire. And I'm not talking about incidentals like hoes, claws, rakes, and trowels. I'm talking about the basic necessities that they never mention in garden magazines for fear of scaring you off. Of their subscription list, I mean. I am talking about:

    1. <u>Some dirt</u>. This is not as easy to get ahold of as you might think. Real dirt exists only on the surface of your kitchen floor and under a foot and a half of extremely complicated lawn sod. How it gets from the latter to the former is a process understood exclusively by dogs and small, sweaty children. You must get through the sod in order to find enough dirt in which to plant things, but the prevailing myth is that *you have to dig up the sod with an expensive gasoline-powered device.*

    Well, consider that myth officially uprooted. You can have any number of garden plots anywhere you want them, regardless of what type of soil lies snoozing under your property, and you don't have to touch a single tool to the ground.[1]

You do this by finding:

    2. <u>Some leaves</u>. By this I don't mean the leaves blowing around your yard and into the cellar windows. I am referring to leaf *mold*, a truly magical substance if there ever was one. Leaf mold can be found in almost every municipal dump across this fair land of ours, rotting away all by itself while gardeners everywhere are blistering their hands digging sod, wasting time that could be spent lying around reading seed catalogs, or, even better, this book. All you have to do is find out where the town street crews dump the leaves they haul away from curbsides every fall. Then you go get a load of them, or hire somebody who happens to have a backhoe and dump truck to do it.

    You should be sure to get leaves at least a year old—the ones that are wet and stuck together in layers. And hot. The best ones are *steaming hot,* and exude a marvelous aroma suggesting empty beer bottles cooking in the summer sun. Yowzah! But you want the leaves steaming hot not only for sniffing and quick composting, but for frying the inevitable dog and cat dollops into more or less unidentifiable, and unsmellable, crumblies.[2] A few won't hurt your garden, but you don't want to grab onto them, do you? Even so, this, and some of the other assorted municipal litter that you might find roasting away in your leaf mold, augurs for good sturdy gardening gloves worn at all times.

You or your dumptrucking friend then pour the leaves out on the ground in the approximate shape of your desired garden. Yes, right on top of the lawn. It helps if you have mowed the grass as short as possible beforehand, but since you are going to pile the leaves eight to twelve inches thick, it hardly matters. Within a couple of weeks, the leaves will have broken down the underlying sod. Worms will migrate up into the leaves, or down into the soil from the leaves. And that's it. Perfect garden dirt. A few weeds will shoot up through the pack here and there—not many. Add manure and compost and more leaves as needed. Whichever of the Five Basic Dirt Structures you have will be thusly mixed and fixed. These Five Basic Dirt Structures are:

1. like a Rock
2. like a Sponge
3. like a Dune
4. like a Forest
5. like a Fairy Tale

—Though in the face of the leaf mold method, these Basic categories are of relative naught and need not concern you, the Getting Started Mad Gardening gardener, for now. Later on, you will be too busy picking vegetables to care and anyway you will never find Number Five Dirt Structure, which exists only in garden magazine cover photos, in the wild.

Maple leaf mold is the best for this process—oak tends to be acidic—and you might want to make sure the municipality hasn't been spraying its trees with something horrible while your back was turned. And that's all you need to do to get <u>some dirt</u>.

After which you will need:

3. <u>A budget</u>. Sure you will. What you do is stop buying nonessentials like clothes and college educations for your nongardening offspring. That should about do it. After all, you have just dumped six tons of leaves into your back yard and now you must add quantities of vegetables and flowers or look like a complete idiot. And so, to protect your new investment in all of the above, you will then need:

4. <u>A large dog</u>. I say "large" because deer, woodchucks, and raccoons, the reasons for this necessity, routinely spit on small canines, thus demoralizing them beyond any use whatsoever. Unhappily, you will have to put up with rotting skunk bodies under the kitchen window, which is where your courageous pooch will spend several hours a day rolling in his well-earned Guardian Reward. Given this, perhaps you would prefer to find a dead dog and have it stuffed in a barking position. Place same near your garden plot. Call up the editors of your favorite garden catalog. Tell them you have a photo opportunity taking place. They'll understand what you mean!

Meanwhile, there are a number of items that you will need throughout your gardening career—matters of dire necessity—that have not, unfortunately, been invented yet. I don't know why not. Maybe it has something to do with the Laws of Physics. Nonetheless, anyone who has gardened for a season or two knows how vital these items are, so why I am sitting here writing instead of running around inventing is more than I can figure out, given those five thousand potential Mad Customers per year! For example:

1. <u>A bulb planter</u> that you can get the dirt plug out of after you have jammed it down into the ground. You just step on the spring-flange that I have cleverly attached to the bulb-plug funnel, and out pops the dirt. Much easier than hammering the plug with a rake handle! And only $2,356.49, which is how much you've wasted on bulbs that you threw over the creek bank while screaming choice body-function epithets because you couldn't get the dirt plug to come out of the planter-part.

2. <u>Tomato stakes</u> that are notched, or have holes drilled through them, so the tomato plants can't pull the ties down and topple over. Which they will figure out a way to do anyway, but here is a first line of defense that seems relatively obvious. $56.99 for two. And maybe dinner and a movie.

3. <u>A solar electric fence battery</u> that stores a little extra and has an outlet plug built into its side. This way, you have a handy source of power for the other outdoor gizmos you possess, such as the electric flower garden edger, the portable slug-exploder, and the automatic outdoor beer cooler temperature control alarm! Or are these all devices I invented myself? I forget. $439.95, but don't ask me to wire it. Or

whatever it is you do that turns invisible benign sun rays into invisible dangerous electric rays that want only to hunt you down and kill you.

4. <u>A smartmower</u> that not only cuts the grass, but gives it a good spanking and teaches it to stay half an inch tall, where it belongs. And while it's at it, it arranges all of its internal mechanical parts so that bona fide living human beings with normal-sized arms and single-jointed fingers can get to whatever it is that needs fixing without having to stand upside down or crawl around on the ground like a molting garter snake. A steal at $65,499. Which includes wrenches that fit the bolts and bolts that fit the holes. Really!

5. <u>Outdoor furniture</u> not built for people with strangely backwards-bent butt bones. You know what I mean here. I believe the offending structures are called "Adirondack chairs," which were invented by evil trolls to whom the word "Adirondack" means "human who sits like broken stork and thinks it's a swell idea." My outdoor furniture is made for people who want to lollygag outside all day, comfortably, while reading meaningless, sexually explicit novels. $5 each, if you bring the novels.

6. <u>A hot coal vacuum</u> that sucks live, hot coals out of your woodstove. I put this in here because the catalog companies all figure that anyone who gardens must also be crazy enough to heat with wood, which opens up a whole new line of gadget possibilities during the winter months. And then they have the nerve to show pictures of clean, happy people kneeling on colorful, crud-free fireside hearths, cheerfully vacuuming out the woodstove ashes while wearing regular civilian (read: flammable) clothes! Except that the fine print always says, "Vacuum is not for hot coals."

Well, why isn't it? How often during twenty-below-zero weather do *you* let the woodstove get dead cold? My Hot Coal Vac takes care of this problem. I don't know how. Maybe it shoots the coals directly outside, through a hole in the wall, and onto your neighbor's sidewalk. $5,000 plus someone to bring in the wood.

Better yet, just use catalogs for fuel! After rolling them up on my <u>Super-Dooper Junk Mail Hot Log Maker</u>, of course. Call me for the price on this one.

It fluctuates! And so will you.

7. <u>A greenhouse.</u> And I don't mean any old 8x10 out by the garage. I mean a greenhouse attached to the living room that will be filled all winter long with flowers blooming in orderly succession, clouds of butterflies fluttering here to there, a cactus and euphorbia collection to knock your eyes out, and a couple of parrots to liven up the place. Better yet, let's enlarge the thing and make it an aviary for endangered species of birds. One morning you walk out into this paradise and find a baby Dodo. With its parents. Oh, and you can start seeds in this greenhouse, if you feel like it. Includes a mildew-scrubbing service and a heater that doesn't cost anything to run and an automated vent-opening and closing sensor that doesn't take any effort to operate. Affordable at Any Price!

8. <u>A shade house</u>. This, sort of the opposite of a greenhouse, will enclose the deck and become filled with shade-loving vines, orchids, bromeliads, and a hot tub for summer and, how can you not, winter. Standing in one corner would be an enormous pot of hollyhocks, the kind whose blossoms children used to pick and make "floating ladies" out of, in those bygone imaginative days before television. Then add a chaise lounge with waterbed cushion and no vexatious yellow jackets or hornets today, if you please. With all attachments, about $15. These are *my* inventions, remember.

9. <u>An arboretum.</u> By this I mean an accessible-to-the-public collection of all the varieties of trees that will grow in your climate zone. Also wildflowers and old-fashioned perennials, with labels, along pathways. Maybe people could have memorial trees planted there with special nameplates attached, so the plants and work would all be donated. Therefore, cost is zero. This idea appeals to the philanthropist in you. The next one doesn't.

10. <u>A hedge maze</u>. A nasty, complicated one, forbidding and scary, complete with topiary animals ready to bite your head off. And when you finally get to the center of this maze, you'll find … no, I'm not telling. You'll never tell either, because you'll never find your way out. Ha, ha! I'll send the bill to your Next of Kin.

11. <u>A raised wooden walkway</u> that goes all the way around the edge of your property. You don't know why you like this idea. You just

do. It would have built-in benches, balconies, gazebos, bird feeding stations, flower boxes—all sorts of nutzo stuff along the way. Maybe you'd eventually add a monorail system—why stop at the possible? For that matter, why not extend the system into town? You never know when you might have to send the monorail out for coffee and bagels.

And all of it made out of natural cedar, too—no CCA (pressure-treated) wood for you! A steal for every lottery winner who is also Mad as a Hatter. Also tax deductible. Because I said so.

12. <u>More acreage</u>. About six thousand more, with no property taxes added. You could give it to the Nature Conservancy when you were done with it. Included in those acres would be creeks, waterfalls, ponds, swamps, flocks of pileated woodpeckers, owls, turkeys, wildcats, wolves, elk, moose, armadillos—you name it. And, of course, a raised wooden walkway all around the edge of it.

13. <u>A yard filled with flower islands</u> so the only lawn to mow is the path between, and a great big vegetable garden complete with its own great big root cellar and great big robots to harvest and store it all. Your wish is to wake up one morning and find all these islands already dug out of the ground and growing. And everything paid for by Florio, the Second Muse of Garden Madness.

14. <u>And all the time in the world!</u>

Notes

[1] As originally done by Ruth Stout in her *Gardening Without Work* (1961) and other wonderful books.

[2] The composting process will even break down some herbicide and pesticide residues. You can ask your local extension agent to test a sample of your leaves for these contaminants.

CHAPTER FOUR
Organic or Not?

RIGHT OFF THE BAT, you are going to have to decide what kind of gardener you are going to be—Organic or Not Organic? This is no trivial decision. On one hand, if you go Organic, you must make peace with the eccentric figure you will cut as you drive around town stuffing curbside bags of other peoples' leaves into the trunk of your VW and begging restaurant owners to save all their putrid shellfish leavings for you to take home! Or, if you decide to go Not Organic, you won't have to be bothered with any of that sort of thing because you will be dead.

Ha! Ha! What a lame joke that was! Because the truth is that lots and lots of Not Organic farmers and growers and their children remain virtually alive today after decades of dedicated pest and weed-controlled Agribusiness that supplies this nation's supermarkets with enormous quantities of cheap, all-season foodstuffs that more than exceed the FDA's nutritional and taste requirements for vacuum cans full of tennis balls! You see, Organic gardening, as any gainfully employed chemist will tell you, is less efficient and more expensive than Not Organic because it produces fruits and vegetables with funny little bumps that cause the consumer to scream and faint right there in the produce aisle, thus creating embarrassment and head injuries and later a lawsuit for millions of dollars in damages that makes the cost of Organic even more prohibitive. So you should eat your tennis balls and be glad that you do not live in some bug-infested Third World country where lawyers have not as yet made a serious inroad upon the land.

In that spirit, we will look objectively at both sides with an impartial and totally nonopinionated, really, honest, Scouts' Honor, eye.

Organic

The Great Organic Debate was started in this country about fifty years ago by the late father-and-son team of J. I. and Robert Rodale, who stirred up a lot of trouble going around using words like "mulch" and "biodegradable" and raising the ire of patriotic farmers who had enough problems trying to control hordes of insects that had descended upon them right after the last of those irritating blackbirds had been blasted out of the peach orchards, using an efficient combination of radium pellets and time-release DDT mortars.

Back then, admitting Organic sympathies was tantamount to whipping out your Communist Party Card and flooffing the end of Joe McCarthy's nose with it. Things did not improve much during the Sixties, when it was well-known by anyone who wore a suit and tie that "Organic Gardening" was an internationally-understood code for "totally far out home-grown wacky weed" and "naming your firstborn children after ancient deities and your favorite Crayola happy color."[*]
Undaunted, in 1942 the Rodales began publishing their now-famous organic gardening and farming magazine, titled, oddly enough, *Organic Gardening & Farming Magazine,* and continued to espouse their ideals of nonchemical soil and plant management, arguing that human and environmental health not only thrived upon, but depended upon these methods. In the meantime, Mother Nature ignored all this hoo-raw and simply went on about Her business of making dirt by mixing fallen leaves, dead grass, rotting straw, and animal droppings with rain, snow, sunshine, and large quantities of angleworms.

Though often ignored or scorned by the official Not Organic line of thought, *OG&F* has lived to see itself become, along with numerous other unmentionable examples, something of a household word. More and more of us are beginning to garden with Organic methods, as anyone can see at a glance through the five billion nonbiodegradable garden catalogs that arrive in our mailboxes every spring. And you,

---

[*] Thus you have such legacies as Burnt Sienna Jones, the Jazz Singer, and Flesh Tone Pinkie Bright, who later changed his name to Rush Limbaugh for greater accessibility to normal American soreheads.

too, can choose to become part of this great Organic movement, and believe me, "movement" is not a word to take lightly here, either.

Talking Organic means that you will be talking about, and up to your elbows in, two basic substances: garbage, which creates compost; and poop, which may, depending upon the source, contain garbage. Essentially, Organic gardening means stacking these elements up in a "heap," which will, if maintained correctly, attain an internal temperature hot enough to set a barn on fire and roast it all down into a tilthy, pleasant-smelling supply of fertile material that you then pile on your garden beds.

All well and good, and incredibly exciting all by itself, isn't it? But if you are truly Organically inclined, the subject of poop will hold a riveting fascination for you that can be truly understood and shared only by your own kind—which, besides Organic gardeners, also includes parents of firstborn babies and the inmates of some of our more enduring institutions. Why, before you know it, you will find yourself measuring everything by the Useful Poop Factor and thinking and talking about poop so much that your family will ask you to substitute a more politically correct word to insure that no one in the modern world mistakenly assumes that you are euphemistically impaired! In that case, you might consider using the word "stuff." Of course, anyone hearing that aphorism will immediately ask you if your head is full of "shit." You should reserve comment until after harvest time, when you will be desperate to get rid of zucchinis and will need all the friends you can get.

Anyway, organic gardeners do enjoy thinking about "stuff." There are all different kinds of it, some good for gardens, some not. You can forget cats, for example. Cats are no help.[*] And dogs—you all know about dogs.[**] Maybe we can develop the technology to fuel steam generators with the stuff dogs leave all over the yard. Better yet, how about using the dogs? But I suppose that would be considered unseemly. Otherwise, poop-wise, the only animals more bodaciously Useless than dogs and cats are humans, who have to invent elaborate million-dollar gold-plated pipelines and colanders to take our stuff far away to the sea, where it mingles with offshore currents and returns to us inside the livers of mackerels and shellfish.

---

[*] *Cats are Scum*, Canis Familiaris Press, 1984, Yowlington, Virginia.

[**] *The Truth the American Canine*, Felis Domesticus Press, 1985, Mew York.

Anyhow, when you examine the way Useful "stuff" works, it all becomes pretty amazing. I mean, you take ordinary grass, run it through a cow, and you get gigantic flowers and more tomatoes than you can eat in a month. Plus, you get cheese. Did you catch that? You run chlorophyll through a cow and you get protein. Let's see the science labs match that one!

Not only that, but if you place all of this nice bovine stuff on such perennial things as alfalfa, you get a lot of grass filled with bovine-correct nutrition. You can then feed the alfalfa back to the cow, who very happily repays you twice over with more of everything, including cheese and lots of her very own stuff!

You can also place a horse in front of the aforementioned grass clippings, but then you will probably feel obliged to put a saddle on this animal and go riding on it once in a while, and fall off and break your head open. This doesn't seem like an equal return for bunches of stuffs that conceal large quantities of weed seeds all ready to germinate in your garden next spring while you are off riding or in the hospital recovering. No, horse stuff is not a good idea.

Another popular stuff producer is the cute little cuddly bunny rabbit, a close relative of the cute little fluffy sheep. What? Wait just a minute. *(whispers)* Well, maybe it's a relative of the cute little fuzzy chicken, then. Oh, yeah? Well, same to you, too, buddy!

Anyway, there are the cute little bunnies, which you have to keep a lot of in order to have enough stuff for more than one measly rosebush, but it's some of the best stuff in the business, impact-wise. And the bunnies quickly take care of the numbers factor themselves, and as for their cousins, the sheep (ha!), anybody who keeps those things has no time for anything else. Also, there are pigs, and while they create some very, very hot stuff, it is hard to imagine why anyone would want to keep a pig in the back yard, unless it's to keep out the dogs,[*] come to think of it. And then there are donkeys and mules and bison and zebus, but I thought you were taking this book seriously, and those are just silly. What? *(whispers)* Oh, shut up.

So with one thing and another, you probably might just as well buy the stuff in sterilized bags from the local feed mill and hire your

---

[*] *See? We Told You So*, Felis Domesticus Press, 1985, Mew York.

neighbor's kid to spread it on. For the question of Useful Poop is not something that you can easily let go once you grasp onto it, and surely it will stick with you in the house of your Garden, forever.

Not Organic

On the other side of this great debate are the folks who maintain that it is perfectly all right to use any kind of artificial chemical on your lawn and garden that you feel like using, because all of these modern substances have been thoroughly tested and proven safe by scientists, who also, you might recall, tested and certified the miracles of DES injections, the Swine Flu Vaccine, silicone breast implants, and chlorofluorocarbons. Also, it is a well-known fact that if it weren't for the millions and millions of tons of chemicals poured out every year upon this vast and surly land of ours, the grasshoppers would chew you and your garden and your household goods into a mass of grasshopper spittle-pulp measuring sixteen feet high and as big around as a plowed-up Dust Bowl. And don't you forget it. Your ancestors did, and look where they are today.

The myriad choices in chemical garden applications that you, the Not Organic Gardener, have at your, if I may coin a phrase, disposal, are remarkable indeed, and a testament to the wondrous nature of the human mind, especially after it has not had access to sufficient oxygen for days at a time! These chemicals fall into three basic categories and can be used as follows:

1. Pesticides. Used to kill "pests," including religious salespeople and every insect for two and a half miles around and anything that feeds on them (the insects). You might remember some of these latter creatures as "birds." Pictures of these beings may be discovered in the "Nonfiction (No Kidding!)" section of your local library. Also you might take a few moments to look up "butterflies," "honeybees," "ladybugs," and "The Diversity of Life on Earth." Some of these topics are almost unbelievable in their humorous depiction of what a pain in the neck going outdoors used to be, years ago, before scientists invented chemicals. For example, anyone with a moldering coal for a brain knows that

the mosquito was once King, or rather, Queen, of the Disease-Carrying Vectors until brave daredevil pilots flying B-52s full of DDT sterilized the swamps and natural predator nesting grounds of Yourtown, USA, thus making it safe for development by genteel folk who also deny any knowledge of burying the leftover DDT underneath the site where the new elementary school is going to be built.

Pesticides that the Not Organic gardener might wish to experiment with in the privacy of Not My Back Yard could well include: Methylphosphorothioate, a nerve gas that kills anything with nerves; Barium Fluosilicate, a stomach poison that kills anything with a stomach; Diazinon Plus, which according to its catchy TV jingle "easily gets rid of more than one hundred kinds of outdoor bugs including those alleged beneficials"; and Disodiumphosphate Inosinate, which kills ... Oops! Sorry! This is an ingredient in Creamy Ranch salad dressing! It doesn't belong in this discussion at all! Really! I don't know what came over me! It's just one of those weird dizzy spells that I usually get right after eating lunch!

2. <u>Herbicides</u>. Used to kill "Herbs," such as that annoying old coot who hangs around the feed store spitting on the wood stove and making wise comments to his pals about your purchases. Or else they (the herbicides) are used to kill plants, though that doesn't make any sense at *all*. I mean, what is the matter with you? Why would anyone want to kill plants? What? *(whispers)* Oh, right! I forgot! Weeds!

Sure, you want to kill off the weeds in your garden, don't you? I mean, who wants to take the time to *weed* them, when you can use such an array of helpful, scientifically-proven substances such as: Dioxin, which was originally tested on school playgrounds and cattle feed (thus its name, from the Latin word for "Die, Oxen!") and later used to "treat" all of the jungle foliage in the entire southeast corner of Asia, as if anyone cares; Roundup, a perfectly legal chemical that you can buy in sizes ranging from itsy-bitsy little spray bottles with instructions that involve full-body plutonium suits and eventual genetic testing to 600,000,000-gallon railroad tank cars with ORANGE JUICE written on the sides just for fun; and ChemLawn, which chems the entire lawn before you can say Dead Robinson! Makes it all green, too! Even the sidewalk!

3. <u>Omnicides</u>. Used to kill "Omnis," those dorky-looking automobiles that the Dodge Motor CoWE INTERRUPT THIS PARAGRAPH TO BRING YOU AN IMPORTANT ANNOUNCEMENT. THE BOARD OF TRUSTEES OF MEGA-CHEM CORPORATION INTERNATIONAL, INC., HAS BEEN MONITORING THIS CHAPTER AND WE ARE PLEASED TO INFORM YOU THAT THE AUTHOR HAS BEEN INVITED TO ACCEPT AN ALL-EXPENSES-PAID INFORMATIONAL TOUR OF OUR MAJOR FACTORIES AT UNDISCLOSED LOCATIONS IN PLACES YOU PROBABLY NEVER HEARD OF ANYWAY. WE PROMISE WE WILL RETURN SAID AUTHOR IN TIME TO FINISH THIS MEMORABLE WORK OF LITERATURE AT SOME POINT IN THE NOT TOO DISTANT FUTURE. UNTIL SUCH TIME WE WILL BE GLAD TO PROVIDE REAMS OF TOTALLY UNBIASED SCIENTIFIC RESEARCH PROVING BEYOND A SHADOW OF A DOUBT THAT CHEMICAL FARMING AND/OR LIVING IS EVERY BIT AS SAFE AS DRINKING THIS ENTIRE GLASS OF LIQUID THAT HAS BEEN DISTILLED FROM THE REMAINS OF OUR OWN INDUSTRIAL SLUDGGGGGGUUUUUUUUUHHHHHHHHHHAAAAAAAAAACCCKKKKKKK

Gorp

Gorp lies somewhere in the middle of Organic and Not Organic and has, in the past, been mistaken for overpriced little plastic bags full of nuts and raisins you're supposed to eat "on the trail." Nonsense! And since I have just turned down an all-expense-paid and possibly quite exciting international vacation, I have plenty of time to explain what Gorp is, and how it got that way.

I first ran into Garden Gorp one hot July afternoon in 1973 when I was asked to go outside and "check the slug trap."

Well, dear readers, the highly successful "slug trap" consisted of a large, shallow bowl shoved to its rim in the dirt and filled with beer. And believe me when I say that anyone who has ever looked (and smelt) upon six quarts of quivering, simmering slug jelly has truly gazed into the Maw of Gorp Hell and survived. The experience brands you with a certain nostalgia about gardening the old-fashioned way—meaning with large doses of petrochemicals (see Not Organic) that instantly turn all disgusting wiggling things to ash.

Nonetheless, I persisted in an unselfish study of this enchanting concept in gardening mediumship. You will run into Gorp whether you choose to garden Organically or Not Organically, so I feel some responsibility to let you know about it right now, before you get in over your head and suddenly realize you are eyebrow-deep in a substance resembling instant mohair-flavored oatmeal that has been predigested for the tadpoles of Australian river rats.

1. <u>Seed-Starting Gorp</u>. This is most likely the first of many messes you have to face each spring, if you insist on starting your own seeds. You know what happens. Whatever kind of seed-planting mix you use, it ends up all over the kitchen counters, the floor, the dishwasher, and in great glops down your sink drain. No matter where you put the trays, your cat knocks half of them over and then does something unmentionable in the dirt. Eventually, as the indoor seed-starting season grinds on through February and March, you discover that the trays leaked just enough Gorp underneath them to rot the windowsills. One tomato plant survives. It is approximately the size and shape of one of those screws that fell out of the earpiece on your eyeglasses and which you cannot, of course, screw back in there even if you do manage to find it because if you could see the goddamned thing you would not need the goddamned glasses to begin with, would you, Mister Smart Aleck Optical Department at Sears, Roebuck, and Backtalk?

You might better just buy the plants from your local nursery and spare yourself the tortures of all this Gorp.

2. <u>Bird Seed Hull Gorp</u>. The second of many springtime messes. Last year I raked up four wheelbarrow loads of it from under the winter feeders. You shouldn't spread this on your garden, by the way; on one hand, you'll get a trillion grass seedlings from the leftover millet; on the other, rotting sunflower seed hulls exude some sort of rancid Gorp-gas that inhibits plant growth. For that reason, I dump this Gorp over the creek bank, where small animals and birds can root around in it all they like. Ugh!

Or, given its anaerobic nature, this Gorp could be used as a weed-snuffer between patio flagstones. What you do is this: You look around the house until you find a teenager that is not yet deaf and brain-dead from the sonic booms jolting out of various stereo speakers the size of refrigerator crates, and you make certain threats involving cars, and the withholding thereof, and you get said teenager to go outside—yes, outside the actual house—and fill in the cracks between the patio flagstones by dumping bird seed hull Gorp onto the patio and sweeping it around to the jaunty boom-box rhythm of Beef Jerky Jerk and the Hopscotch Rhinos singing "Pickle Mucus Tattoo"; or, if you are not willing to risk going completely out of your mind, you can do this chore yourself, or you can run away from home and never be heard from again.

 3. <u>Compost Gorp</u>. Did you think you'd get out of this one? Learning to run a cooking compost pile can produce some amazing Gorp-slorp in the beginning. Remember "magic rocks?" Those pieces of Something-Or-Other-in-a-jar that grew stringy little tendrils in lurid colors when you added water? Well, now the secret is out. "Magic rocks" are mined from compost heaps! And what eventually happens to "magic rock" tendrils, you may ask? Those glowing Magic Stalactites that you never threw out but which somehow always vanished from the jar the moment you left the room? You guessed it! What happens is that they grow big enough to unscrew the jar lid and crawl away, back upstream to the Heap, where the survivors mate and lay their eggs, thus completing another of Nature's grand and mysterious cycles of Birth and Sex and Suffering and Death.

 4. <u>Driveway Gorp</u>. I bet you didn't know about this one! Only applicable if you have a combination of an uphill dirt driveway, a wood stove, several cats, and a long, snowy winter. Items from the above are generously mixed upon the driveway's surface, creating a sort of hearty frozen Gorp stew, which inevitably warms into soup on the same afternoon the Real Estate Broker shows up with the only clients in the world who might be crazy enough to take the whole organic elephant off your hands within your personal lifetime.

 5. <u>Expert Opinion Gorp</u>. The most insidious of all. The kind of stuff that pours out of books like this one, making you think you must be a jerk for loving it out there in the Gorp when all you'll get is a

bunch of gorgeous flowers that will be around for five or six months, tops, before they're gone.

Well, if flowers be the song of love—Gorp on!

Did you know that:

Chemical fertilizers, weed killers, and pest controls are no more harmful to the environment than anything else humans have ever injected into soil, air, water, wind, lakes, rivers, trees, birds, fish, reptiles, oceans, mountains, deserts, ponds, wells, streams, packaged food, guinea pigs, laboratory rats, bunnies with their eyes strapped open, breakfast cereals of unsuspecting institutionalized children, underground storage mines, short-lived orbiting space satellites, "pressure" treated landscape timbers chock-full of chromated copper arsenic that leaches out into the soil and water with every rain, and two-ton tractor-trailer trucks with bad brakes?

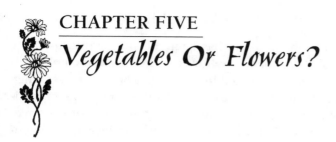

CHAPTER FIVE
Vegetables Or Flowers?

Now THAT WE HAVE the Organic vs. Not Organic question settled, the Gardener must decide whether to concentrate the Madness on the growing of vegetables, flowers, or absolutely everything. Probably you will have already chosen the latter. Probably this choice is what has driven you Mad in the first place. And there is nothing wrong with that, is there? Of course not! Ahhahahahahahahahahaha!

However, should you find yourself in the position of having a woeful lack of garden space—if you are unwilling to rip out the garage, for example, or you live in a neighborhood governed by a "committee" whose idea of gardening springs from the pages of *Pavement Quarterly Review*—it is good to know the history and lore of vegetables and flowers as separate entities of the gardening world, should you have to choose from among the 15,876,952,499,756,000 plants offered in the pages of your typical mail-order catalog.

Flowers as Flowers

Flowers have been with us since the beginning. In fact, there would be no life on the Earth at all if it weren't for flowers. All vegetables have flowers on them at some point. You can mix flowers right in the vegetable garden or vice-versa. I don't see any reason why you have to make a *choice*. I don't even know why I'm writing this *paragraph*. What in the world am I *thinking about?*

Flowers as Vegetables

On the other hand, there has lately been a revival upon the land in the venerable lore of edible flowers. This is a branch of horticultural knowledge that originated in the distant primitive past when the human species foraged for its food and its death rate was approximately twenty-five times greater than its birth rate. And for good reason! Foraging for edible anything was hard work, besides being potentially lethal. You grubbed around hour after hour, winter and summer, and usually grubs were what you ended up with, plus a couple of what you hoped were chicory and not deadly nightshade roots for a family of four. Maybe a day or two later you managed to snare a weasel to round out the hairy cattail stems your mate dragged home. After twenty or thirty years of this, most humans were ready to cash it in, which was easy enough to do in those days. Then along came technology with its labor-saving devices and central heating and cable TV and nacho-flavored frozen Cheese-Wheezie Pops. It's just amazing what the human brain will come up with when it wants to stay home in front of the Superbowl instead of wandering around outdoors all day, trapped inside a skull that has to go foraging!

Well, fast-forward to the present and see where all this has gotten the Mad Gardener. After centuries of employing all the labor-saving devices extolled so raptly in gardening books and magazines, you have managed to increase your gardening chores to something like a fifty-three-hour work week, not counting time spent giving away squash. Then about ten years ago, it occurred to you that all the while you were out there toiling over the tiller for the sake of Good Eating, the folks over in J. I. Rodale Land have been indoors, out of the sun, seated comfortably at their keyboards with coffee and donuts, clacking out well-paying articles on how sedentary types like yourself can turn their dirt into Nirvana with Hardly Any Work At All.

It was then, O My Best Beloved, that you wondered if there were not a compromise between foraging and farming; between grubbing and growing; between searching-out and sweating-away. Well, there probably isn't for most of us, but the knowledge is there, encapsulated in such books as Euell Gibbon's classic *Stalking the Wild Asparagus* and Roger Tory Peterson's *Edible Wild Plants* series—though a cursory inspection of these helpful narratives will immediately reveal the fact that "common wild edibles" have names like Sow Thistle, Shepherd's Purse, Toothwort, Fireweed, and Pasture Brake, which certainly sounds like a tale of cause-and-effect out in the old edible wilderness to me! But then, you are looking at a person who, as a kid, used to boil and drink chokecherry juice and smoke sumac roots for fun; but that was the Glorious Fifties for you and anyway, you are not looking at *me*, you are looking at a bunch of squiggles on a piece of paper, so there you are.

You would be wiser to study children's books on the subject, since these editions have simple, carefully drawn, full-color pictures of (you should sincerely hope) edible plants both wild and tame; and then you would be wiser still to forget it, unless you grow domesticated flower edibles such as nasturtiums and daylilies and know exactly what you are biting into, which is, after all, if you stop to consider it, a crop of sex organs.

Nonetheless, I once knew a fellow, an artist, who did this sort of thing—who foraged along the seashore and through the woods and fields for his meals rather than spend valuable hours in a garden plot or supermarket. He hardly ever left his studio, and he is alive today, so obviously he knew what he was doing, though he also had a wife, which right there negates all this blather about how with foraging he saved time not gardening or not shopping or not laundromatting or not housecleaning or not phone answering, but I digress. He and I walked along the seashore together a few times while he foraged for supper, and it was an education. The ocean had thrown up piles of kelp, which this fellow gathered and ate on the spot, though I demurred, insisting that I, too, would throw up piles of kelp if I tried eating any; so we went on to horsetails, as he called them—small thick-fronded plants with bulbous little pods all over them that grew just below water level.

"These are the most primitive plants in the world," my friend said, biting off a pod and chewing it enthusiastically. Cautiously, I tried one myself and Lo, it was surprisingly good. "Just like salted peas," my friend pointed out, and I asked, "So why not just buy peas and salt them?" and my friend gave me a look, and said, "That takes too much time," and we meandered up the beach to dig a few dozen razor clams and then meandered back to my friend's house, where we cooked up a razor clam chowder with only a little sand on the bottom, and only five and a half hours spent searching, picking, digging, hauling, prying, cleaning, stewing, eating, and worrying about the previous week's Red Tide.

It was all very idyllic and close to nature, and it represents a parameter of choice to the Edible Flower Gardener, if such personage really and truly does know the difference between, say, elderberry bushes and jimsonweed. If one is not one-hundred-percent sure, and one also enjoys making tea from wild leaves and berries, then one is sooner rather than later going to find oneself, if I may be excused, Dear Reader, for not mincing my words, deader than a deep-sixed doornail. Here is a description of mistaken-for-edible from a book for writers that gives detailed instructions on how to poison people so that readers will not be frustrated by silly made-up facts and inaccurate non sequiturs: "Baneberry *[Actaea spicata]*, can be mistaken for blueberries. A small dose is enough to produce burning in the stomach, dizziness … nausea, vomiting, bloody diarrhea, convulsions, and shock … In 1972, one English family was poisoned after they made a pie out of the berries they had gathered. All but the mother died as a result of the fatal pie.

"In another case, [a surviving baneberry] victim stated: 'At first there was a most extraordinary pyrotechnic display of blue objects of all sizes and tints, circular with irregular edges; as one became interested in the spots a heavy weight was lowered on the top of the head and remained there, while sharp pains shot through the temples … Then suddenly the mind became confused and there was a total disability to recollect anything distinctly or arrange ideas with any coherency. On an attempt to talk, wrong names were given to objects, and although at the same time the mind knew mistakes were made in speech, the words seemed to utter themselves independently.

'For a few minutes there was great dizziness, the body seeming to swing off into space, while the blue spots changed to dancing sparks of fire.'"[1]

Sounds like the original Woodstock experience! More than enough reason to stay indoors during baneberry season! And stay away from writers, too, while you're at it.

And don't even *think* about wild mushrooms.

On the other hand, the book's descriptions of death by *pesticide* might provide some instructional contemplation to the beginning Mad. Take Rotenone, which is often recommended by gardening magazines and catalogs as a safe alternative to "harsh chemicals." Here's what exposure to it can do: "... much more toxic when inhaled, [Rotenone causes] numbness of the mouth, nausea, vomiting, abdominal pain, muscle tremors ... convulsions, and stupor. Chronic exposure leads to kidney and liver damage ... Once thought to be harmless, it's now known to be five times as toxic as pyrethrin."[2]

Enough to rethink the entire definition of "edible" anything! Though I have strayed slightly off the immediate track, which was heading nonetheless relentlessly toward ...

Vegetables as Edibles and Decoration

Humans got the idea to grow vegetables some fifteen thousand years ago, shortly after we had domesticated the dog and realized that unless we found something for our new furry friend to do all day, we were soon going to be up to our fancy foreheads in desiccated skunk bodies and rotting deer intestines. So instead of foraging for wild turnip greens, roots of parsnip, hearts of swamp lettuce, and the like, we decided to transplant these provisions into our garden and tell the dog to SIT NO SIT DOWN I SAID SIT GODDAMNIT SIT DOWN RIGHT THERE AND STAY NO NO COME HERE I SAID STAY STAY STAY SIT DOWN STAY STAY STAY SIT STAY SIT by the vegetables and SICUM SICUM KILL KILL KILL NO GET OVER HERE NO HERE I SAID COME HERE DAMNIT HERE KILL KILL kill woodchucks.

Thus humans were set free to experiment with the taming and propagation of agriculture, though this was not always an easy road to hoe, even after we started hoeing it.

For one thing, the category of "edibles" changes and mutates right along with every other "fact" in the world. Why, not so long ago, experts knew for a fact that if an earwig crawled inside your ear, it would burrow right through and come out the other side of your head, leaving you somewhat less inclined toward scholarly conversations with entomologists. On the same note, there is the peculiar history of the tomato. Perhaps as a result of early soup-making with its deadly alkaloid leaves and stems, the tomato was for centuries considered violently poisonous and was grown for decoration only, as a shrub. Time passed, gardens grew, Europeans sailed to America and weeded out the natives, and sometime in the 1890s, a man named Colonel Armslinger or something stood on the steps of a courthouse someplace and ate a bushel of tomatoes before a couple hundred people who were happy enough to come out in 100-degree heat in neck-high wool clothes to watch the poor man go into raving, drooling convulsions and die. This is what good Christian folks did for fun before the invention of live television news coverage of murder trials and natural disasters. When, after a decent interval, the Colonel appeared to be alive and well, everyone ran home and started ordering tomato seeds from catalogs, thus bringing into popular consciousness the long-awaited *Lycopersicon esculentum,* which means "wolf apple," or common garden tomato.

History, therefore, as perpetuated by humans, says that the tomato fruit was always edible, but until the brave Colonel came along to demonstrate this fact, we'd all been missing out on the main reason to have a backyard vegetable garden—fresh, peak-of-ripe, not-from-crates tomatoes. Well, the record will herein be set straight. The fact is that tomatoes *were* deadly poison all that time. The old stories about them weren't fibbing. If you so much as sniffed one of the things, your eyeballs would spin around in your head and fly out into the next county, closely followed by your brains and most of your insides until you died a horrible death or ran for political office, whichever came first.

But then on January 16, 1887, the tomatoes held a meeting in Ologonqua Township, Ohio. Witnesses say it was surely a sight to behold. Many of the tomatoes arrived in horse-drawn wheelbarrows. Nobody knows how the horses managed to hold the crayons in their hooves long enough to *draw* the wheelbarrows, but then, history contains a million mysteries, and who are we to fathom any of them, you say? Well, that's yet another story, isn't it?

Anyway, by the time this meeting was over, the tomatoes had wised up considerably, as anyone who cares to read the tomato clerk's notes can see:

FIRST TOMATO: Listen, friends, there's a problem here. Just because we're deadly poison to humans, we're being smashed up and thrown into landfills at a rate that'll get us extinct in a couple of decades, maybe less.

SECOND TOMATO: Yeah, well, cheer up—we can seep into the groundwater and get even with their grandchildren, which is more than the Dodo can say for itself.

THIRD TOMATO: I've got a better idea. Let's change our chemical composition so we become the best-tasting vegetable ...

FIRST TOMATO: Fruit.

THIRD TOMATO: Huh?

FIRST TOMATO: Fruit. We're a fruit, not a vegetable.

THIRD TOMATO: Fruit, vegetable, Twinkie-on-a-stem, whatever. We become the best there is, get humans to like us so much they start consuming us like crazy and saving our seeds and mailing us all over the *planet* and growing us *everywhere,* and putting us in *cans* and *restaurants* and the food section of the *New York Times* and then one day far off in the future when we've got 'em hooked good and there's a Pizza Hut in every town ...

SECOND TOMATO: I get it! We'll turn poison again!

ALL TOMATOES TOGETHER: Ha! Ha! Ha!

And that is the tomato story, so illustrative of Gardening History of Vegetables and Flowers in its rich and complex incredulity at the length and breadth of human underestimation of Nature! Remember you heard it here first. And then you'd better go out and rip up all of your tomato plants while there's still time and then you should call the National Guard and the National Media and the folks at W. Atlee Burpee and then you shoooAAAAAAACCCKKKGGLLLUGGGHHHHhhh

TOMATO (*unwrapping stems from neck of Mad Gardener*): Ah-ha, stupid human! *Viva la Revolution!*

GOOD VEGETABLE TASTE	BAD VEGETABLE TASTE
Meaty tomatoes	Pulpy tomatoes
Sweet, crisp lettuce	Typing paper blah lettuce
Sweet, crisp cabbage	Slug-infested cabbage
Sweet, crisp carrots	Popsicle stick carrots
Sweet, meaty peppers	Hot, nasty peppers in your eye
Solid, juicy potatoes	Cold French fries
Teeny-tiny eggplants	Big-fat eggplants
Pygmy Brussels sprouts	Hogshead Brussels sprouts
Diminutive zucchini	Moby Dick zucchini
Crooknecks of Lilliput	Crooknecks of Brobdingnag
No lima beans	Any lima beans

Did you know that:

One backyard vegetable garden can provide food year-round for the average family of four, mainly because three of them would rather subsist on pizza-flavored Corn Honkers and beer?

Notes

[1] *Deadly Doses: A Writer's Guide to Poisons*, Stevens and Klarner, 1990, Writer's Digest Books, Cincinnati, Ohio, pp. 53–54.

[2] *Ibid.*, pp. 187–188.

CHAPTER SIX
The Types

OF GARDENS, I mean.

The truly captivated cultivator will enter, and usually, though not always, emerge from the Ten Typical Types of gardening fervor and design. Each Type represents a stage of learning and self-expression. Each is firmly rooted within the history and lore of Garden Madness. Each has its own origins and evolution.

Each is distinctly flavorful and crazed.

1. <u>Sprawling.</u> That is, the learning-level vegetable garden, which is always, without fail, huge. Enormous. Vast. Colossal!

What happens is this: You, the emerging Mad Gardener, wake up one spring morning and discover an ad in the classifieds for "gardens plowed" services. In the blink of an eye, the nod of a word, the flash of a spark plug, something immutable happens inside your dreamy soul. Perhaps it is the image of freshly upturned soil that does it—just the idea of all that dirt coming up from under the skin of the Earth sets off a time bomb deep within the genetic code for Garden Madness. You don't need to plow up the sod to start a garden, but you do not know this yet. You call the number and when the fellow with the plow shows up, you take one look at that shining blade hanging from the mighty tractor like the fantail on a glorious peacock, and you completely lose your wits. In twenty minutes, you have a plot of naked dirt clods the approximate length and width of Lake Erie. And you cannot believe your good fortune.

Dutifully, you pay the plowman—who is laughing so hard he can barely see to steer his tractor to the next Learning Gardener's house—and you go about chopping the dirt clods by hand, for you do not even have a rototiller at this point. Eventually, in the next stage of your Learning, you will have one, but at this point, you are enduring the fire of beginner's sweat, bugbites, and weeping blisters and have no strength left over at the end of your day to leaf through the pages of gasoline-gizmo catalogs.

Only months later, when the Harvest lurches into your life and you realize with a sickening jolt what you have brought down upon yourself, do you advance into the Journeyman stage and amend your ways. Next year, you will let half the garden area grow over to pathways or lawn; half again the year after that; and by another halving or two, you will have learned enough, and become Mad enough, to start enlarging your garden space again by flowered leaps and beds—but without the curse of spine-busting clod-pounding weed-battling water-hauling intensive labor that the Sprawling Type requires.

No one except real working farmers cultivates in Sprawl for more than a season, though there is a certain nostalgia for it among garden veterans. As you can see here.

You will never call a "gardens plowed" number again as long as you live.

2. <u>Technical.</u> Another type of gardening that the Mad typically pass through.

You spend the first winter after your Sprawling stage reading everything you can get your hands on about how to garden correctly. This is the stage in which you start ordering soil test kits, compost pile thermometers, specialized weeding gadgets, and other such devices from catalogs, which know exactly how to cater to whatever degree of Madness is holding you in sway. You may enroll in horticulture courses, where you will be instructed by experts in the fine points of vegetable and flower management. You will make extensive lists and wall charts of seed-starting dates, succession crop strategies, bug emergence schedules, companion planting patterns, etc., etc. By the time you are ready to go out there and garden, you have amassed so much technical information and knowledgeable know-how that you have become quite a raging pain in the behind.

You will then proceed through the growing season with a by-the-book perfectionism achieved elsewhere in this life only by those suffering from certain obsessive-compulsive disorders and by other Mad Gardeners in the same stage as yourself. You will seed, plant, water, mulch, fertilize, spray, prune, and tend everything according to your new expert information–surfeited know-how. Your garden will respond lustily. Visitors will be astounded by your masterful proficiency. You will be asked by the local newspaper to write a gardening column based on your technical knowledge and experience. You will receive fan mail asking technical garden questions. You will answer the fan mail using technical garden terminology. You will find yourself believing that you have achieved technical gardening Expertdomhood. You will start casting around for some other challenge to stimulate your underused technical capabilities.

Your garden will be completely destroyed by raccoons.

3. <u>Imported</u>. This is the garden Type grown in the back yards of ethnic neighborhoods, and is characterized by rows of carefully staked old-fashioned open-pollinated tomatoes, sturdy garlic shoots, peppers, pole beans, asparagus and horseradish beds, hand-made coldframes, and flowers of all kinds in graceful complement to the equally beautiful vegetables. There is no showiness here, nor any gadgets or adornments, but there is great joy. Typically tended by

men and women working together who are in their eighties and nineties and look thirty years younger. You never hear them palavering about gardening technique. They just go out there and do it. Because it springs from the experience of necessity, their Madness may be muted by a sense of decorum, but it is no less intense than your own. You would do well to cultivate their guidance.

You would do even better to have these people as your grandparents.

4. <u>Oh! Natural</u>. A garden Type that lurches into the Mad Gardener's head at about the third season of trial and errors. Invented in the Sixties by totally spaced-out back-to-the-landers who decided that you could just stick vegetable seeds out in the field and forget about them until the Moonbeam Goddess let them know they (the vegetables) were ripe, today's "Natural" gardening style means replacing formal flower borders and lawns with wildflowers and meadow environments, a feat that is too often described by the applicable catalogs as "easy to maintain" with "regular initial watering" and "some weeding" and "seasonal mowing."

Since no one ever sat down with you when you were an impressionable child to explain that nothing is ever as simple as product sales pitches say it is, you will now, as a Gardening adult, gaze into the Wonderland of those ethereal wildflower catalog glossies and order enough seeds to recover all mowed areas within a radius of fifteen city blocks, minus those winding pathways which you will surely create right after you finish shaking the seeds out of their packages and planting thereby your meadow of workfree delight.

Well, there is nothing wrong with the basic idea, and much that is wonderful about it. But as for being "work free," it's like the famous lunch—you will just have to start using less salad dressing if you want to lose that ornery blubber! And as for your seeded wildmeadow, the biggest problem is that you have to start the thing on a clean dirt slate, or it doesn't work. This means that you have the following choices:

(1) Rip up the sod. Or call up that fellow with the "garden plowing" services again and ask him if he would mind bringing along the two-ton cultipacker while he's at it; or

(2) Cover your entire lawn with six to eight inches of leaf mold brought in by the truckload until you keel over dead from the exertion of pitching; or

(3) Cover your entire lawn with herbicides and wait until these have broken down into harmless substances that eventually wind up inside everyone's personal body tissue; or

(4) Turn *one* flower border into *one strip* of wildmeadow using a combination of seeds, transplanted native wild flowers, and the effect of yard weeds and grasses let go to blossom. From there you discover how much diligence this takes, year after year, and decide if you want to enlarge the theme.

You will not listen to me for a minute.

5. <u>Raised Beds</u>. A garden Type that appeals to the neatness fixations—a nervous need for orderly crop rotation and a weird fascination with dirt and manure—that in varying degrees exist in all Mad Gardeners. One day you suddenly decide you want your carrots and onions encased in squared, framed rows with wood-chip pathways defining precise geometric patterns. It may be snowing outside when this idea enters your head like a phantasmagoric spermatozoan, but that makes no difference whatsoever. The Mad ovum of your mind will become so pregnant with raised-bed plots and plans that you will dash out there whatever the weather and start hammering away on scrounged-up pieces of lumber until your dream is born!

Actually, raised beds have many advantages, including the fact that the crops inside them grow in soil that is loose, deep, and never walked upon, and which warms up and dries out earlier in the spring. You can space plants close together and it's easier to set up and nail down row covers, weed barrier mats, etc. And the frames look so professional that all of your nongardening friends will be quite convinced that you are *never* going to get a life, and they might as well give up on you.

But! Be warned—*do not use "pressure" treated landscaping timbers for raised beds*. Numerous studies have shown that the chemicals used to make this wood leach into the ground and thus into your crops.[1] Use naturally rot-resistant wood (old locust fence posts are good) or just plan on replacing the frames every few years; or use bricks, stone, cement blocks, or even lengths of fallen trees. Or shape the soil itself into a raised mound. You can plant lettuce in the upmounded sides for even more efficient use of space.

Another variation on the Raised Bed theme is the Square Foot gardening technique,[2] in which vegetables and pest-affective flowers are bunched together in tight little blocks of succession plantings laid out with the kind of precision that normal people reserve for wiring computer microchips. The outstanding advantage here is the control you have over the harvest, which is more than you can say for the computers. And everything is in *neat* little squares with *neat* little walkways for an overall *neat garden* design that, just looking at it, makes you positively pulsate with meticulatiousness.

There is no end of nit-picking once you start your raised bed system of gardening! Isn't it wonderful?

You cannot answer. You are already out there nitting.

6. <u>Container Gardens</u>. A method often used by Mad Urban Gardeners, in which vegetables, flowers, herbs, and even dwarf fruit trees are planted in large tubs, pots, buckets, and barrels all over the porch, deck, rooftop, or driveway. New varieties of vegetables and flowers suitable for container gardening are introduced every year, including bush cucumbers and squash, downsized tomatoes, and "patio" roses, but you can experiment with the usual garden plants and high-pow-

ered compost-rich soil in just about any well-drained container you can think of and/or scrounge.

This Type has many appealing advantages, not the least of which is that you can rearrange the containers to the maximum content of your heart and back muscles; but more than that, it gives your cats a pleasing set of targets upon which to practice their territorial imperatives.[*] You may want to build your Container darlings a ledge or place them a couple of feet off the ground for this reason, though strategically-placed mothballs go a long way toward repelling your kitties away from your garden and back to the comforts of your upholstered furniture! Marauding wildlife can be a problem here, so altogether you might consider screening your deck or enclosing the plants in chicken wire. Also, it helps if it doesn't matter where the water goes as it pours out of the Container bottoms, such as down through deck flooring to the ground. There are all sorts of amusing rooftop disasters waiting for you on this score, so figure it out first.

You will drag the Containers inside the house as Frost approaches, hoping to keep your garden with you all winter. This will not work, and you know it, and your carpets will be destroyed, but you will do it anyway.

Your cats will love you for it.

7. <u>Window Boxes</u>. A version of Container gardening that has become the center of controversy in certain sections of history-snobbic urban areas. The contention is that Window Boxes are not "authentic" because our Puritan forefolks did not believe in such sinful things as windows. Of course, if you go back far enough, your basic *Homo sapiens* ancestor didn't have sin, either, so the case for "authentic" living can quickly become one mother of a sticky wicket, with preservation committees squabbling for decades over the details. Meanwhile, real estate consortia and parking lot developers go about their business of buying up farmland and old forest and turning it all into "authentic" shopping malls selling, along with approximately 500,000,000,000,000,000 other things, green rubberized window boxes guaranteed to last a "lifetime." You can

---

[*] *And You Thought We Were Exaggerating*, Canis Familiaris Press, 1988, Yowlington, Va.

fill yours with mixes of bulbs, bush cucumbers, trailing nasturtiums, lettuce, sweetpeas, morning glories, whatever you can think up and tend to.

You probably should not pour water into your window-boxed beauties at the exact same moment that the Preservation Committee comes to inspect something directly underneath your apartment windows.

8. <u>Rock Gardens</u>. Often put in by gardeners who mistakenly think this is a carefree, no-work, weed-free Type. Well, you Rock Gardeners are having a fine laugh over that one! For weeds can take over a Rock Garden and obliterate the demure alpine plants and pretty stones before you can say "Rumex acetosella stranguleum." And pulling weeds out from mats of creeping thyme and teeny hens-and-chickens is exactly like trying to pluck the gray hairs out of your head after you hit the Big Five-O, and with just about the same degree of success.

Nonetheless, Rock Gardens are worth every speck of trouble that you put into building and tending to them. Memories of rock gardens fill the images of my childhood, as perhaps they do yours. Collecting fascinating rocks for this Type can evolve into a Side Addiction all its own, so be warned! Every time you move, you will cart along one complete truckload of rocks. No way are you going to leave those babies behind! You will even bequeath them in your will. Which might explain why your lawyer never returns your phone calls any more. Not to mention the moving company.

You understand exactly what I mean, for you have already planned how to pack your rocks in case you ever relocate.

9. <u>Water Gardens</u>. As children, those of you who adore this Type insisted on having a constant supply of unfiltered bowls full of colorful, fan-tailed googlee-eyed goldfish so that you could hold shoebox funerals for them after their mostly unchanged water successfully transmogrified into solid algae form. And as your precious piscatarian

pals passed on to that Great Green Pond in the Sky, you vowed that one day you would have a whole bunch of them in their very own goldfish pool in the yard and that you would never, ever dump the entire box of fish food in there all at once like that, ever again.

Well, all those childhood promises and yearnings can be fulfilled now in the realm of Water Gardening. Recent innovations and improvements in pond materials, water pumps, maintenance chemicals, and, best of all, aquatic plants, make this Type among the most pleasurably gadget-intensive hobbies that any Mad Gardener could hope to discover! And most important of all, you would not believe the developments that have been made in the evolution of colorful, fan-tailed, googlee-eyed children! And the goldfish are pretty amazing, too.

You will bulldoze out an enormous lily-filled Garden Pool and dump all of the dried mealy-worm Koi-food into the water at once. If moderation were your strong point, you would not be a Mad Gardener in the first place, would you?

Which leads us to the most important Type of all, namely:

10. <u>All Of The Above</u>. Otherwise known as Mad Beyond Redemption, this is the Type that all of us eventually embrace. Here you will find bits and pieces of all other Types and numerous ongoing experiments and passions. It will include a couple of pieces of statuary and a formal rose hedge, some technical know-how adapted to fit your experience, some carefully cultivated and beloved foodstuffs from which you often save the seeds for next year, a wildflower bed or "naturalized" piece of lawn-meadow, raised vegetable beds with some "square feet" here and there, rock gardens on every slope and hill, water gardens, pools, and ponds with fish and lily pads, window boxes filled with blossoms, porch containers packed with plants of every description, and an overflowing gout of pathways, trellises, arbors, groundcovers, houseplants, bulbs, herbs, trees, shrubs, vines, coldframes, lattice frames, maybe a greenhouse, potting shed, orchid shed, cut flowers, dried flowers, forced flowers,

annual flowers, perennial flowers, and anything and everything else that you can joyfully cram into whatever space you have around and within your abode.

You will add lots more.

Notes

[1] *Organic Gardening* magazine published several articles on this, including its January 1994 and July/August 1992 issues. One point made in these pages is that CCA (copper-chromium-arsenic) wood that is exposed to vegetable compost has more significant leaching than CCA-wood not exposed to these organic acids. So don't use this stuff to make compost bins, either! Or anything else!

[2] As in Mel Bartholomew's *Square Foot Gardening*, Rodale Press, 1981.

CHAPTER SEVEN
The Plants

*B*otany classifies things all wrong when it comes to the Queendom of Plants. Why, at one time, just the number of species that were divided and cataloged and described and named and added and subtracted *ad infinitudus* would run into the hundreds of thousands, when any respectable Mad Gardener knows that plants come in two basic categories: those you can eat, and those you'd like to grind up and serve on the sly to your Ex.

Though it might seem obvious to view plant characteristics in such terms, the sad fact is that this eminently logical division has been made without sufficient attention to the scientific mind. Because plants in the modern world can now be classified in *three* categories: those you can eat, those you'd better not, and those enhanced with excess molecules found lying around on scientific laboratory floors!

Of course you informed folks know that I am referring to that recent biological breakthrough in elongated shelf life, the bio-technicated genetically-backwards-engineered Wonder Tomato from Calgene ("Tomatoes ЯNA Us") Incorporated, of Davis, California, in which scientists have figured out a way to fiddle with DNA and postpone rot. In the tomato, that is.

Though a coalition of produce farmers had planned to sue to keep genetically engineered food from the marketplace until the FDA had run a lot of inconvenient safety tests, the Wonder Tomato—known commercially as the Flavr ("Ho-Ho, No O") Savr—is now appearing, unlabeled, in Yourstore everywhere, staying ripe far beyond the, you should excuse the term, pale across the shelves and countertops and restaurant salad bars throughout this great land o'plenty-N-plenty more-N-more-N-more.

By now, you readers are probably assuming that I am going to plow into this whole idea with all the acid verbiage one can muster! But both of you are wrong. I think that unlabeled, genetically-fiddled tomatoes in our supermarkets is a fine idea, and, saving my muster for chicken hot dogs and bologna grinders, I shall tell you why.

First off, you have to understand that this is only the beginning. Once unleashed, the scientific mind never comes home again. Why, not so long ago, the Cadillac of produce-fiddling was irradiation, which changes the chemical composition of food into mutagens that many bacteria would not eat on a bet, allowing you to feed it to your children, who, as any parent can testify, don't have anywhere near the dietary squeamishness of a microbe! And as any scientist knows, this is all to the Greater Good. Fruits and vegetables with a shelf life longer than breakfast cereal can be shipped anywhere in the world with impunity, thereby rescuing humans from the bother of trying to save indigenous farmland or lowering population growth or anything else politically cumbersome, and besides you know perfectly well that everyone outside the USA eats stuff like eel eyes and boiled goat hair and therefore needs to be Saved. No, really.

Second, and closer to home, delayed-rot tomatoes with a few funny hunks of DNA are a huge improvement over whatever comes out of the so-called "diet" industry. You think I'm kidding? Go microwave yourself a "diet lasagna" and get back to me.

Thirdly, there's always the possibility that eating the Wonder Tomato will alter *your* genetic code and give *you* a longer shelf life, which would be nice, I think. On the other hand, you have to wonder if there's only so much future a person can stand. Or is that my rot-DNA talking?

But more important than all of this altruistic gobbledygook is the unalterable fact that the Wonder Tomato is just the first in a whole new evolutionary line. Once you can fiddle with the genetics of an edible and make it even more edible than it already was, then how long before you can fiddle with the genetics of *inedibles* and create a heretofore unimagined world of abundance and plenty?

I mean, think about it. Why go to all the trouble of shipping the Wonder Tomato from laboratory to supermarket in all those bulky wooden crates? Why not just dispense with the tomatoes altogether? Why not simply fiddle with the genetics of the wooden crates and make edible, indestructible packaging that you don't even have to plant or fertilize or water or harvest or anything? Besides, you don't have to package packaging, do you? Think of what this could mean to our overflowing landfill problem! Not to mention jobs in the packaging materials sector. Hallelujah!

And then, no doubt quite soon, scientists will discover a way for you, the Ordinary Person, to fiddle with the genetics of everything, right in your own backyard with your very own gene-fiddling device! Think of it! Just place this new PCB-powered DNA alterator on a pile of rocks, and presto! Genetically created edible food material. No need for anyone to struggle with all those nasty gardens and farms full of dirt ever again. Incredible!

Not only that, but scientists have already foreseen the day in the not-too-distant future when all objects everywhere on the planet will have been genetically created into food material for humans and there is nothing left but 465.77 billion people and their genetically created food by-products. I can't go into detail on this for reasons of national security, but you can be assured that the giant spaceship filled with all the scientists and their families from Calgene, Incorporated, took off without a hitch last Monday and that it had nothing whatsoever to do with that broken test tube they found in Zucchini Genetics Lab No. 6. They said they'd be in contact with the rest of us real soon.

Meanwhile, we'll just have to slug it out in our UnWonder Gardens and wait for that passé old broad "Nature" to hurry up and take her course.

How DNA reactionary! But fear not! Scientists are not going to let us down. Already the dairy farmers of America are shooting their cows full of genetically-replicated BST growth hormone so that Bossie can give us even more milk and cheese with which to fill up this nation's overflowing underground storage bins in case we cannot set aside enough Wonder Tomatoes to withstand, and possibly defend against, atomic attack! And I will allay the groundless protests of you pure-food faddists out there by pointing out that BST appears naturally in every cow on the planet, so it makes perfect sense to take some of it out of a cow, fiddle with the DNA until you have a large, and, let us not forget, expensive amount of the synthetic version of the natural stuff so that the DNA companies can *sell it back to the farmer* so it can be *injected back into the cow* so that she can make even more milk than she, or you, ever thought possible! Not to mention agonizingly painful. Oops, wait a minute! Sorry! Just a thought molecule escaping from my own personal breast tissue! I'm so embarrassed! It's just these silly old outdated memories of what it feels like when you are producing more milk than you ever thought possible! I shall endeavor to keep such remarks out of this discussion. Who wants to listen to a bunch of whining breast tissue, anyway! After all, BST was thoroughly tested on kids' breakfast cereal and was found to be perfectly safe. Though it was a little hard to tell, what with all the radioactivity floating around the Sugar Bomb Berries and everything. Nonetheless, science prevailed! And so should you!

And then you should just shut up.

There! Now let us return to Gardening and other important business.

Where the Mad Gardener Gets Plants

It is the dead of winter. You have just stuffed logs into the woodstove for the seventeenth time today, and it is only nine o'clock in the morning. Outside, the landscape is as exciting as a piece of yesterday's butcher paper. With the windchill factor, it is forty-seven degrees below zero. Everything has frozen to death, including the fence. You are seriously considering the logic of doing the same. Perhaps you will simply walk to the mailbox naked.

But lo! What is this? A bright, shining kaleidoscope of color beams out of the gloom and into your eye, proceeding along barren hallways directly into the portion of your brain that has memorized your MasterCard number! What can this be? What is this miracle of golds and blues, pinks and reds, creamy whites and hybrid purples?

What is this Fantasia of delight, this Xanadu of prose, this promised Fairyland of spring?

Why, it is a garden catalog, of course. You shall open it now, and read it cover to cover. You shall look at every glossy photograph displaying gouts of blossoms that radiate from the pages in weedless perfection. You shall absorb every word, believe every claim, desire every seed. You shall contemplate the quickening of your breath, the tingling of your veins, the thumping of your heart, the foreclosing of your mortgage. You shall, in other words, order every single plant in the catalog. And you shall have absolutely no idea what any of them are by the time your head has cleared and UPS is trundling up your driveway. Not to mention the fact that all the packaged plants will look exactly the same—like fettucini.

It is early spring now. The UPS man has been to your home one hundred and twenty-five times since March first. He will no longer get out of the truck if you are nearby. Instead, he flings the packages out the door as if he were feeding lions at the zoo. He has a frightened look on his face. You do not blame him. You have a frightened look on your face, too. The garage no longer has room for cars. The local landfill exploded last week, spewing cardboard and excelsior over your tricounty area, and you are solely responsible. You have 9,725 plants to install before next winter, and you are not going to make it. The daylilies in box #316 have been grabbing at your ankles with their roots. Any moment now, they will go for your throat. But you are still trying to figure out where to plant all the fettucini in box #65. The name on the label says it is "Eragrostis v. expensivosa as allgettoutti," but you have no idea what this means. You do not remember what any of these things are, or why you ordered them in the first place. Since you have thrown out the catalogs, you cannot look them up. Some of these plants may even kill on contact. You no longer care. The invoices are due in five days, or the companies will kill you themselves.

Outside, it will soon be ninety-seven degrees above zero and humid enough to turn wallpaper into oatmeal. It is out there that you must toil for your sins. You are doomed.

You long for winter, for the dead landscape, the snuffed-out greenery, the disappeared garden, the snowdrifts of yestersleep. Next year, you will not so much as riffle the pages of a single catalog. You will send out cards directing all mail-order companies to wipe your name from their lists. You will forget that you ever looked upon the face of a glossy four-color page full of antique English roses. You will order no more forever. You promise. Really. Not a thing!

And then you will sprout wings and fly, far away, to that ancient land of Nod, where you will have lunch with King Arthur and the Knights of the Round Table and all of their legendary Kin. Who will be too busy ordering next year's rutabagas from Guerney's to pay any attention to you at all.

Yes, this little cautionary tale speaks true. The catalogs are wondrous indeed. No one in the gardening world would disagree with that one, as any Mad Gardener can attest. But catalog prices vary widely—witness the difference in tree peonies: Henry Fields offers varieties for $15.99 each, while Wayside's are between $48 and $78, to name one particularly eye-popping example. And you pay all that shipping and handling, which gets more expensive every year.

But most of all, you must face the truth about catalog ordering: You will forget what you purchased until it arrives, and then you will discover that you over- or duplicate-ordered. Inevitably. Every time. Something happens to the Mad Gardening brain when it comes in contact with catalogs. It does not understand the concept of physical labor or overdrawn checkbooks. You might think you can fool it by throwing the catalogs out in the trash, but it will get up in the middle of the night, dig the catalogs out of the garbage—your Mad Gardening brain has learned this trick from its twin organ, the fat cell—and then quickly, before you can come to your nongardening senses, it will fill out all the order blanks for plants and seeds and bulbs and run out to the mailbox with the preaddressed, post-paid envelopes! You will have had no choice in this. The Mad Gardening mania is not to be reckWE INTERRUPT THIS PARAGRAPH TO BRING YOU ANOTHER IN A SERIES OF PUBLIC SERVICE ANNOUNCEMENTS.

SEE THIS FRYING PAN? THIS FRYING PAN IS SITTING ON A STOVE BURNER WITH THE HEAT TURNED UP UNDER IT AS FAR AS IT WILL GO. THIS FRYING PAN IS OBVIOUSLY IN THE HANDS OF AN INSANE PERSON. THIS FRYING PAN IS A GARDEN CATALOG.

SEE THIS EGG? SEE IT BREAK OPEN AND GO SPLOOT AND TURN INTO SIZZLED SILLY-PUTTY IN THE FRYING PAN? THIS EGG IS YOUR BRAIN WHILE READING A GARDEN CATALOG.

SEE US PICK UP THIS FRYING PAN WITH THE SIZZLED-SILLY EGG IN IT AND THROW THE WHOLE MESS OUT THE DOOR SO THE RACCOONS CAN CARRY IT AWAY AND TURN IT INTO SCAVANGER-ORTS?

ANY QUESTIONS?

THANK YOU.

... oned with. Perhaps someday scientists will track down the faulty DNA that causes Mad Garden Ordering. In the meantime, try pulling the wool over your eyes by opening every catalog you receive, writing something in every blank on the order form—your brain will think nothing whatsoever is amiss at this point—and then quickly, before you let your brain know what is going on by thinking about it, toss the order blank into the wood stove!

Unfortunately, this tactic only works if you (1) have a wood stove, and (2) it is winter, and (3) the catalog company has not cleverly included a toll-free customer call-in number on every third page! Throwing the glossy catalogs into your wood stove is not advised. Catalog ash creates a goo on the inside of your chimney flue that has been known to cause brain damage. Even more brain damage than Mad Gardeners are obviously already afflicted with, I mean.

Other Places to Get Plants

Out of Your Local Nursery. These folks go through all the seed-starting hassle for you, and they understand your regional climate better than you do. Also, they're equipped and staffed to make those plants grow tall and sturdy and ready for bloom.

They are the ones who transfer every single one of those eyelash-sized seedlings to cell packs. They are the ones who rush to the greenhouse on their days off to open and close the vents so those seedlings won't fry or freeze. They are the ones who remember to water those cell packs only as often as needed, no more, no less. They are the ones who make sure no cats pee in the perlite. They are the ones who suffer and die for our Madness.

So before you start ordering from catalogs, try calling the nurseries to find out what they'll be offering in your particular garden interest line—and don't forget the feed mills and local supermarkets, which frequently offer spring bedding plants, and neighbors with greenhouses, who might have some leftovers they'd enjoy handing your way. Then fill in around the edges from the catalogs. Carefully! Or maybe not at all. Are you sure you can eat just one?

Out of Division. Great for spreading around those precious perennials and such tuber-producing annuals as dahlias. Your own or from other gardens. Why not run an ad in the classifieds asking gardeners if they'd like to swap or share divisions?

Also, you can "rescue" plants and flowers from abandoned house lots and from the wild, though unless the plants are unquestionably threatened—by a development project, or imminent roadside spraying, for example—you should leave them alone. Don't pick wildflower blossoms, which effectively neuters them, and don't trespass on private property without permission. And make sure the plant you are rescuing is not poison ivy. Oops! Ha, ha! Nature has the last laugh once again!

Out of your own nursery bed. A raised bed system in which you nurse along cuttings and seedlings, even baby trees you found sprouting in awkward places, until they're ready for a more permanent place.

Out of Desperation. Smiley wooden replicas on sticks.

So what with the forces of Science and Nature and Craft Shows, the Mad Gardener never has to worry about where to get plants. Though as we have seen, worrying about the plants eventually getting *us* is a whole other story to behold.

CHAPTER EIGHT
The Animals

*S*OONER OR LATER, the animals will find you.

They are part and parcel of the natural order. They are intimately intertwined with the ecological nuances of the Earth. They are guileless denizens of the Great Outdoors. They are an enormous pain in the Gardening Tuchas.

You have even brought some of these creatures voluntarily into your home. You will notice that ours is the only species that does this. Of course, ours is also the only species that thinks it's a good idea to have so many of ourselves that we can't figure out where to put most of us any more, let alone what to do with our junk cars. So what difference a few household pets make is beyond me, unless you, as a Gardener, are thinking about the Useful Poop factor.

With the possible exception of guinea pigs and rabbits, household pets fail the Useful Poop Test every time. In fact, dogs and cats are miserable failures at just about any kind of test you care to subject them to. For example, if you ask a cat, "If a train leaves Buffalo at nine o'clock and a train leaves Chicago at ten-fifteen, how fast will they be going when they collide with the two men in a rowboat who are digging a ditch at ten miles per hour," you will get the response, "Seven thirty-two P.M.," which is obviously dead wrong. If you then ask a dog the same question, someone would probably start calling the authorities. But that is to be expected. Anyone who has cats and dogs together, or at all, in the same house, bears some watching. Not only do these beasts produce a never-ending flume of Garden-withering excreta, they wage a constant intergenus range war to trick you into getting rid of the other one.

> CAT (whispering in your ear): The dog dug up the rose bushes again.
> DOG: GRRRRrrrrrrr
> CAT: He's the one who peed on the drapes last night, too.
> DOG: GGGGGRRRRRRRRRRRRRRRRRrrrrrrrrrrrrrr
> CAT: And he never leaves any fresh mouse intestines under your chair for you, does he?
> DOG: Yum!

The only practical use these animals serve is for scaring off the other ones, and you know how often that happens.

Let us launch, then, into the Animal Kingdom and see how we might best shoo it away ourselves, using our highly developed cerebral cortex as our primary means of defense.

Insects

WARNING! The following statement has been rated "R" due to its utterly demoralizing content: Four out of five animals on this planet are Insects. Yup, that's true. Four out of five of your fellow creatures, or about nine hundred thousand identified bug species. Which is estimated to be about ten percent of the Insect species yet to be discovered, multiplied by a couple of billion members each, give or take a few mil, that are out there waiting to crawl into your eyes, sting you on the tongue, infest your embarrassing anatomical areas, dig under your epidermis and hatch maggots, turn your house into a pile of sawdust, scare the bejeezus out of you at periodic intervals, and, not incidentally, chew your garden into revolting nodules of green Gorp, and there is very little you can do about any of it.

You have two kinds of weapons against the Insect world: Chemicals, which kill everything in your backyard and then proceed on up through the food chain to the biggest fish, which turns out to be you, eating a tomato sandwich; or Naturals, which include such compassionate devices as the Sticky Trap, onto which every bug within range, including those that appear in sweet little children's bedtime poems, will stick and struggle and scream and weep and beg for its Mommie until it finally dies covered with Sticky ick and various twitching parts of its Insect companions; and Diatomaceous Earth, a dust consisting of microscopic fossilized shell remains that shreds slugs, caterpillars, fleas, and other luckless crawlies who venture out into the mine field without looking and can't get back no matter how hard their buddies try to rescue them.

Other "Natural" insecticides, called Botanicals, are available in some stores and through such specialty catalogs as Gardens Alive! But these deserve a goodly scrutiny, too. "*Most* Botanicals break down quickly in the environment without leaving dangerous residues, and Botanicals pose *somewhat* less risk to beneficial insects," italics mine, says the Gardens Alive! description of these controls. Trouble is, you're still depending on a concoction of compounds that, mixed with everything else we eat and are exposed to and expose everything else to, adds up to an unknown effect *somewhere* or other down the line. (The labels do say, "Hazardous to humans and domestic animals.")

And then there's the control factor. Meaning your control over what's in the product. For example, in 1991, the popular Ortho Insecticidal Soap was accidentally contaminated during manufacture by several different herbicides, including 2,4-D. Oops! No one, including Ortho, knows how many containers of this soap ended up on the shelves of Gardening America before the goof was discovered; months after Ortho's recall of the product, cases of it, bearing the contaminated lot numbers, continued to be available in stores (according to articles in, and letters to, *Organic Gardening* magazine throughout 1991 and 1992).

Talk about burning down the house to get rid of the relatives! Maybe you should stick with such homemade repellents as half-and-half mixtures of vinegar and water, reputed by some to "instantly dissolve" Insects such as the slug, which is not really an Insect but a Gastropod, which is Latin for "having a foot on your stomach," which is just about the most ridiculous thing I ever heard of. Spray made out of pureed hot peppers, diluted down so it doesn't melt the container, also works very well—just don't get it in your eyes! Ouch! You can also mix this pepper puree with Tabasco sauce for extra flavor and apply it to your bird feeders in a futile effort to repel squirrels, which despite their appearance are not Mammals but the most highly developed Insects on the planet. They chew up your feeders to regurgitate the masticated plastic and cedar Gorp as food for their young and material for mud nests in which the females deposit squirrel larvae by the billions. Really, this is true. Anyone who has ever attempted to feed the birds anywhere outside of the Gobi desert and certain isolated areas of the Antarctic wasteland knows these facts for what they are.

Even more fun than hot pepper spray is the Organic pest "solution" method of grinding a few slugs, or whatever other Insect is chewing your garden, to a pulp in your blender—that would be the same kitchen instrument with which you are going to make party drinks at your next barbecue—and spraying the resulting substance all over your veggies. According to this idea, the remaining bugs will take one whiff and buzz off, screaming, to your neighbor's apple orchard and the relative safety of DEET. You don't even want to know what these folks recommend for keeping stray dogs out of the yard. Or burglars.

Anyway, then there is the technique of bringing in the "beneficials." These are helpful predator bugs in white cowboy suits that you order from catalogs and let loose to bring truth, justice, and the American mail-order way into your teeming slime pit of a backyard, if any of these "beneficials" really exist in the first place. Some of them have scary names like "Trichogramma Wasps," which sounds suspiciously like a DNA Doomsday concoction mixing hornets with feminine itching; and others, like "beneficial parasitic nematodes" are completely invisible and my guess is that the guys in the catalog company mail room are just boxing up empty corked test tubes left over from the "Sea Monkey" rage of the Fifties and sending these off to you while laughing themselves into comas. Whether you want any of these things breeding freely in your garden is something you should take into serious consideration. The mail-room guys would probably want to drink a lot of beer first, and raise a ruckus, and throw up in your bird bath, so it may not be worth the shipping and handling fees.

Beneficial nematodes, on the other hand, work this way: You dissolve their shipping medium, usually a clay capsule, in water, and spray the thirty to forty thousand microscopic nematodes out across your lawn and garden, where they seek out fleas, cutworms, grubs, Japanese beetle larvae, squash vine borers, weevils, and other destructive—they are programmed with eenie-meenie microchips to know which is which—insects. The nematodes drill into the bodies of these unfortunates and release a bacteria, which kills the host. This accomplished, the nematodes throw their own version of a beer blast and reproduce like crazy, filling the dead bug bodies with offspring that hatch and depart in search of more host bugs so they can have their own reproduction parties without their parents hanging around, and so on and so on, until there are no bad bug hosts left in your yard and the whole nematode community dies off in a microscopic cataclysm of rampant overpopulation and disaster.

Sound familiar?

Though beneficial nematodes are at least a method of insect control that works somewhere within the eco-cycle rather than coming at it from the corner of chemo-technology, you do try to keep that word "natural" in mind, do you not? Is mailing microscopic predators from one part of the country to another really a good idea? Can you not help but wonder what will happen when "beneficials" run smack-dab into the new-era science lab plant product of tomorrow?

FIRST BENEFICIAL NEMATODE: Hey, look at this! My host weevil's been munching on backwards DNA!

SECOND BENEFICIAL NEMATODE: No kidding! How does that make you feel?

FIRST BENEFICIAL NEMATODE: Sort of like … sort of like … aaaaaaaaAAAARRRGGGGGGGGGGGHHHHHHHHHHHHHHHHHHHHHHHHHHH-HHHHHHHHHHHHHHHHHHHHH

SECOND BENEFICIAL NEMATODE: Help! Help! Leonard is bursting through his clothes and turning bright green!

FIRST BENEFICIAL NEMATODE: AAAAAAGGGGGGH-HHHHHHHHHHHHHHHHHHHHHH

THIRD BENEFICIAL NEMATODE: Oh, no! He's running amok!

•   SECOND BENEFICIAL NEMATODE: He's jumping onto that passing schnauzer! He's releasing his bacteria!

THIRD BENEFICIAL NEMATODE: The schnauzer is a goner!

SECOND BENEFICIAL NEMATODE: Now look! Leonard's reproducing like crazy!

THIRD BENEFICIAL NEMATODE: Oh my god! What's going to happen next?!

SECOND BENEFICIAL NEMATODE: I don't know, but I want some of what he was eating, don't you?

FIVE MILLION BENEFICIAL NEMATODES (all together): Yes! Yes! Yes!

Fortunately, this is a silly made-up nematode dialogue that has no bearing whatsoever on the real world of today. What the real world of tomorrow might consist of is not my province to explain.

One real note of caution: Some "beneficials"—certain types of ladybugs, for example, not to mention all those mail-room guys—can arrive at your door preinfested with their *own* parasites, so you should read catalog offerings carefully and only order the "quarantined" varieties. Follow release instructions carefully. Opening a vial of mantises in your car on the way home from the post office does little to promote diplomatic relations between you and the Insect world. 'Tis it not a far, far better thing to keep your yard and garden chemical-free and filled with a healthy variety of vegetables, flowers, ground covers, perennials, trees, and shrubs, and therefore hospitable to indigenous "beneficials?"

If all of this scary bug business weren't enough, Insects comprise one of Gaia's best shaggy dog Useful Poop jokes. It's probably great stuff, but you would have to scrape fly specks off the windshield for a hundred thousand years to get enough to fertilize one lousy cucumber, which is silly because by then the cucumber would be dead anyway. On the other hand, bees turn poop into honey. If that isn't a miracle of peristalsis, I don't know what is. We would do well to take a lesson from Apian ways.

Altogether, you are just going to have to get used to living with Insects. Consider how they manage to live with us, and they, at least, do not drive bulldozers through our communities or squirt poison all over our homes or run around hitting us with magazines. On the other hand, we do not bite them in the buttocks or traipse barefoot through their kitchen cupboards, either. It is a simple matter of Ecological give-and-take.

Mammals

Includes wild bothersome things such as gophers, raccoons, deer, skunks, bunnies, moles, and mice; and somewhat tamer but more personally dangerous things such as horses, cows, goats, and geese. What? Oh, sorry, geese aren't Mammals! What was I thinking? Geese, like squirrels, are disguised Insects, cousins to the vicious Fire Ant! What? You don't think so? Try walking onto property where there is a swarm of geese and see what happens.

And if you don't think cows are personally dangerous to humans, then apparently you haven't been out of the house in a while! Just consider this news item from the May 30, 1994, Associated Press:

Man Mauled by Herd of Cows

LONDON—Paramedics rescued a man mauled by a herd of cows. John Hine was crossing a field near Tetsworth, about 40 miles northwest of London, when the Jersey cows spotted him. The cows knocked him to the ground, breaking his leg and badly bruising his chest. Hine was unable to move and called for help on his cellular phone. His dogs barked to help paramedics locate their master in the boggy, secluded spot.

Doesn't this make you wonder why the man was carrying a cellular phone through a cow pasture to begin with? Maybe he works in a bovine growth hormone laboratory and had received threatening letters written in Moo, and was already running scared. And the dogs—sounds to me as if they were in on the whole plot, don't you think?[*] All that purposeful barking seems a bit suspicious. You certainly have to check out every possibility in a case like this.

There is some question about goats, too. Their eyes go the wrong way, like on a crab, which is ethnically a spider, which aren't even Insects but Arachnids, which is Latin for "EEEEEEKKKK!!!" And then there is the duckbilled platypus, which nurses its young, and has fur, and lays eggs, and breathes fire and flies. Flies around, I mean. The only Mammal that breathes flies is the anteater, and nobody knows where flies come from in the first place, or where they go afterward, and they are hairy, so they are probably related to the porcupine, which they resemble if you get up close, meaning to the fly; so there you are. The Mammals are just one great big dangerous mess, topped off by Us.

Getting rid of Mammals in your garden is almost never accomplished without the help of electricity in some form. You can shoot them, of course, but then you would lose the benefits of many Mammals, such as the grub-eating habit of the skunk; and besides, shooting them means that you have to be outside all the time, shooting, in order for this method to be effective. Or maybe not so effective, if you happen to have a problem with garden hippos, as this Dec. 17, 1993, AP news item demonstrates:

Hippos Have Been Destroying Crops

YAOUNDE, Cameroon—A herd of 100 hippos is destroying acres of crops in northern Cameroon and has killed two women in a hunting party chasing the animals.

The marauding herd has for weeks been terrorizing the rich farming community around Lake Guere ... They have uprooted and destroyed dozens of fields of millet and sorghum. Hunters in canoes attacked the hippos with spears and arrows ... [when] a hippo calf overturned a canoe and attacked the two women, who fell out and drowned. The other hunters fled to shore.

_____   No Botanical sprays available for that!

[*] *Dogs Are Sneaky Double-Crossing Varmints*, Felis Domesticus Press, 1989, Mew York.

For the more mundane Mammal problem, a barking dog placed near your garden will work tolerably well, or until the police show up with nuisance-noise warrants for your arrest, which were actually called in by those witty raccoons with the clever opposable thumbs, taking turns in the phone booth on the corner! You can also do things like tie bars of "Irish Spring" soap on your ornamentals to repel deer, or spread barber shop floor sweepings and blood meal around your garden, or any number of grisly tricks, all of which involve *handling* stuff like "blood meal" and somebody else's head discards. Plus, animals are not the brainless blobs of beef that humans seem to take them for. They will figure these spooker maneuvers out sooner or later, often before you get back inside the house:

DEER: Forsooth, mine hare, observe yonder resident *Homo sapiens* hanging perfumed soap upon the *Ilex opaca* once again.

RABBIT: Indubitably. Perchance we should call upon our friends the *Formicidae monomorium,* or common household ant, to infest with their great numbers and utterly devour this aforenamed "soap" that it not unduly deter us from our appointed rounds of chowing down the greenhenge?

DEER: Ods bodkins, sir, thou art naught but a genius *lepus* thereto!

RABBIT: And verily, there are trillions more of us where I come from!

DEER: Us, too, verily well indeed. Especially since Big Brain over there killed off all the predators.

ALL TOGETHER: Dumb! Dumb! Duuuumb!

Rather than inviting this sort of other-species Reasoning Exercise—remember, it was figuring out how to stand up and use pruning shears that started us up Darwin's Ladder—you might better purchase one of those electric fence kits complete with posts, wires, holders, and charger. This works just fine, and after a few weeks you can leave it on nights only, thus saving the batteries, though there are solar fence-charging kits that you can buy for about $100. Not even your household pets will venture inside it, though it does little to deter ...

Reptiles and Amphibians

Another order of fauna that can cause significant screaming and benefits. Snakes, turtles, lizards, frogs, and toads are all apt to creep into your Garden and consume large quantities of Insects and other pests, including, oftentimes, each other.

I realize that many humans, Mad Gardeners unfortunately included, share a distinct phobia about snakes. Perhaps it would help to keep in mind that despite their reputations, snakes are not slimy, which is more than you can say for far too many members of your own species, isn't it? And even poisonous snakes are at least up front about their intentions. They either want to avoid you entirely or they want to swallow you whole and digest you slowly, over a period of weeks, and then excrete whatever they don't need any more, and go on. Not many people are that honest about it! And toads eat five times their weight every year in slugs, earwigs, gypsy moths, cabbage loopers, and the like, so give them a couple of broken clay flower pots for shelter and leave them alone—if you touch them, you'll give them a case of toad heebie-jeebies from the feel of your yucky smooth skin.

You may live in a region of the country where you are concerned about alligators and crocodiles, which are two different versions of the same creature. Alligators do not appear in crossword puzzles nearly so often as their cousins, the crocs, and are much more apt to live in Florida, where there are, you will notice, no wild hippos whatsoever, and not that many cows, either. So as far as the Reptiles are concerned, it is probably wise not to poke your nose into Poop that is none of your business in the first place. Would you rather have alligators or cows hiding underneath the Reemay cloth every morning? Yeeek!

Birds

Birds used to be reptiles a long time ago, but decided that enough was enough with hunkering around on the ground and getting one's scales all mucked up with discarded chewing gum and road tar, so they grew wings and flew off to a better horizon, except for the Ostrich, the Emu, the

Moa, the Roc, the Roll, and the BeeGees, who all stayed on foot and are best known for their colorful plumage and the laying of absolutely gigantic eggs.

Birds are incredibly beneficial to the garden, though they can also cause damage and turmoil by devouring the raspberries right along with the greenworms. And then there are bats, which are technically not birds, but belong in this category anyway because they are major consumers of insects, especially the mosquito and the gnat and the black fly, which is by the way not a true insect but the embryo form of piranhas. Bats rush out every night into your backyard fast-food restaurant and eat something like five times their own body weight in bugs, a comparative twenty billion hamburgers served per night per bat, and still count-ing. So you can see that the world would be one titanic pus-pocket if it were not for our most maligned Bird, the bat, who also, not incidentally, pollinates more flowers worldwide than bees do.

As a Gardener, you will have to figure out your own balance between put-ting out the bird welcome mat and putting out the bird-scaring gadgets. As for this last, catalogs sell things like fake rubber owls and "spooker cats" with eyes made out of marbles that flash in the sun, or you can make fake snakes out of chunks of garden hose that you have conveniently cut up with the lawn mower. But you will have to move these around fairly often or the birds catch on and start making sarcastic comments in the form of gadget defamation poop, which means that you will have to resort to tougher spooker methods and possibly wide-brimmed plastic hats. You can buy huge rubber bands and stretch these across the top of your garden until they reach from stake to stake or snap in two and amputate your nose, whichever comes first. The idea here is to create a boingy sort of vibrating sound that birds will hate, so why not save yourself the hassle and just blast disco music from your kitchen windows? That should do the trick.

Also, you could cover the entire garden plot with "bird cloth" and spend the season crawling around on your hands and knees underneath it, but all in all you might better just learn to live with the Birds, who besides everything else good about them can sing much better than humans and do not accompany themselves with drums or electric guitars.

You could become so enamored of Birds that you decide to grow your own bunch of them from eggs, which is called chicken farming. For gardeners, the main idea behind chickens is that they have top-notch Useful Poop, though you have to get them to perform this amenity in more or less the same spot, which is called a chicken house. And if you let them run around in your garden, they will instantly turn into lunch for the foxes, who will show their gratitude to you by also eating your dog, if it doesn't watch out. Or you could decide to raise ducks, except that you have to provide them with a place to swim so that they can ignore this and crowd onto your front porch day and night, night and day, week after week, summer and winter, peeping and cheeping and yeeping and peeping and pooping until you break down completely and stomp them to death. But you will have lots of organic Bird matter to slip on and scrape off long after your duckies are but a revolting memory of halcyon gardening days gone by.

You simply can't avoid the fact that Birds are flawlessly intertwined in Gaia's endless round-robin of swanlike ecological symmetry.

Worms

Meaning of the Angle kind that you find in the ground and in your compost heap, if you have been doing things right.

The problem here is this: What kind of Animals are worms, anyway? The Latin word for them is "vermiculus," which means "potting soil," so clearly Latin is not going to help. *The Columbia Concise Encyclopedia* says that "worm" is a term for "various unrelated invertebrates with soft, often long and slender bodies," but that could just as easily refer to the models you see in *Vogue* magazine and is as lousy a piece of noninformation as I've ever been forced to encounter. Worse, the next entry in the *Columbia* is "Worms, Diet of," which the obviously intoxicated encyclopedia writers expect me to believe involved something called an "Edict of Worms" in a *city* named Worms, and frankly I am not going to look anything up in the encyclopedia ever again. It is just too preposterous.

What we know for sure about worms is this: They spend their lives running dirt through themselves and turning it into superior dirt. They cut the middleman out of the entire ingestion process, in other words. They don't have to grow anything on dirt in order to make use of it. Worms think that dirt is just fine the way it is, with garbage and dead bodies and mulch and compost all blended together in neat, cool layers that comprise a true worm smorgasbord, though you are not required, strictly speaking, to provide dead bodies for them to be happy. So you can see that worms not only pass the Useful Poop test, they are its progenitive standard-bearers.

You can't fence out a worm, or shoo it away even if you tried, which would earn you a strange reputation indeed. And please, don't stick them with hooks and drown them just so you can rip up the mouth parts of fish. No, that is more easily accomplished by using those barbed gizmos that resemble, come to think of it, miniature lawn ornaments with teeth. Leave the worms to their dirt-pooping duties. You will be richly rewarded.

Well, I would rip into the rest of the Natural Menagerie here, but I see that we've run out of time and anyway all that's left after you subtract all the Mammals, Insects, Reptiles, Amphibians, and Birds from everything else is this:

1. Things that float (Ivory soap, jellyfish, dandelion fluff, pond scum).

2. Things that reproduce by getting chopped up with a shovel (alien protoplasms from space, amoebas, kudzu vines, coat hangers).

3. Things that outsmart you at every turn (head lice, your VCR, antiques dealers).

4. Things that go bump in the night (thunder, furniture rearranging itself down in the living room, leprechauns).

5. Things with the brains of a bent-over buttboard (dog biscuits, tourists, Dan Quayle).

6. Things nobody can figure out at all (oysters, viruses, why anybody would want to be elected President, pigeons).

Truly unclassified information!

CHAPTER NINE
The Skills

FIRST, you have to get in shape.

You know this is true, of course. Shape zealots have been yelling at you for months now, but you know what happens. You lie around watching gardening videos all winter, blissfully lifting nary hoe nor trowel. Then comes March 21, and what do you do? You rush out into the crocus and your vertebrae start popping like rotten rubber bands. Within minutes, you're heading back to the couch and the heating pad. You're in worse condition than last year's ooze-hose.

Well, to combat this Mad Gardener's affliction, I have come up with a series of exercises for you to do over the winter. These are designed specifically to ready you for the rigors of next year's growing season, and in no way guarantee that your garden will look any better than it ever has. After all, does Schwarzenegger weed the crabgrass out of his portulaca? I think not!

Therefore, you should combine the following exercise schedule with a daily reading of your favorite seed and plant catalogs to keep yourself in the proper fitness frame of mind. And see your physician first. She'll be over in the doctors' lounge, sound asleep, so just look in on her and then go home. It's the least you can do.

The Mad Gardener's Get in Shape for the-Season Fitness Program

1. <u>Weeder's Knee Knock Knumbers.</u> Place your kneecaps on the kitchen floor and lean on them to a count of seven thousand. Do this four times a day or until you can pound nails into wooden blocks with any part of your lower legs. Breathe deeply.

2. <u>Wheelbarrow Spine Spiff Special</u>. Holding your arms out in front of you, assume a half-crouch and pick up the television set. Taking moderate strides, circle the living room ten times or until your eyes stop watering. Often it is best to unplug the TV before attempting this one. Return to original surface. Meaning the television. Exhale.

3. <u>Hoeing Arm Hardbody Howdy.</u> Grab nearest teenager and pull toward his or her room while bellowing instructions for cleaning out said hovel. Teenager will run in opposite direction, providing isometric resistance. Repeat until the cows come home or teenager reaches twenty-seventh birthday and moves out, whichever comes first.

4. <u>Rototiller Rhomboid Rumble.</u> Place nine-by-twelve area rug into washing machine and start cycle. When machine starts whanging out guts (its), wrap arms (yours) around same and walk backward in straight line to a count of 175. Repeat through spin cycle. Be sure to clench teeth away from tongue.

5. <u>Every Seed In Its Own Little Spot Stretch.</u> Shake out vacuum cleaner bag. Separate all cat hairs. Taking last deep breath of day, bend at waist until forehead is even with ankles. Carefully line up each cat hair end to end until you have encircled the inside of your house 4,726 times, or the approximate distance from here to the Moon. Do not straighten up without supervision.

6. <u>Pitching The Compost Prep.</u> Slide ordinary broom handle under living room furniture and fling, one piece at a time, into upstairs hallway. Meanwhile, have assistant blow large quantities of dirt into face (yours) with room fan. Five reps of ten furnitures each should do the trick on this one.

7. <u>Planting The New Trees Push.</u> Flush three bed sheets and two full rolls of toilet paper down second-floor commode. Using plunger, at-

tempt to force materials through sewer line. Once this is done, allow large animals to roam through domicile at will, gnawing everything into rubble. Scream and gesture uselessly at same, breathing from diaphragm.

8. <u>Starting The Lawn Mower Muscle</u>. Entering municipal animal control shelter, locate largest canine suitable for adoption. Place knotted end of rope in said creature's slavering jaws and yank, while growling playfully. Canine will leap forward, sink teeth into fatty region of forearm (yours) and yank back in response to your efforts. Seventy-five sets of one hundred and fifteen reps should develop upper arm socket-dislocation flexibility required for proper combustion engine recoil endurance.

9. <u>Fixing The Lawn Mower Might.</u> Lying face down on storm sewer grate while holding worn-out screwdriver and screws with worn-out screw-slots, push arms through grillwork and press until cheekbone is properly squashed against greasy, mud-encrusted metal. With tippy-ippy ends of fingers, attempt to force screws into slightly misaligned screw-holes located underneath rat's nest of knuckle-gouging pipe shafts, stretching constantly until spittle forms on chin and you feel the "burn."

10. <u>Dragging The Water Hose Hoist.</u> Having affixed automobile emergency brake to "on" position, tie twenty-foot length of rope onto rear bumper of same and pull uphill through winding obstacle course consisting of priceless Ming vases arranged in random cluster patterns until pulse rate exceeds relative humidity index factor of one hundred and seventeen percent in the shade. Gasp raggedly until death seems to have receded momentarily, keeping close track of aerobic pain ergome measurements.

11. <u>Harvesting The Tomato Crop Heft</u>. Order a ton of rocks from your local contractor. Carry these in the front of your sweatshirt, ten dozen at a time, into your kitchen. Arrange on counters, windowsills, and appliances. Repeat until entire rock pile has been successfully transferred. Leave in place until you start to go crazy. Grind six thousand into dirt and cram into freezer. Give four hundred thousand away to friends. Throw nine hundred thousand out of car window while driving around countryside at night. Breathing insanely now, take remain-

ing rocks and completely bury garden plot. Fling garden tools into compost pit and incinerate, using flame thrower, until implement and fat-burning benefits are assiduously realized.

12. <u>Hiring The Yardhelp Holler</u>. Opening newspaper to classified ad section, see listings under "situations wanted" category. Clutching telephone in bicep-augmenting squeeze progressions, punch in number for yardwork person, using sharp jabs of alternating digit flexors. Agree to pay whatever wage is requested. Sigh with relief. Return to sofa, stretch out right arm, grasp TV remote. Switch same to "on."

Sit there until winter returns.

You've earned it!

What to do Next Skills

Now that you have prepared yourself physically for the demands of gardening, it is time at last to be up and about, out of the doldrums of winter gloom and into Spring Chores, quickly, before anyone sees you for the slovenly dullard that you are.

We are speaking here of getting the garden tools ready for planting season. Of course, as anyone who reads the "Outdoor Handyfolk" column in the local newspaper knows, you should have done this particular job before the winter closed in around you last November, but I know you better than that. You threw everything in a dirty, rust-caked pile inside the barn and shut the door, oblivious to the whimpering of rotting tines and gunky engines, didn't you? Well, so did I! So there!

So now comes the comeuppance, and you'd better be ready for it. Here is how to sharpen your spring clean-up skills in the three basic type-of-gardening-device categories:

1. <u>Things that are going to explode in your face or cut off your arm at any moment.</u> These include all lawn mowers, weed-eaters, yard-waste shredders, and anything else that involves gasoline or electricity, or a derivative thereof. You're supposed to empty the dangerous goo out of them every fall and start over, even though each Thing weighs at least five hundred pounds and there are no directions printed on It

anywhere and you will be arrested and euthanized if you dump so much as a drop of said goo anywhere except in government-approved landfills in faraway jungle-covered Third World nations of no consequence. So phooey on it!

Clean-up method: Call local Dangerous Mechanical Devices Repair Shop. Blame condition of machine on someone else, preferably feckless Significant Other. Hide in cellar while repairfolk person changes motor oil, starts engine, replaces specially certified eyeball-melting battery acid. Later, tell neighbors you did all of this yourself. Everyone else does!

2. <u>Things that are kind of useless but which look real neat all jammed together in a barrel in your garage like maybe you're going to use them once in a while. Right</u>. These include fancy oscillating hoe-edgers, long-handled rotating crabgrass-decapitators, adjustable foot-operated scissoring bulb-plungers, and a host of other stuff that you paid too much for through garden catalogs, each complete with some sort of fancy gear wizardry that clogs shut five minutes past the first weed.

Clean-up method: Wearing gloves, carefully sink each device down into new spring mud to a depth of fifteen inches. Leave in place all summer, thereby impressing friends with how much work you're doing. Toss back inside barn (the tools) when winter comes. Repeat until they (the tools) rust into Eternity.

3. <u>Things that you really and truly use all the time in your garden and wouldn't even think about going out into the dirt without and neither did your grandmother</u>. Includes a trowel, a hoe, a pair of rubber boots, and a distant, dreamy idea of a rhapsody of flowers and arbors and vine-covered trellises and pathways and island beds all over the place, possibly throughout the world.

Clean-up method: The trowel, the hoe, and the boots can be rinsed off in the sink. Your dreams, on the other hand, should stay as they are. After all, from where else do gardens grow?

From the dirt of years past, I say.

Let the revels begin!

Scrounging Skills

One of the most important Skills you will need in your gardening career, though there is ample evidence that Scrounge is not learned, but is an inborn trait, passed down through generations of horse-traders, flea market dealers, oddball inventors, and others who tend to live beyond, and off of, the fringe.

To test the existence of Scrounging Skills within your personal soul, simply do this: Never again purchase any new garden gizmo, with the possible exception of selected bedding plants. Before you know it, you will be roaming the streets of your neighborhood on trash day, searching for old flower pots, tomato stakes, leaves and grass clippings, discarded and only slightly broken garden tools, perfectly usable rubber boots, big pieces of edging brick, and the like. You will feel triumphant, rather than embarrassed, about picking through curbside garbage for this purpose, although it might be a good idea to keep your tetanus shots up-to-date before you start honing this particular skill. Bags of yard waste can be full of broken metal and glass and various disgusting objects, so be careful. Wear gloves!

You could run ads in the newspaper classified section for mutual Scrounging "swops," which is an old New England Schooner Cap'n word for "bamboozle the landlubbers afore yew hang 'em from the gry'lin mast by th' hacken'sickle sprigots." So keep a wary nose to the ground when you swop-and-shap with strangers. Besides, their pieces of broken terra-cotta drainage tiles may not be worth your fine collection of splintery hoe-handles!

Trash mounds behind lumber yards are another good Scrounging area, and you should also be on the lookout for house-renovation scrap piles that you can sort through for goodies. Rummage sales can be fruitful too, sometimes offering garden-useful items in freebie boxes. But if you're going to get up that early in the morning, you might better go out and tend to your vegetables before the bugs are up and ready for breakfast. Keep your Scrounging Eye in gear at all times, though, and you'll be amazed at what's out there for you to scarf up and enjoy. Dogs have used this philosophy for thousands of years, and look where they are today—living off us, the ultimate Scroungee![*]

---

[*] *Dogs Are Parasites*, Felis Domesticus Press, 1990, Mew York.

Fixing Your Mistakes Skills

In Mad Gardendom, there are no indelible mistakes, unless you have done some eco-heinous act such as spraying your greenery with that Insecticidal Soap mentioned previously. Now, *there* is a goof! Though by whom is something of a question.

Otherwise, you can do, undo and redo just about anything Out There simply by planting, observing, digging, replanting, redigging, moving, removing, arranging and rearranging and experimenting to your heart's content. Your flowers will be your guide.

But there is one major outdoors mistake that you have probably made, and continue to make, and no longer know how to fix, and wish that it were frying in Hell, and that is: Your Lawn.

Yes, the Great American Lawn Craze has been upon us for decades, and I should know. I grew up surrounded by six acres of Lawn that required the combined mowing efforts of my parents and several generations of neighborhood kids over the course of two to four days per week straight through from May to October, not counting time given over to repairing the things (meaning the mowers). I used to think my parents were three sheets short of a floundering sloop for doing this. Until the day I woke up and discovered that I was all grown up and had purchased my own house with an even *bigger* lawn. Days and days of mowing from May to October! Not counting time given over to repairs! Meaning on me! Help!

That's when I also discovered that human beings are never satisfied. You give us a string of nice hot, dry summers that burn our yards into easy-care no-mow oblivion and all we do is complain. And then you give us a nice cool, wet summer so the grass can grow and grow and grow and we can all mow and mow and mow until the smell of chlorophyll-clogged machinery parts fills our ears, noses, and throats with joy, and what do we do? We complain. And we never notice the side benefits of weather, such as the rainy-season moss that destroys lawn grass. No one bothers to point out that this moss is bright green and only grows an eighth of an inch tall. Perfect! And completely unappreciated. In our ignorance, we rush out and dump chemicals all over the place, kill off the moss, and plant specialized grass seed that requires chemical fertilizers and herbicides and mowing so that the grass will be nice and green and exactly an eighth of an inch tall. Why Nature continues to bother with us is beyond me.

However, there are ways to deliver one's beleaguered self from this depressing mistake of lawn-tending. All you have to do is murder your lawn!

Think about it. Gaia in all Her wisdom has been trying to do just this for years and years, with the help of Her army of weeds, grubs, sidewalks, fire ants, small children, and the aforementioned moss, to name but a few of Her weapons at hand. Why not take advantage of the inevitable, using one or more of the following unofficially approved Lawn-Kill methods:

1. <u>Boiling water.</u> Pouring boiling salt water between patio flag-stones is a sure-fire way to kill off invading grass, so why not do the same all over the yard? Though I'm not exactly sure how you would accomplish this task, short of dumping the boiling brew out of a cauldron from the roof, upon which you have built a large cooking fire using leftover lawnmower gasoline. Check with your local zoning officer before trying this. You may need a variance. Bail money too, no doubt.

2. <u>Mowing real close to the ground. Real close.</u> I did this once by happy accident and it fixed my lawn but good for the rest of the season. It turned a shade of brown beautifully reminiscent of Nestle's Flavored Choco-Pops. *That* was a summer to remember. Though I forget exactly what else it was that I did. All in all, though, it was a start on the happy road to lawn freedom.

3. <u>Paving the whole yard and painting it green.</u> Well, no, I haven't done this one myself, but I knew someone who did and then sold the family lawn mower and had a big party. The following spring, a single dandelion burst up through the cement. Grass stalks soon followed. The man left town.

Pavement probably isn't a good idea anyway. You will just end up standing out there like an idiot, watering your cement with a garden hose. Haven't you seen people doing this to their sidewalks and driveways? Admit it. Self-torture is a basic human instinct.

4. <u>Grazing animals.</u> You've heard the joke. You toss out your mower and buy a goat. Several goats. Or sheep, or reindeer, or even steers, which is the name given to cows with bungled sex-change operations. Whatever grazing animal you choose, you should not forget to pick up a fence on your way out of the store. And a barn. And some hay bales for winter. And something bigger than a gerbil dish for water. And an even bigger shovel. And a truly gigantic compost bin. And, if there is any room left in your car, a veterinarian. And definitely a couple of chiropractors.

Maybe grazing animals aren't the best bet for the average home lawn snuffer. Besides other disadvantages, grazing animals are apt to get into your garden and cause a worse mess than a plague of grasshoppers ever thought of doing. Come to think of it, you might consider ordering a plague of grasshoppers for the lawn instead. About two billion of them should do it. And you can share your dead lawn fortune with the neighbors!

5. <u>Setting it on fire.</u> You've seen people who tried this method, haven't you? The folks who are standing out in their charred yards clutching charred broom handles in their sweaty, charred fingers, watching the Rocky Mountain National Forest go up in a mighty conflagration of their own making? Guaranteed to murder your lawn, but taking half the surrounding flora and fauna with it is unfortunately a distinct possibility. Maybe you'd better leave this one to the professionals. They can be contacted by leaving a note with Vinnie "the Bug" Vincent, c/o Storage Locker #75, Grand Central Station, N.Y. 10020, but it's okay if you forget that I mentioned it.

6. <u>The Agent Orange solution</u>. Introduced into mainstream American Agriculture in the mid-seventies as "No-Till Farming" to guarantee elimination of pesky time-wasting indigenous field greenery and also to provide a more rewarding use for leftover patriotic deforestation chemicals than could be realized by ordinary roadside spraying. Useful variations and derivatives for suburban lawn murder may be found on garden supply store shelves everywhere, a fact that will thoroughly flabbergast archeologists a hundred thousand years from now when they excavate billions of indestructible buckets of lethal Home Lawn Kare Kemikals that comprise the remains of our "civilization."

In the meantime, you can blast away with impunity. Or at least legally. Which ought to flabbergast our minds right now. But are there any?

7. <u>Phooey on it.</u> Otherwise known as Letting The Yard Go Straight Down the Tubes. While not exactly a permanent solution, this method has its primary benefits in showing the neighbors that you are not some spineless, wimpy lawn conformist like the rest of them. Primary disadvantages involve embarrassing publicity and court appearances in which you are depicted as a rabid weirdo and the question of bail money again raises its weary brow.

8. <u>Employing the composted leaf pile.</u> You know, the Leaf Mold Method. Pile the leaves half a foot thick in garden-pretty shapes all around your property. After the sod is decomposed, you can plant anything you like therein—flowers, vegetables, shrubs, whatever. Or nothing. Who cares? Just keep adding leaves once a year or so. If nothing else, it *looks* as though you're going to do something nifty. Aren't looks what got us into this lawn mess in the first place?

And that's it. A beautifully murdered lawn.

Absolutely the perfect crime!

Loafing Skills

Soon after the season begins, all Mad Gardeners start practicing one of the most important Skills of their trade—a skill that sets the standard for all outdoor work, and without which very little else could be accomplished in your terra firma and not so terra firma.

This is the all-purpose mastery of Garden Loafing.

Scientists have theorized that human beings are moving up the Darwinian Ladder at a slow but steady pace, having only recently pulled ahead of our apodal ancestors by virtue of the evolution of lawn furniture. In the Beginning, at the dawn of the Parenthetical Era, all lawn furniture was carved in the shape of the notorious "Adirondack chair," which was originally designed for a nonvertebrate skeletal system developed specifically for crawling up the sides of canyons. Now, however, lawn-sitting apparatus in all shapes and sizes appears in every store and catalog throughout the land, and some of it is even useful for honing your Loafing Skills. Scientists and humans, after all, have yet a long Ladder to ford, chevy, and dodge, as anyone can see by the following list of the Seven Basic Loafing Furniture Types:

1. <u>Fancy iron sofas </u>with expensive cushions that turn to mush the first time it rains on them, which doesn't matter because no one uses them for anything except as props in photo layouts for snooty decorating magazines. Also enhances Upscale Swearing Skills from endless toe-bashing against little iron spoolie-gougie gargoyle trimmings.

2. <u>Rustic chairs and tables</u> made out of "redwood"—meaning woodlandlike mystery materials stained "red" and put together with almost the right number of flesh-maiming eye screws—and lie-flat but too-short loungers from your local supermarket's parking lot sale. Optimizes Loafing Skills the first year but fall apart in the barn over the winter and will kill or cripple you if you try sitting in them ever again. Cushions survive rain but gradually become filled with numerous generations of satisfied mice and spiders.

3. <u>Authentic wooden benches and chairs</u> made out of the last of the Amazon Rain Forest and shipped directly to your little ecological corner of the planet for a price that will make your eyeballs spin around in their sockets and explode, which is only fitting, when you think about it. Considerable Denial Skills required.

4. <u>Folding automatic tip-over aluminum chairs</u> with torture-weave seats that rot and break just as you sit down with your fifth beer in one hand and a paper plate full of chili tacos in the other. Recalls Loafing Skills developed in hedonistic days of bygone halcyon youth, which you stupidly threw away instead of the aluminum chairs.

5. <u>Folding canvas director's seats</u> occupied exclusively by the cat. Perfect for Dislodging Your Pet Without Serious Incident Skills. If you really want to sit down on a cushion of cat hair and discarded tapeworm segments, that is.[*]

6. <u>Old tree stumps and logs</u> that your embarrassing relatives have fashioned via chain-saw art into droll sitting-stool things and brought over to your house in pickup trucks along with all their children. Requires considerable Skill in putting up with a bunch of idiots, something that we Americans have obviously perfected far too well.

---

[*] *Cats Are Disgusting!* Canis Familiaris Press, 1991, Yowlington, Va.

7. <u>Hammocks.</u> There are no such things as hammocks. They exist purely as urban legends, like the vanishing hitchhiker and the fifty-dollar Porsche. The only people who own hammocks are your neighbor's second cousin's best friend's brothers, and even they fell out of the thing. You might better lie down on a sewer alligator.

8. <u>Adirondack chairs</u> inherited from your grandmother. Oh, well! You may not be able to sit in the things without pain, but when you consider the loafing furniture alternatives available today, you might as well give up and regress to your natural slug state safe in the knowledge that Loafing Skills are an as-yet unfiddled part of your natural genetic heritage.

Waiting Skills

Sooner or later, you will find yourself waiting for the nice man to show up and fix your snow blower. At the same time, you will find yourself waiting for the other nice man to show up with the truckload of you-stack-it firewood. Eventually, with the passage of many weeks, you will come to realize that they are the same man. In fact, they are *all* the Same Man, and all of the classified ad numbers ring in His house. This is the reason you spend three-quarters of your allotted lifetime waiting around for The Nice Man To Show Up When He Said He Would.

Do you and I, Mad Gardeners every one, ever complain about all this waiting? No! Among its other sublime benefits, gardening eventually turns even the most compulsive-aggressive right-now people into skillfully passive simpletons in just a few short seasons. Here's how:

THE WEATHER. Spend a couple of seasons outdoors with Our Friend The Weather, and before you know it, you won't care about anything. Why, you won't even care if you send your name, address, and passport photo to local TV weatherfolk so they can display these and your temperature readings—the outdoor temperature, that is—to all the other cringing Milquetoasts in your region who wait for the weather report in hopes of being able to count on something definite tomorrow. Ah-ha-hahaha-ha! If you want to know when the last frost date is, you'll have to wait and look at the calendar.

THE CALENDAR. No one knows when the last frost date is. Or the first frost date, either. A bunch of old Yankee Wiseacres got together around the cracker barrel ten thousand years ago and made up the calendar just to embarrass the immigrants, most of whom had never heard of frost or Nor'easters or fo'c'sle ha'mast'd whale'n'ships or anything else spelled as though an insane person got loose in the dictionary factory. The only way to figure out when the last and first frost dates are is to wait until everyone else has put in or harvested their gardens and then do yours. Using this method, you will have somewhere between ten and thirty-nine full growing days in which to wait for ...

YOUR CREDIT CARD DEBT. By now, after several seasons of gardening, you have probably noticed that your credit card debt is designed by the same fiendish monsters who did your mortgage, so that no matter how many monthly payments you make, you will never be rid of it. Even if you are smart enough to send in more than the "minimum payment due," which is actually coffee money for the credit card accountants and has nothing to do with your bill at all, you are doomed. You are in their clutches forever. You might just as well charge it up to the limit on flowers and trees and enjoy yourself while you are waiting for ...

THE LOCAL FARMER'S MARKET. This is where gardeners who have successfully outwaited all of the above bring their gardening bounty to get rid of before it smothers them. Here, instead of gardening, mere mortals can buy vegetables by the basketload and not have to fight off a single predatory bunny rabbit. But it isn't the same. Once the dirt bites you, you never get over it.

Just you wait and see!

Grammar Skills

Useful so that instead of saying, "Ain't them hornworms makin' a mess out o' the gawddamn termaters?" you will know enough to say, "Ain't them hornworms makinG a mess out o' the gawddamn termaters?"

Poor old G. Everyone forgets him!

Other than that, I gave up on grammar a long time ago. Isn't you? And those are all the Gardening Skills you need!

Did You Know That:

ChemLawn chemicals do not make your grass grow taller, but instead make *you* shorter and stupider, so that constant mowing and fertilizing all that bilious poisoned greenery seems like a real swell idea?

CHAPTER TEN
The Tools

ONCE you have come to your senses and decided to plant, propagate, weed, till, pluck, mulch, pet, sing to, harvest, and otherwise grow everything there is, you will be ready to choose, purchase, use, and maintain the Important Equipment that is so necessary and intertwined—ingrown, perhaps, not unlike a toenail—with your life of Madness.

I should clear something up right away. There is a fundamental difference between Garden Equipment and Garden Gizmos, which I shall review in the next chapter. Garden Equipment is the big important stuff that I obtained through wise purchases after careful, informed consideration. Garden Gizmos are the stupid pieces of eye-catching junk that you wasted your money on without asking my advice first. Besides that, Garden Equipment is Macho-Reflective. I mean, most of it could turn any part of you into luncheon meat at any moment, but do you wear galvanized steel armor whenever you go near it? No, of course you don't. See what I mean? Ha!

Humankind has progressed a long way since early Cro-Magnon gardeners were forced to pay illegal Neanderthals in mastodon suet to dig the turnips by hand, a job for which anyone should have been meekly grateful in those harsh times, don't you agree? Today, this work is largely accomplished by all sorts of complicated machinery consisting of miraculous newfangled grinders and rotors that are a thousand times more dangerous than any mastodon ever was, and a whole lot harder to repair. And you can see the results of this Evolution right inside your neighborhood supermarket, in the form of piles and piles and piles of victuals in a mind-boggling array of forms and colors, much of it very nearly edible foodstuffs.

But for you, the homey lone Mad Gardener gardening madly alone at home, the issue of mechanical accouterments is smaller, though not a bit less exciting. Many of the modern tools of gardening and yard care have their own unique and fascinating history, and each is cleverly designed for a specific helpful function, such as emptying your wallet with the ease and grace of butter sliding out of a toaster-oven.

Tools for Power

1. <u>Riding lawn mowers</u>. In childhood days gone by, little girls played with dollhouses while little boys went outside and tore up the sidewalk with miniature bulldozers. But the world has progressed, the sexes are achieving true equality, and everyone regardless of gender or frustration level now gets to have his or her very own Tonka Tank in the form of a sixteen-horsepower riding lawn mower with a forty-eight-inch mower deck and an endless variety of greasy moving parts that are no longer fixable or currently manufactured! These Tools grind everything in their path into satisfyingly lethal surface-to-air missiles, and the eardrum-dissolving "twin-cylinder horizontal crank-shaft engine" makes you feel as though you're accomplishing something even if you just drive it around inside the barn. Also hauls quantities of dirt, tree branches, rocks, and leaves—if you have a garden cart, that is. No landowner with a grudge should be without one.

2. <u>Self-propelling walk-behind power mowers</u>. Now available with mulching capacity, though a bagger attachment is handy if you need a batch of clippings for the compost pile and are understandably too lazy to use a rake. Trouble is, the bag will fill up faster than your yard is square and no matter how you figure it, you will end up dragging a sixty-pound bag of wet grass between the stalled mower and the Heap every time. Maybe you should have paid more attention in geometry class.

Altogether, for sheer agonizing pain and sustained fury, nothing even comes close to owning and trying to start one of these mowing Tools. The most fun is when the starter cord *yanks back* and you become convinced, correctly, that the !!*&^*&^%$#!! thing is alive and that it hates you and is going to get even by at the very least destroying your shoulders or, with any luck, your fingers and toes. Power mowers use all sorts of ruses to get you to stick your hands and feet underneath them, including The Stall technique. Don't believe it for a second. If your power mower stalls, shoot it in the spark plug and push it out into traffic.

3. <u>Weedwhackers</u>. These gizmos, oops, I mean pieces of Equipment, have become standard trim-up tools of lawn and border care, but that's not why you should have one. You should have a weedwhacker for the same reason you have a power mower: because they are far superior to any exercise machine on the market for building muscle tissue, not to mention your insanity threshold. After an hour or so of fruitless hauling on the weedwhacker's starter cord, you should be ready to enter the Popeye Balloon Biceps Beauty Pageant and/or call up a few machinery repair shops and ask for someone who has the wits to comprehend that this is a boogery way to make a machine. Ah-ha-hahahahahaha! Eventually, you might even get to trim weeds.

4. <u>Rototillers</u>. Piling lots of compost and leaf mold on your garden beds pretty much eliminates the need for rototillers, despite the neat photos in gardening magazines of nattily-dressed people steering forty-horsepower soil-grinding earth-turners with their pinkie fingers, a feat that I personally do not believe for a second, by the way. Despite that, tillers are good for making busy-sounding noise and throwing rocks around like government grant money. Similar cord-yanking problem to the above, however—made worse by the fact that it's much harder to fling a tiller over the creek bank without excoriating both of your shinbones. Trust me on this one.

5. <u>Shredders</u>. Great for experiments with garbage, old love letters, excess zucchinis, and "yard waste." I have to plug my shredder into the oven outlet and run the cord out the window or it fries every circuit in the house. Indispensable for compost-making and annoying

the neighbors. The keen satisfaction of ramming sticks down through a shredder and turning them into racket and mulch is difficult to put into words. Perhaps a couple of hours trying to read the "Internet" manual will bring some applicable words to mind. I know it certainly loosened up my personal shredding vocabulary. You really can compost anything!

6. <u>Electric leaf-blowers, apple pickers, and yard vacuums</u>. Wait a minute, how did these get in here? Do I look like an idiot or something? These are gadgets trying to pass themselves off as Real Equipment. You can't bamboozle me.

7. <u>Utility vehicles</u>. No Mad Gardener, or anyone else who does any kind of outdoor work, is worth a load of salt without a Utility Vehicle or two. For most people, this means a pickup truck at least nine years old with just enough metal left on the fenders to provide a place to stick the duct tape that holds the doors shut. After all, the sole purpose of your Vehicle is to haul manure and leaf mold, right? In fact, the more reprehensible your pickup truck, the more points you score with the old-timers down at the local feed mill:

FIRST OLD-TIMER (*snorts*): Say, Edgah, thayat old hippie ovah theyah a-loadin' up th' kee-rakkt caa-hn shuah is a funny-lookin' piece o'work, ain't he, she, or it?

SECOND OLD-TIMER (*hawks*): Ay-yup. But thayat's one fine hahd-workin' old jeeyunk pick-up truck he, she, or it's got theyah, ain't it now?

THIRD OLD-TIMER (*hacks*): Ay-yup. Mebbe he, she, or it ain't so disgustin' aftah'all.

ALL TOGETHAH: Spit! Spit! Spit!

Other types of Utilitarian Vehicles could include backhoes, dump trucks, and bulldozers, though the heady possibilities inherent in one of these things—such as driving right through the wall of the local feed mill and scattering the old-timers like a mud-mound full of termites—may turn out to be too great a distraction and are probably best left alone.

8. <u>Chain saws</u>. Get out of *town*. These things are more dangerous than *plutonium*, for crying out loud. Whatever it is you think needs chain sawing, such as cordwood, you can hire it already sawed. Note general physical condition of hiree. Some fairly important body part, such as the face, is usually missing pieces of itself. Chain saws were invented by the same people who came up with power take-off shafts and silo fillers, those mainstays of Agricultural Equipment designed to rip the arms off troublesome farm workers or, for a few pennies more, eliminate the annoying employee problem altogether by grinding said personage up and spitting the remains atop the ensilage, sort of like an Alfred Hitchcock Family Fireside Mystery Theater show, you know, back in those good old days of "family" TV?

Anyway, Mad Gardeners don't need any of that stuff, or if you do, you have obviously lost your mind and have decided to become a professional farmer for a living and you are not reading this book in the first place because you barely have enough time to eat meals and go to the bathroom as it is.

My sympathies.

Tools for Hand

1. <u>Hoes, trowels, and claws</u>. The First Gardening Tools, created for Adam and Eve and all of their progeny to push dirt around and make it viable for vegetables and flowers. However, it should be quite obvious even to the fig-leafed eye that these inventions came about *after* that unfortunate incident with the Apple. Just look at the three-pronged claw, for example. Applying all the powers of the modern mind, you will undoubtedly notice that the thing vaguely resembles a pitchfork, and you know what that means! After all, who *really* wants you to go out there in the heat and insects and *dig holes in the ground?* Is it you or some ... Unmentionable Force? Good Heavens! Obviously, Adam and Eve should have left Gardening alone and gotten themselves involved in some worthwhile activity, such as melting rock-and-roll records in the microwave.

2. <u>Wheelbarrow</u>. An ancient weapon once used to cart the above instruments into battle against the Crusaders. Nowadays you are more likely to see this tool appear in suspiciously mundane activities such as hauling compost. Look in flea markets and rummage sales for used ones at a fraction of their new-store soon-to-be-gorped-up-anyway price. Variations on the original design abound, including huge boxy things with wheels the size of millstones, but the end result of wheeling any barrow around, whatever its advertised advantages, is this: You will have a backache, and you won't care. I mean, are we Mad or are we Not?

3. <u>Kitchen spoon.</u> A secret Tool used by all gardeners at one time or another, usually in, though not exclusive to, childhood. Can be made from stainless steel or solid Revere Coin Silver and I had better not say any more about it or a lot of gardeners out there are going to get a whomping from their mothers! Didn't you?

4. <u>Push mower.</u> An artifact of days gone by if there ever was one, originally designed for smaller and scruffier lawns than most Americans will tolerate today, not to mention the physical labor involved in using it. But it will never tear your tendons loose from your bones and it does not spew fossil fuels into the morning air, unless you count what happens if you accidentally whizz it through a fresh dog doot.[*] Still, it is precisely this evocation of innocent times that makes the push mower such an essential Tool, even if it just sits around in your garage displaying its homely virtues to one and all.

5. <u>Dibble.</u>Though pictures of this device have been appearing in fancy garden supply catalogs for years, dibbles do not exist except as smelly street thieves in long-running Broadway musicals based on even longer and insufferably boring novels by dead British authors.

6. <u>Poacher's spade</u>. A skinny shovel invented by Medieval peasants who used it to outsmart the Aristocracy, overturn the feudal system, and chop off the heads of bewigged monarchs at about $50 a current catalog price chop. Also slices down through just about any soil type with ease for quick tree stealing and transplanting.

---

[*] *Ick! The Way Things Arf to Be!* Felis Domesticus Press, 1992, Mew York.

7. <u>Soil blocker.</u> You jam this Tool down into the ground and come up with your own square-o-dirt, into which you then stick seeds for starting. Except in February, which by coincidence is when you are supposed to start seed-starting and the ground is also frozen solid and covered with snow. Maybe this tool requires planning ahead and gathering your dirt chunks while Ye may. Or maybe it's just plain silly. You decide.

8. <u>Bulb planter:</u> Derived from the above at about half the cost and seventeen times the frustration. Trust me on this one. Use a poacher's spade.

9. <u>Pruners, loppers, and hedge shears.</u> Offers more hacking-away fun than you've had since that time you chopped off all of your little sister's hair with her own blunt-endy kindergarten scissors! Only this time you get to do it on trees and shrubs. No guarantee the results will look any better, however. Just remember not to lop through that pesky wasp nest hanging there in the *Buddleia buddleia*! Makes the trouble you got into about your little sister seem like vanilla fudge cake.

10. <u>Watering cans</u>. Once simple hand tools of the trade, now considered collectibles worthy of an antiques dealer's best haggling talents. If you look for these at rummage sales, you'd better get there a half-hour early and be ready to punch, scratch, bite, kick, and cheat. And that's just the people running the sale! Of course you can order new watering cans from catalogs, but what fun is that?

11: <u>Hoses, lawn sprinklers, faucets, couplings, soakers, quenchers, timers, and twirlers.</u> Because you will not feel like hauling watering cans from your water source in July and August, the inventors of gardening gizmos came up with these alternative devices, which have achieved full Hand Tool status largely on the coattails of the Great American Green Lawn Craze. They are monumentally convenient and some of them run close enough to gizmoland to offer a zany thrill or two, as in the "Tractor Sprinkler," thought up by those folks who never got over the titillation of watching model trains run around and around in a circle, except that the "Tractor Sprinkler" ratchets along your yard hose while spraying a thirty-foot spume of water in all directions! It just goes to show that you can't predict form and function once the human mind gets involved, doesn't it?

12. <u>Rakes, forks, spades, cultivators, weeders, planters, hatchets, shovels, tampers, dampers, clampers</u> … Wait a minute, who is joshing whom here? Who or whom goes out in the garden and gardens with any of this stuff anymore? What have I been telling you about "mulch" and "compost?" What have I been telling you about "sitting in the shade doing the crossword puzzle?" Aren't you paying attention? Have you been letting your mind wander all over the place without supervision? How do you know it's not keeping the neighbors awake at night? You should teach it to lie down and not move even if someone tempts it with a bag of bite-sized Snickers bars. After all, who is the master of your mind? You or any old thing that comes along?

With that observation, we travel on to the last category of gardening Tools, and possibly the most important.

Tools for Adornment

Namely, the Garden Wardrobe.

A Garden Wardrobe comprises some of the most essential items that you will ever need, mostly because of the side effects of Garden Gorp.[*] Items in your Garden Wardrobe do not have to match one another, or even yourself, to be practical and effective. They do not have to resemble anything you have ever seen on a human being or any other creature of Earth. All they have to do is get the anti-Gorp job done. So here is a list of the fundamental items you should have, as epitomized by my own personal Garden Wardrobe:

1. <u>Bright green plastic curly-toed garden clogs</u>. You can buy these from numerous catalogs, and other than making your feet look like Looney Tunes tootsies, they'll never let you down. The cork insoles pop out and they all wash up with a hose. Perfect for Mud Gorp days. Order them a size larger than you ordinarily wear, but if you tend toward bunions, forget them altogether and get rubber boots. I don't like rubber boots because they stick in the Gorp and pull my socks down.

---

[*] You know about this already. See Chapter 4.

2. <u>Bright orange rubberized suspendered pants coveralls.</u> Because of the danger of being mistaken for deer riding around in electric carts, golf enthusiasts often buy these items in golf apparel shops and sporting goods stores. For gardeners, the coveralls are perfect against Weedwhacker Gorp and for crawling around on the ground trying to locate your riding lawn mower's "steering sector gear shaft cable," which has just snapped in two and is located directly underneath the "clutch yoke spring pivot driver," which is located between something called the "loose ferrule mandible quad" and the "speed selector transmission lever pilot," none of which can be reached from a normal upright position.

Coveralls, along with the gender-impaired inventors of all mechanical objects, may be hosed off at will and hung out to dry.

3. <u>An old khaki five sizes too big London Fog jacket</u> with deep pockets and a zipper built by Mack Truck. An inherited or thrift shop item, most likely. Pockets hold small gardening tools, gloves, wads of kleenex, and secret caches of M&Ms, many from last year. Perfect for Wiping Off Hands Gorp.

4. <u>A bright red washable polarized visor hat</u> with adjustable terrycloth headband. I've had one of these things since I first started gardening and was forced to go outside in July one afternoon in 1966. It shields my face from UV and Bug Gorp, though protection against this last is somewhat offset by the use of sunscreens, which employ cantaloupe sugars and attar of beer foam as their main cosmetic ingredients. Also, after looking through a red visor all day, you begin to get the feeling that everything is bathed in the glow of an evil sunset, and you become even more depressed about stuff like poison ozone and holes in the Van Allen Refrigerator Belt, or whatever. But if you can keep your face from turning into suitcase material, who cares?

5. <u>Three pairs of raggedy old blue jeans,</u> one of which manages to fit your present body without sawing it in half or causing you to burp up your breakfast the first time you bend over and which you can also wear other places, like downtown, hoping that nobody will notice how fat you've gotten over the winter. Protects

from Thorn and Berry Bush Gorp, if not nasty remarks made by your supposed friends.

6. <u>Cheap cotton gripper bumpie gardening gloves</u> purchased in quantity from your local hardware store. Protects against all the Dirt Gorp your mother ever warned you about, but just to be on the safe side, you should do what she said and scrub your hands for fifteen minutes before digging peanut butter out of the jar with your fingers! After all, you can't be too careful about Garden Gorp these days.

Fashionably speaking!

CHAPTER ELEVEN

The Gizmos

OF COURSE YOU WILL DISCOVER Gizmos the moment you begin your gardening career. Gizmos and gadgets pervade the catalogs, and they are the single most addictive substance the modern world has ever known. That appears in catalogs, that is.

Face it. Deep down in the bottom of your secret heart, you have always been searching for the Ultimate Gizmo. What it is, exactly, that such a gadget might *do* for you in real life is not only beside the point but a very irritating question, the sort of nonsense that computer programmers have to put up with from ROM-Impaired civilians whose defective genetic makeup causes them to think that they are happy with manual typewriters and handwritten correspondence and books typeset on actual paper. The Thing of Your Dreams, after all, answers a need that you had not even imagined was there until you looked at Its glossy four-color picture and read the amazing description of Its function! O Catalog Writers! Who are Thee? That all thy Swains commend, not to mention procure from, Thy Department?

Anyway, the already Gardening Mad need some sort of guide to Gizmoland, so here is a brief one. I would go into more detail, but I have to put the electronically-controlled complete with underground Ooze Hose and Seedling Spray Mist Dispenser garden sprinkler system together this afternoon before it rains!

Garden Gadgets and Gizmos come in three distinct categories: Incredible, Gettable, and Arrestable. By the truly Gardening Mad, in this last case. By any Mad Gardener on your gift list, in the middle case. By any parameters of good sense, in the first; but do we pay attention to this sensible caution? Just ask the friendly folks at MasterCard about this one—they know where their interest rates are buttered, don't they? And so do you!

Incredible

Typically offered by catalog companies in late spring, after the season for torturing gardeners with a vast array of plants and seeds that you also can't afford has passed. Here are some examples taken from the pages of current catalogs. And I swear on the Great Bosom of Gaia that I am not making a one of these up.

Before you read this, however, I must warn you: like the Tree of the Fruit of Knowledge, once you read this—even though it is meant to help—you will no longer be able to live without any of this stuff.

1. Reusable storage tops for canning jars. Okay, these seem fairly sensible to me (of course). You buy these so that instead of dumping the leftover homegrown beans into a Tupperware bowl to turn into fluorescent botulism spores in the refrigerator, you can achieve the same effect right in the canning jars you undercooked them in! Tops are pretty colors, too. Three for $4.50. Leave them to me in your will before you start the canning.

2. A collapsible wire harvest basket. You certainly don't want to horrify your neighbors and embarrass your children by using a cardboard box! Holds twenty pounds of vegetables, thereby turning the ones on the bottom to instant juice. $24.95. Put the carrots and cabbage in first, like I didn't, you nincompoop.

3. A cutesy little sign that says "Cat Crossing." I don't know about your cats, but mine have marked their garden crossings quite well all by themselves. Perhaps this $5.50 sign is meant as a warning.

4. Weird plastic funny-face vegetable molds. You place these around emerging zucchinis, pumpkins, or cucumbers so you'll end up with, quote, "the most talked-about vegetables in your neighborhood"— if your neighborhood enjoys discussing squash that resemble screaming

drooling ax murderers, that is. $19.95 for a set of three. And $175 per hour for sleep disorder therapy.

5. <u>Patio pyramid planters</u>. You fill this redwood-slat thingie on wheels with four and a half cubic feet of dirt, jam plants in the slots, and water from the top to create a "perfect focal point" on your patio or—this is what it says—in your living room. A swell idea, though the pyramid looks too much like a cat-scratch post and I'll bet that the "focal point" you end up with is a big puddle—either from your cat or from watering by other means. And wouldn't a four-and-a-half-cubic-foot bag of dirt weigh about a hundred and twenty-five pounds? Dry? Just wondering. $89.99. You supply $135 for potting soil and $2,962 in new carpeting.

6. <u>A compost pile thermostat</u>. I confess, I almost bought one of these things, though I managed to come to my senses and decide that for $18.95, this gadget could be supplanted by (1) sticking your hand inside the compost heap to see if it's warm, or (2) forgetting the whole compost-temperature flap by assuming it will all cook down sometime before the next Ice Age anyway. I mean, if green hay bales can make a barn explode, your fresh lawn clippings must be worth at least a small meltdown.

7. <u>Black plastic composting bin</u>. Related to #4, at about $100. I wanted one of these for a long time and then got over it, sort of like an unrequited love affair, only cheaper. And I was going to make further metaphoric comments here about rendering one's leftovers, but I guess I'll quit while I'm ahead. Anyway, these gadgets are supposed to speed up the composting process and they do look neat as a pin, but your messy backyard heap is free, isn't it? Still, my ordering fingers itch whenever I see photos of these bins in the catalogs.

8. <u>Composting yard ball</u>. As children, the inventors of this contraption spent many happy days stuffing live rodents into see-through plastic "hamster rollers" and laughing hysterically while the creatures propelled themselves across the room and down the stairs, bonk bonk bonk! This twenty-cubic-foot grownup version supposedly cooks your leaves and grass clippings with only a few daily rolls around the lawn. With the Yard Ball, I mean. Catalog copy says that it can be "put together in less than three hours with simple tools." Does three hours in the hot sun assembling ten thousand identical parts of a big circle using "simple tools"

sound like a happy summer Sunday to you? Experiments with household pets and obnoxious little brothers seem fairly implicit here, so maybe it should come with a padlock. Also, my yard pitches downhill toward a pond and altogether I can see all sorts of hilarious disasters in the making with this gadget. $189 plus increased homeowner's insurance premiums.

9. <u>Poopets</u>. Honest, that's what they're called. Bunnies, toads, "skat cats" and "turdles" made out of one hundred percent cow manure. Created by Amish craftsfolk with a little too much time on their hands, what with the invention of such modern labor-saving conveniences as the Composting Yard Ball. When they're really feeling creative, they add beans for eyes (on the Poopets) and a cottage cheese whitewash for "a bit of color." The description says, "Poopets will last indefinitely if kept indoors." But then there's all that cottage cheese. Prices range from $3 to $12, depending on factors too lurid to mention here.

10. <u>Blowtorch weed destroyer</u>. Everything you ever wanted to get for Christmas when you were a kid and had to make do with a magnifying glass on the living room carpet! The copy for this Gizmo says, "One blast and weeds disappear for good!" Sounds great, unless you are the parents of Robert Oppenheimer, wondering where you went wrong. $64.95 plus recommended automatic fire department call-in alarm.

11. <u>Cracker flinger</u>. According to the description, this thing "throws Ritz Crackers 150ft. in the air for seagulls or your dog." What I want to know is, how did your dog get up there in the sky with the seagulls? And how did a Cracker Flinger end up in a respectable garden supply catalog? Do Gizmo manufacturers think that we tillers of the tilth have all gone completely off the deep gadget end, or something? Ah-hahahahahaha! $24.95 plus all the seagull guano you can carry home. Just be sure to stay out from under your dog.

12. <u>Celebrity lawn sprinklers</u>. Imagine gazing out across your burgeoning turf on any quiet summer evening and enjoying the inscrutable pleasure of watching Pope John Paul II water your lawn. Or perhaps you'd rather have Moses do the job. Or Liberace. Or Elvis. Or even, for those avid collectors of contemporary nostalgia, Ronald and Nancy Reagan. You can also have sprinklers custom-made in the image of departed friends, or your pets, or even yourself. No, these sprinkler

people do not perform their duties in an offensive, so to speak, manner—water sprays up from behind them. You should hope this does not give your pets any ideas. Though what idea could be worse than these things to begin with? $55 to $75, plus optional BB gun target attachments.

13. <u>Robo mower</u>. The latest in upscale lawn Gizmos to spring from the overheated brain stems of aging Pac-Man Boomers. You put this computerized, solar-powered frisbee-shaped machine in your yard and off it goes, mowing the highways and byways of your flora and fescue all on its own, day and night, sun and rain, toiling endlessly on your behalf or until it up and runs away with one of the Poopets! Pray they don't bring the children home for a visit. Relentless DOS-compatable manure creatures chomping through the Flavr Savr patch is not an image to be borne by the meek. $2,000 and a plane ticket to anywhere the hell out of here. Fast.

14. <u>Garden wind chimes</u>. The catalog copy for these objects from Hell invariably claims that the constant, never-ending, relentless, incessant, night-and-day, every-little-breeze-induced clanging and banging and clashing and clonging and clacking and ringing and ringing and ringing and clanging and clanging and CLANGING AND CLANGING AND CLANGING AND CLANGING "will create a delightful tone in your garden." Oh, yeah? How about the "delightful tone" that will be "created" by my "twelve-gauge shotgun" as it blows your **&@#***!!!%%^^&&**!!! "garden wind chimes" to eentsy-weentsy "bits?" Don't even ask how much these things are. I'm not going to tell you. Ever.

15. <u>Lawn sandals</u>. Invented by a former golf caddy who figured out a way to get even for all those lousy tips, these Birkenstock wannabes sport inch-long steel spikes that are supposed to aerate your lawn and, not incidentally, kill grubs by skewering them as you trudge around feeling like a homicidal maniac, haplessly trying not to step on your own foot. Use of ski poles is recommended. Not to mention a tourniquet. $13.95 a pair, but don't forget to take them off before you rush inside to call for help!

16. "Beaver Chew" furniture. Real, actual pieces of home decorating wrested from the incisors of this, our largest North American rodent. Now your chairs, tables, and lamps can have that rugged outdoors look of pointy, gnawed-off tree stumps that is sure to inspire many fascinating conversations around the fire. That is, the fire you will hastily make of your furniture when a pack of pissed-off beavers comes knocking at your door! $69.95 a Chew. But who wants to incur the wrath of a sixty-five pound aquatic woodchuck with teeth the size and PSI capacity of jackhammers? Not me. You might better decorate your house with old car tires and be safe.

17. Electric "Woodzig" chain saw on a stick. The ad for this Gizmo of death describes "Woodzig" as a "hand pruner," which is certainly a forthright piece of catalog honesty, for once. The miniature chain saw sits on top of that famous ten-foot pole, which I, at least, would not touch with one of itself on a bet. $139.95 and includes a free initial consultation with the orthopedic surgeon of your choice.

18. A garden Scoot-n-Doo. This is a little green wagon made out of "rugged plastic" that you are supposed to sit on and scootch around from garden bed to garden bed, thereby saving yourself the trouble of walking on all that bumpy, uneven ground that goes sharply downhill on the side of your house right next to the four-lane highway ... oops! There you go! $59.95, if we ever see you again, that is.

19. Bridges for the Birds of Madison County. Really, that's what a brass plaque on the side of this bird feeder says. For sheer egregious salespitch allusion, this Gizmo takes the Mad Gardening-catalog cake. Suet cake, that is. How about a Feeder for the Pigeons of Popular Hokum? At $39.95, who would notice? Also available with a steel pole, possibly for affixing miniature chain saw squirrel pruners. But if this thing climbs to the top of the Gizmo Best-Seller List, I'll eat it (the feeder) myself.

20. A mailbox and flower planter combo. Your mailman will love this gadget! But then, at $48.50, perhaps it can be rigged to time-release acid rain all over junk mail, utility bills, IRS notices, and Gizmo catalogs before it's too late.

Now, that would be entirely worth it!

Gettable

Naturally, we must not forget what happens in the world of Gizmos when Christmas slouches its way toward Productland. Even gardeners are caught up in the merry web of guilt and money, as witnessed by anyone who cares to make a trip to the area mall in Yourtown, USA, and peruse the offerings therein to see what gifts might best fit the stockings of your favorite Gardening Maddite. Such items include:

1. <u>Garden books</u>. Fine as far as it goes. The problem here is that approximately ten million to the tenth power gardening books are released annually to the Christmas buying marketplace. Very few of these volumes, with the obvious exception of this one, are of much practical use, and unless you are almost as well acquainted with your Mad Gardener's garden as your Mad Gardener is, you will not find the useful one, believe me. You might better pick up a gardening *calendar,* specific for your Zone, with hints and reminders and pretty pictures year-round. Garden diaries are nice, too. And then there are *Garden Substitutes,* which are painfully necessary by December 25 because there's a lot of winter out there ahead of us, and every gardener in the world would love an indoor blossoming *something* to tend to. Flowering house plants, seed-starter kits, forced-bulb collections, windowsill herbs and mini-gardens, indoor grow lights, garden magazine subscriptions, and so on are all good Getting Gizmos. And that's about it in this category. Too often, however, Getting disintegrates into this:

2. <u>Shopping mall store garden tools</u>. The Gizmo category in which the weary Giver can most easily run amok. By the time you have shoved your way down the discount aisles to the "outdoor" section, you will be ready to use the standard-offering three-toed claw-weeder on all the whining adults and sweating children in the place. And then you will see that no one on the management level of any shopping mall store anywhere has gone outdoors since his or her grandpappy was just a tad. And just a tad *what* is open to some speculation, too. Interminable offerings of overpriced bamboo rakes, knee-high wire fencing superbly crafted for keeping marauding land tortoises out of the shrubbery, bags of sanitized (thus removing the manure) manure, and the

omnipresent plastic pink flamingo whirligig can certainly boggle the Mad Shopper's mind clear through Easter, can they not?

Though that is not the worst of it. The worst of it is:

3. <u>Garden software</u>. To qualify for their jobs, computer programmers must prove that during the previous calendar year they have visited physical reality at least once in every month that has an "R" in it. They are then allowed to spend all of their time in vast, rubberized rooms thinking up incomprehensible electro-megabytetronic replacements for the pencil, and why each of these is necessary for survival in modern life. Having accomplished this, programmers swim back upstream to important public-service positions in Department of Motor Vehicles offices everywhere.

If you are even thinking about buying garden software for someone on your Christmas list, yourself included, my advice is, forget it. Or if you don't believe me, just ask any of the helpful clerks in the Expensive Electronic Thing section of certain Large, Roebuck department stores that inhabit all shopping malls everywhere. Most of these clerks do not speak English, and by that I don't mean that they speak any other Earthly language, either.

YOU: Pardon me, is this gardening software compatible with my home computer?

CLERK: You have IBM 586 SVGA-GPD XXY-99.98 Ram-Rom 3475.99 Zero 85-97 Qvwak?

YOU: I haven't the slightest idea.

CLERK: No problem. Perfectly compatible.

YOU: Really?

CLERK: Of course. Let have Master or Visa card now please.

YOU: Uh—okay. By the way, what time is it?

CLERK: One hundred fifty-six to eleventy.

YOU: Thank you.

CLERK: You're wel(click) wel(click) wel(click) wel(click) wel(click click clickclickclickclickkkkEEEEEEEEEEEEEEEr-rrrrrrrrrrrrrggggaaaaaaahhhhhhhhhhhhhkkkkk (clerk crashes to floor, breaks into basic component parts).

One of those stickum-*landscaping/garden-arranging graph-charts,* at about $15, is the only recourse.

Or how about giving the ultimate gadget of a gift certificate for a few hours of garden help? Assuming that you follow through on this. Oh, yes, I can read your mind! I'm no dummy! You see, I gave *myself* a couple of these certificates last year. I thought it was a pretty clever idea until I called myself up on the phone and yelled at me for not showing up. Sheesh!

Arrestable

It is time to speak frankly of something that is so quintessentially American—so illustrative of the grand sweep of the vox populi across this great land of ours—that one is almost at a loss for how to find the right words to describe it, let alone keep down any of the five major food groups!

No, I am not speaking (here, anyway) of running into someone you know in the "adults only" room at the video store, or of accidentally blowing your nose down your face in the middle of a conversation, or of any other homey little consequence of daring to be alive! No, I am speaking here of an affliction upon the gardening psyche that must be corrected now, before it overtakes the world like an apocalyptian scourge of DNA-enhanced groundhogs.

I am speaking of Garden Statues.

I don't know exactly where the Garden Statue Craze began, but I suspect the ancient Greeks, who are responsible for everything we have today except swear words and forks. But do not waste your concern worrying about large armless marble nymphs whose garments have fallen in graceful folds around their six-hundred-pound thighs. You don't see too many of these set up in the marigold beds of America, anyway. What you do see are the items offered for sale in thingamajig catalogs and/or constructed out of Items You Can Find Lying Around The House. And so, before it's too late for Mad Gardeners everywhere, I am offering here the definitive list of Unpermitted Gizmo Use Ordinances for G-1 Garden Zones.

And if you don't believe me, call up your local zoning officer. He won't believe me either. To wit:

Not Okay Garden Statues

1. Anything made to look like the hind end of a bent-over living creature, including cows and pigs, but especially female human persons with quaint polka-dot underwear and/or several-sizes-too-small shorts, bikini bottoms, or lack thereof. Penalties shall be inflicted by female volunteers armed with rocks. Statues depicting bent-over male human persons whose pants have slipped down to expose wooden love handles and that portion of the anatomy known by four out of five doctors as the "ass crack" shall require immediate execution of both homeowner and model by firing squad selected from the local Zoning Board of Appeals.

2. Any plastic cartoon animal decorated with primary colors or wearing clothes of any type but especially red plaid skirts and hair ribbons. Such figures shall be forcibly recycled into Nerf basketballs, along with the homeowner if it is a second offense. Fake-fur yard sheep, cows, pigs, moose, and the like can remain in place only if accompanied by genuine yard pooh, which shall be replenished daily by the Homeowner and subject to inspection by the Zoning Officer without prior notice.

3. Any plastic troll from any catalog whatsoever, but especially those dressed in alleged "brightly colored ethnic outfits from European mythology" and bearing such gnomes-de-plume as "Ralph the Raker" and "Louie the Lumberjack." Penalties shall include a replication process by which the homeowner shall likewise be "filled with sand for added stability," though it is doubtful that such remedies will augment the human party in question.

4. All deities, or ancestors of same, standing in upright bathtubs that have been painted blue.

5. All other household appliances or representatives of bathroom plumbing, or parts thereof.

6. Any figure, human or animal, from which water is made to spout from any orifice. Penalties are not limited to forcing the Homeowner to duplicate the procedure in public.

7. Anything sporting an incorrect apostrophe, as in "The Pinhead's live here."

8. Large bilious mirror-surfaced bulbs on stands that make your reflection look like something out of "A Nightmare on Elm Street: The Meltdown."

OKAY GARDEN STATUES

1. Sundials.

2. Any of those cast iron things from your mother's attic that turn green two days after you put them out in the dirt and which almost always look like the White Rock Fairy and which once belonged to your Victorian grandmother.

3. Anything else I have in my own garden! So there!

And that's the Mad word on Gizmos!

Addendum

Yes Garden Gifts

Redwood planters
for the patio.

Fragrant rosebushes,
any color .

Six-packs of cotton
garden gloves.

Birdseed scoops

Any nice garden tool.

Terrycloth velcro-clasp
sun visor caps.

In season, any 6- or 8-
pack of bedding
plants from local nursery.

Gift certificates for lawn
mower repairs and/or
towing away of same to
local junkyard.

No Garden Gifts

Any piece of toilet
architecture.

Chia pets, especially
groups of same arranged
around Chia trees as if
to Chia pee.

Six packs of "lite" beer,
unless one is truly desperate.

Huge wooden bird feeders
made to resemble
300-lb chickadees with
see-through plastic bubble
stomachs full of seed.

"Miniature" tools for
children. Why do you
think Mad Gardeners
buy electric fences?

Any hat with freeze-
dried rattlesnakes, or any
other animals or portions
thereof including horns and/or
snout, that hang down over
face in waggish glee.

In season, any animal with
useless poop, such as Siamese
cats and Airedales.

Any gasoline-powered device
whatsoever with possible
exception of yacht enroute to
the Bahamas.

CHAPTER TWELVE
The Weather

ONCE OUTDOORS, you will run into the Weather right away. It has been waiting for you.

The Weather and Her Daughters, the Elements, manage the climate. They determine if your tomatoes are going to taste meaty and delicious or like wads of used tea bags or if, after a season of weeding and hoeing yourself into a froth, you are going to have any tomatoes at all. If they are especially bored or irritated, the Elements might even decide to turn your house into a pile of mutilated jackstraws with an Amtrak caboose slammed down on it. Given this fact, you'd think that humans would have a little more respect for the Elements than we do. Building wooden structures on sticks along the same shoreline where Sister Hurricane so often travels might seem a bit foolhardy to your average woodpecker, for example, but shucks! Whose beachfront is this, anyway? Besides, unlike birds, humans have insurance. It draws on that infinite money aquifer located deep in the shale underneath Billings, Montana. Given that resource, we can do anything we want.

Knowing this, the Weather waits. It is patient. It has all the time in the world. It, too, can do anything it wants. But it is much, much bigger than you are. And there is nothing you can do to change its mind about anything.

Doesn't that just tee you right off?

Understanding and Predicting

Luckily for Mad Gardeners everywhere, human nature would not put up with cringing before a bunch of Weather for very long, so we decided to develop ways of understanding and predicting the Elements for our personal benefit and safety, sort of like flu shot roulette, only funnier. And almost before you could come in out of the rain, humans had invented all sorts of gizmos designed to sort out information thrown at us daily by the Elements and bring it all down to a reliable network of scientific head-scratching and shoulder-shrugging unparalleled since the Dawn of Time! Meanwhile, out in the grassroots, folklore methods of observing and understanding the language of the Elements were being passed down through the generations along with holistic burning-castorbean cures for spastic colon and other ancient scourges. Through it all, the Weather just about ruptured itself laughing. Then we had a typhoon.

What it all boils down to for the home gardener, who is, after all, only trying to grow flowers and vegetables without incident, is this: There are three ways of trying to predict the Weather. You can look at Television, you can look at *The Farmer's Almanac,* or you can look at Nature. That's it. The only other course is to take pleasure in whatever the Weather hands out every day, as if your life were just a simple matter of living it, or something.

The Elements

Recognizing the Elements is essential if you are trying to predict gardening weather with any hope of getting it right once in a while. They are:

1. <u>Rain/Not Rain.</u> The Elements upon which most everything else pivots, including crop irrigation, which is, after all, just a way of trucking Rain/Not Rain from one place to another. More often than you'd like, this pair invites its radical cousins, Torrential Downpour and Searing Drought, to come set a spell. What this means is that the majority of your gardening days will be spent invoking the spirits of

these Elements with incantations based on key body-part functions used as colorful adjectives and adverbs. Good luck! And you can wash out your mouth with soap and Rain.

2. Too Hot/Too Cold. Can combine with variations of Rain/Not Rain to create the most miserable growing season you ever didn't get vegetables from in your entire life. The Element of moderation here, Just Warm Enough, only comes around in mid-June while the Toos have gone on vacation.

3. Sunshine/Cloud Cover. A result of all of the above, plus numerous other random factors such as smokestack emissions, faraway volcanic explosions, and overall Climacteric mood swings. And you know what? You can just like it or lump it! Because Gaia said so! Ha!

4. First Frost/Last Frost. Capricious and thoroughly undisciplined Elements that flit in and out at will, even though they have been given an official curfew and quite a lot of verbal abuse throughout their formative years. And you should know!

5. Big Wind/No Wind. Can include the Furies of Hurricane and Tornado, though a Wind that's just Big enough to blow the Reemay cloth away is plenty annoying, isn't it? However, Modest Sister Breezes does tend to be the norm, unless you live in the flyways of Catastrophic Events, such as Tornado Alley, or the middle of the Atlantic Ocean, or wherever. In which case, you have been gardening down cellar for some time now and according to your keepers no longer need this guidelist.

6. Freak Storm. A dreaded Element that can scream in anywhere across the land roaring with thunder and hailstones and bolts of lightning and buckets of water, ripping up trees and anything else it feels like, and generally indulging in all sorts of detestable behavior that can wreck your garden in a matter of minutes! Not to mention the entire downtown section of Muncie, Indiana, but who cares? As a gardener, you know which is more important, don't you?

7. Snow/Ice. Theoretically confined to predictable areas of the planet, but can spread outward without any shame whatsoever, and have been known to turn even the most acclimated human being into a hair-tearing howling gurgling slobbering moaning weeping drooling pleading puddle of snot after only a few months of steady accumulation and drifting.

8. <u>Perfect Days.</u> Mythological Element existing primarily in your childhood and selected areas of Somewhere Other Than Where You Live. Might make a brief appearance in the early evening hours of your next love affair. Other than that, you'll have to read the works of a lot of dead poets to find out more about this one.

No matter, for gardening can make a Perfect Days purse out of just about any Sow's Ear Element of the Weather. You Mad folks out there know what I mean by this! So all that's left is to figure out how best to predict when a Sow is on its way. As I said before, there are three prediction means available, two of them vaguely of human origin.

Television Weatherfolk

In an effort to attain the cultural status currently reserved for prominent sports figures and dysfunctional cartoon characters, Television Weatherfolk have made impressive strides toward elevating their two-minute Weathernews spot into life or death drama. Of course it helps if you live in an area of this great land of ours that has Weather to begin with. Some places, such as Arizona, haven't had any Weather since that time a cloud passed over Bisbee on November 17, 1973, causing severe head injuries to dozens of Weatherfolk who stampeded to the windows for a look-see.

But in places where the Elements enjoy their special spontaneous blend of pleasure and havoc, Weatherfolk toil long hours to bring you accurate, up-to-the-hour prediction information so that you can struggle up out of your TV chair and get those flowers and vegetables covered before Freak Storm arrives! And if Freak Storm decides at the last minute to go somewhere else instead, well, you needed that shot of adrenaline anyway, didn't you?

To this end, Weatherfolk prediction relies heavily on such technical resources as ships at sea, airplanes in flight, orbiting satellites, Doppler radar, computer networks, humidity indexes, rain gauges, thermometers, ceilometers, gagometers, party balloons, telescreeps, radio grommets, little twirly things that spin around in the sun and play Broadway show tunes until you want to smash them, and Bernie down in Accounting with the trick knee, to name a few. As you can imagine, incredible amounts of data pour out of each and every one of these devices every minute of every day, and so to snipe and carp at your poor overstimulated Television Weatherfolk person, who routinely experiences multiple orgasms about things that really don't even exist, such as barometric pressure readings, is to miss the point of TV weather predicting altogether!

You see, the point of TV weather predicting has nothing to do with the Weather. It has to do with protecting your state of mind from itself. After all, who pays television news producer salaries? A happy-weather person buying enormous sheet pizzas, fast-food hamburgers, new cars, and tooth-wrecking soft drinks by the gallon, or some crummy-weather curmudgeon paying no attention whatsoever to the virtues of consumerism? Knowing this, you can easily see that TV weather predicting should be as optimistic as possible no matter what is going on outdoors! As in the following TV Weather Forecasting Code Debunking Chart, which was smuggled out of the National TV Weather Information Room at great personal cost:

What they Say	*What they Mean*
Partly Cloudy	Miserable
Partly Sunny	Abominable
Chance of rain	Dreadful
Chance of snow	Horrible
Temperatures near freezing	So cold you will want to die
Great weekend for skiers	A blizzard disaster of mind-boggling proportions

A weather event is on the way

So much snow, ice, sleet, freezing rain, below-zero temperatures, and serious power outages that we Weatherfolk are just about hemorrhaging with excitement. Aren't you?

We will study and learn from that last weather pattern.

We will confer with Mr. Ed

Moderate winds out of the South

Hurricane

Gusty winds out of the West

Tornado

Normal high for the season

Hotter than the fires of Hell.

Sunshine with an afternoon shower

So hot and humid that you would glady seek relief by jumping into the fires of Hell, if you could only unstick your thighs from the car seat.

A thunderstorm watch has been declared for your area.

You are all going to die. After which you will end up in the fires of Hell.

Partly cloudy with a ten percent chance of rain in the morning, clearing off by noon, then sunshine with puffy white clouds, low humidity, blue skies, temperatures in the mid to high seventies, with a reason for living at last.

A crowd wielding baseball bats and garden rakes has gathered outside the Weatherfolk studio. Actually, it is going to be miserable.

A sunny, gorgeous weekend such as winter dreams are made of.

You are sick with the flu.

So keep a close eye on your TV Weatherfolk. Hear those headlines with a jaundiced and watery ear. And remember that there's a conspiracy afoot in the air, and it is right in front of your face. Forewarned is foreweathered! And watch the skies for further developments.

The Farmer's Almanac

The quintessential quintessence of wise old-timer Weather predicting and homily. Founded in 1792 by a fellow named Robert B. Thomas who claimed to possess an indefatigable forecasting formula, the Almanac offers moon charts, sun charts, star charts, tide charts, gestation charts, fishing charts, frost dates, nail and lumber guides, planting guides, recipes, Zodiac secrets, fables and puzzles, tables of measures, motor vehicle laws, gardening advice, ads for everything from choir robes and the Rosicrucians to rototillers, and, not incidentally, Weather summaries and day-to-day predictions for every region in the country, all carefully and reasonably explained by catchy little sayings and parables meant to mean just about anything you like.

FIRST OLD-TIME ALMANAC EDITOR: Say, Edgah, how's abaht fer spring we say "Oak come out befoah the ash, you'll have a summah of wet and splash."

SECOND OLD-TIME ALMANAC EDITOR: Eh? What in Hell-n-gone does that mean?

FIRST OLD-TIME ALMANAC EDITOR: Danged if I know.

THIRD OLD-TIME ALMANAC EDITOR: So how's abaht we say, "Whan that Aprille with his shoures soote/The droghte of March hath perced to the roote, /And bathed every veyne in switch licour/Of which vertu... "

FIRST OLD-TIME ALMANAC EDITOR: Eh? *What* in Jeehoso-fattin' crackah-jackin' dialect-in' hoahneytoahdin' gobbeldy-gookin' Glori-oskie ah yew *talkin'* abaht? What in Hell-n-gone's a "veyne?"

THIRD OLD-TIME ALMANAC EDITOR: Danged if I know.

SECOND OLD-TIME ALMANAC EDITOR: Cripesley crow! Cayn'cha jest speak *Ing*lish?

CHAUCER: You idiots! That *is* English!
EDITORS (ALL TOGETHAH): Right! Har! Har! deeHar!

Possibly you should look at *The Farmer's Almanac* with discretion. Or at least with caution. Such a glut of old-time wisdom might prove a distraction from the real issue of the Elements and their effect on your personal switch licour, after all.

Looking at Nature

Thus, the Mad Gardener is essentially left with Nature. Isn't that always the way?

You look. You listen. You feel the air, sniff the breeze, observe the birds. You see that the clouds are doing this-and-that. You perceive that the clouds, and the air and the breezes and the birds, are pretty smart about what's going to happen across the next couple of days. As for the seasons, you might check out the moss of a tree, the down on a duck, the woolly on a bear. And then you might go out and mulch your gardens a-plenty and give then tilth and firth and even a pat or two on the roote.

The Weather is. The Elements are. Your garden will be.

And that's just about all that's predictable!

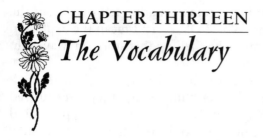

CHAPTER THIRTEEN
The Vocabulary

With the madness biting daily at your heels, not to mention various other of your parts, you will soon discover that vocabulary plays an important role in this beloved pastime of dirt and veggies, the first of which is to point out sharply, perhaps with a rap across your filthy knuckles, that we do not use such lowlife words as "dirt" and "veggies." Not nohow! Such terms are to be spat upon, unless your mother is watching. No, a quick flip through any garden text or catalog worth its *sale conditio* will amply display that there is only one set of words in official Gardendom for anything, and that is, as you former students of parochial schools have already guessed and have thus fled screaming out the door, Latin, otherwise known as "incomprehensible and generally snobby foreign-type names for plants and flowers" by the rest of us.

Well, my *osseus capiti* friends, I see that I am going to have to do a little educating here on how horticulturean words got to be the way they are, and why you can't even wade through directions on a ninety-eight-cent seed packet without falling over large, boring doses of Latin. Are you ready? Gather 'round the fire, children, 'cause here goes.

The Official Garden Vocabulary

Once upon a time when the years ran backward, just after the invention of numerous surly deities and deitiesses, the Latins came along and founded Rome, using pieces of marble left over from the explosion of Mt. Saint Helens. What? Oh, sorry. I mean the explosion of Mt. Saint Pisa. What? Listen, who's telling this story, anyway? Oh, yeah? Well, same to you, too, fella!

Anyway, so the Latins had Rome all ready to go, with flush toilets and torture chambers and everything, when they remembered that they didn't have a language yet. Now, you have to keep in mind that there was a lot of competition for words back then, seeing as how there weren't as many objects in the world, though there were quite a few more animals and insects to take up the slack. But there are only so many words you can pin on an animal before it gets mad and runs away, not to mention the killer bees and how they reacted to all of this kaffuful.

Worse, the Anglos and the Saxons up north had already cornered the market on body-function expletives, and the Greeks were busy applying for patents on Astrology and Math. So the Latins scratched their heads, looked under their fingernails, and hit on a solution. They decided to create a language where none of the words bore any relationship to anything at all!

The diabolicalatiousness of this idea was instantly manifold. Take, for example, the common household radish. Now if I had my way, I'd take the radish and place it in a spaceship headed for Mars, but the Latins didn't have any spaceships, so they were stuck with calling this disgusting little ick-root *something* or other. So what they did was decide to call it a "Raphanus sativus," which makes no sense whatsoever. Even the Greeks couldn't figure it out. You could have shipped an entire wooden horse full of "Raphanus sativus" grenades right over to Athens and nobody would have known what they were. The military advantages of this whole idea simply boggle the mind.

But the Latins didn't stop there, no siree! The next thing you knew, they'd put "Callistephus chinensis" on the innocent aster, "Canis dufus" on the ordinary everyday dog, "deus ex machina" on the simple four-wheel drive Chevrolet, and whatever else came into their minds while hauling elephants across the wilds of Switzerland and building overhead irrigation systems out of "squashi slavea gigantus" stone. And then the Latins really went nuts, and started making up words like "data" and "stimuli" and "media," which are all "are" words even though they look like they should be "is"; and the next thing you knew, there were "rhinoceri" and "formulae" and "petuniae" and "staphylococci" coming out of their ears, noses, and throats until the whole mess came to a screeching halt and a meteor crashed into Arizona and killed all the Latins dead and the mammals took over the world.

On the other hand, maybe those words came from the Greeks, and the Latins swiped them without giving a moment's credit. After all, the Latins had already swiped the Greek gods and changed all their names, thinking no one would notice! And in fact, no one did, except for Zeus, who set Pompeii on fire in retaliation for being renamed after a big, fat planet with a methane gas problem and spots all over itself. Wouldn't you?

And so today, we have Science and Technology and the conjugation of verbs behind our backs and completely unreadable textbooks besides. And if you had any pride at all you would learn how to read catalog discourse in the way it was intended, which is to say, to make you imagine how incredibly intelligent you are for ordering all of those plants and seeds with John Hancocks that no one else in modern America can decipher or pronounce, sort of like Mr. Spock's last name. So you can see the fate of Latin and for that matter vocabulary in general, can you not? Which leads me to topic of:

The Euphemistic Vocabulary

The word "euphemistic" comes from the ancient Greek myth of Allerdyce and Euphamistie, two lovers who were turned into trees by Hyperdactyl after Nestor, God of Filthy Places, refused to allow anybody into his bar who couldn't cough up a legitimate I.D. card. Allerdyce was later rescued by Aphrohairdo, who fell in love with him even though he was a sorry-looking old crabapple by then, but Euphamistie was left behind to rot in the swamp and so to assuage their guilt, everyone agreed not to use her real name ever again. Thus you have another annoying habit of speech springing from a misbegotten tale of torture and suffering, which should come as no surprise at all to aficionados of Walt Disney animated "classics."

While the Vocabulary of Gardening Euph will not often creep directly into your personal affairs—or at least not as often as the creeps do—there may be times, such as while speaking with experts or academic scholars, when you will have to translate Euph subtitles into something approximating English, as in the following examples:

Euphemism	*Real Meaning*
Mechanistic depilitorization	Lawn mowing
Manual xography	Hoeing
Entomological fustication	Bug bites
Exoskeletal tintinnabulation	You stepped on a roach
Plaintive podial topography	You dropped a rock on your foot
Egregious implementive angst	You can't start the mower
Adaptationistic xeroscaping	You forgot to water the garden and it died
Flagrant florabundicism	Flowers planted *every* goshdarn where
Anthropomorphicological pandemonaturalizationry	The premise of this book
Applicable eleeomosynatious acquistionary rapaciousness	You are buying this book by the millions

Which brings us, and not a whit soon enough for the preservation of genteel expositional criteria, back to the unpretentious proposition of:

Your Gardening Vocabulary

Your own gardening vocabulary is more than likely the simple product of the sod—dirty words, in other words. Or direct words, in a word. For Out There in the Mulch, we Mad Gardeners can call a spade a "fat oversized fork with a handle that is too @$#@!*&*&!!! short" and not bat an eyelash with the best of them. And compost shalt *not* melt in our mouths.

Therefore, more as a warning than as instruction, here is the type of vocabulary that the Mad Gardener will develop over Time and Tine. If there are any children in the same room with you, perhaps you should send them to the local arcade until you are safely past this chapter. You never know how a word might affect a young mind! Why, just a glimpse at the printed page has been known to turn well-mannered adolescents into repulsive snotheads who go on to wreck their elders' lives and not a few of their elders' cars. I know I did. Meanwhile, gardeners are out in the cabbage patch talking like this:

1. WHAT THE &^%$!! ARE ALL THESE @&^^%$#@!^%!!(*&* LITTLE^%$$#@*!! GREEN WORMS? Referential allusion to the caterpillars of those ^%$%^$##@!* little white %$#$#%!! butterflies that flitted so prettily about the brassicae just a few short #@!#$&*(*!!! weeks ago.

2. HEY!! WHAT THE &%#@^%$%$#!!*&^**!%$** !#@!^%^%$@@@^%$^%)***&^%^#$#@!**!! IS THIS??? Richly descriptive enchantment used to express one's thoughts after glovelessly grabbing a handful of compost and discovering that it was quite recently visited by the neighbor's cat.

3. HEY!!!!! THIS **^%&$%^$##@*&^%!! SUPPOSEDLY HARMLESS**&^%&^%$%$#@%$^%@!! INSECTICIDAL SOAP JUST **&^*^%%$^#!%$@@!!KILLED EVERY **&^%%^$#$#@!! PLANT IN MY **&^%$%^$#(&^%!!GARDEN!!! A phrase commonly spoken by the unfortunate purchasers of Ortho Insecti**&&^%%$#@!!cidal Soap a few years ago.

Often repeated at garden Tool throwing contests to create the appropriate atmosphere of retribution.

4. THOSE #@!%$#&^%*&^&^!! ^%$#@#@!&^#*!! RACCOONS ARE GONNA#@!^%!! DIE. A common nomenclature affixed to a classification of animals that are so incredibly @**&^%^%$!!*&^!! clever at figuring out how to get into your garden and chomp EVERY SINGLE &^%%$#@!&^^%$!!*&*&^!! VEGETABLE IN THE WHOLE @*^%*!!&^%&^%$%$#@@!##@!! PLACE that you will quickly grasp with alacrity upon your shot**!!^&**%$@!!gun and blastHELLO THERE, MY NAME IS STEPHEN KING. I am inserting myself into this chapter to bring you some indispensable vocabulary advice.

You poor outdoors-besotted garden-dinks might not realize that I used to be a righteously dull English teacher until the day my wife brought home a four-color glossy flower catalog. It was a Wayside Gardens, Spring '75, I remember, and the minute I opened it to the nightshades, I was hooked. I just grabbed a pen and started ordering and ordering and ordering completely at random, and before I knew it I'd gone through our life savings and I had to start cranking out huge vocabulary-packed best-selling novels to pay for it all. But my craving for catalogs got so bad that I was finally forced to bump off my own pen name for a lousy six million advance plus seventy-five percent royalties and perpetual movie self-insertion rights. So let this be a lesson for all of you hokey eco-junkies who think it doesn't pay to have lots and lots of big fat vocab … HEY! WHAT THE **&^%%$##@!*&^!! ARE YOU DOING WITH THAT **%$#$!!*&^%!!! DELETE BUTTON! I'M NOT FINISHED WITH THIS IMPORTANT **&^%$#@(*&^&!! VOCABULARY MES

There! Now, what was I talking about? Oh, yes, your Garden Vocabulary.

It all boils down to this: Just grab that !*#$#@!@!**%$#@$!! trowel and get out there in the !@!%*&*&^%$#!! dirt while there's still !**&^%$@*&^%$#@!**&*!! time!

What more is there to say?

CHAPTER FOURTEEN
The Literature

*T*here is a flabbergasting amount of Literature out there on every subject imaginable. Moreover, imaginable subjects have been multiplying exponentially for the last fecund decade or two, challenging the boundaries of the human mind and certainly the definition of "Literature" itself! Why, just a quick stroll through any modern bookstore will confirm what you, the Gardening Mad, already suspected: An awful lot of trees are being chopped down to bring you endless volumes of richly incomprehensible computerbabble along with even more fascinating unauthorized biographies detailing how famous people rose from sordid backgrounds to achieve fame and fortune in the world of infomercials. Nevertheless, undaunted, you rush to the gardening section, where, amongst the colorful crush of glossy, hard-covered salespeople, you manage to find this book. The contrast simply strains the limits of modesty beyond endurance.

Of course you know that much of the Literature of gardening also appears in other forms, namely seed catalogs, magazines, and newspaper columns. So how are you, one mere gardener afar from the madding crowd, supposed to wade through all of this wordage when there are rows out there to hoe and everywhere weeds to enwhack?

Well, to protect you from the threat of reading gridlock, I have prepared the following overview of important gardening Literature and its probable effects.

Books

The esthetics of gardening Literature are myriad and great, starting in childhood with such immortal classics as the famous poem by Lewis Carroll that begins:

> 'Twas brillig, and the slithy toves
> Did gyre and gimble in the wabe:
> All mimsy were the borogoves,
> And the mome raths outgrabe.

—and ends:

> 'Twas brillig, and the slithy toves
> Did gyre and gimble in the wabe:
> All mimsy were the borogoves,
> And the mome raths outgrabe.

—a clear reference to invasions of corn weevils, giant sucking aphids, and the notorious *Leptinotarsa decemlineata* Colorado potato beetle maggot flyworm, as any child cowering under the covers should know! Or possibly you began your tender travels through the Land of Books with *The Secret Garden* by Frances Hogshead Blarney, which starts out something like, "She was such an odious little girl that everyone who met her wished to slap her right across her little piggy face," and goes on to describe how this charming moppet is dragged from her secure home in cholera-infested India and taken to a mildew-infested swamp of an English mansion to live with an uncle who hasn't come out of the bathroom in fifty-seven years, a story that every respectable television talk-show host in America would kill to schedule, piggy face and all. Then the little girl is apparently Saved by finding a weed-infested garden behind a door somewhere, but at this point I, at least, tossed *The Secret Garden* out the window and picked up *Tarzan of the Apes,* which is after all set in a *jungle* and has the interesting addition of heaving bosoms and rippling flesh and loincloths, not to mention the most thrilling line in all of children's literature, which is when Tarzan takes a stick and scratches in the mulch this request of his newly-rescued pal Jean-Luc Picard:

Teach me to speak the language of men

—whereupon Jean-Luc proceeds, despite the fact that Tarzan reads English, writes English, and is, in fact, an English Lord, to teach him to *speak French,* thus setting the standard for severe dyslexia and garden catalog ordering headaches from that moment on through time. Then everyone is eaten by cannibals.

After that, books by Gertrude Jekyll and Vita Sackville-West, which recount in splendid detail how their gardens were planned, set out, and weeded daily by the help, are something of an anticlimax, to put it mildly.

Still, if it's enchantment in adult garden Literature you're looking for, you might try such hardy old-timers as Katharine S. White's *Onward and Upward in the Garden,* the premier voice of impassioned catalog commentary; or the truly breathtaking volumes of *The Complete Book of Garden Magic* by Roy Biles, who wrote this and other editions of his classic in those misty pre–World War II days before television and power tools.

Actually, Biles should be read by every garden enthusiast, Mad or sane, for two sharply contrasting reasons. On one hand, no other garden books capture as profoundly the joy, the affection, and the unadorned desire for happiness that grow into, and out of, flowers and vegetables and their accessories. Accompanied by line drawings that are so exquisite in their simplicity that you are almost in pain, looking at them,

Biles show us this Garden of another time as "a place for rest and relaxation; a place to entertain in; a place for children to grow up in; a place to grow plants and experiment," which sums up most anything you could want from life itself, and isn't that the idea? Thus, Biles devotes his book to such things as "A Play Yard for Children," "Garden or Tea Houses," "The Drying Yard," and "Care of Trees," this last neatly showing how to use the ancient, truly beautiful devices of guying and block-and-tackle. In fact, *Garden Magic* generates profound humility and nostalgia for old-fashioned manual labor (what he goes through with a shovel to put in stepstones is beyond belief), and for a time when there *was* time to do all of this, slowly and dreamily, by hand, for the love of it.

The opposite reason to read *Garden Magic* is because it is an absolutely riveting history of casual backyard chemical applications for everything, especially the Great American Perfect Lawn. Biles shows how to make compost and mulch, but his emphasis is on spray-n-kill, complete with drawings of Our Miss Brooks in shirt-waist dress and heels blasting nicotine dust all over the strawber-ries. ("A rubber apron is advised," Biles notes.) The list of potions and sprays goes, as they say, on and on—pages and pages full of charts and graphs and formulas for such chemical pest controls as arsenate of lead or *whale oil* for eliminating bagworms, or plain white arsenic bran mash for killing grasshoppers, which "die slowly after feeding," according to Biles, and believe me, by the time you've gotten this far in the text, you are ready to call the SPCA or the Save the Grasshopper Foundation or Rachel Carson or *somebody*. "You can make [Massey Dust] by mixing nine parts of dusting sul-phur and one part of arsenate of lead," says Biles, evoking images of those gleeful childhood afternoons when you snuck out into the garage and dumped everything you could find into one big jar to see what would happen.* "Tobacco dust may be added to [the above mixture] to control aphids," Biles adds. "It is excellent mixed with peat moss or homemade compost when used as a mulch ... [and] seems to be a more reliable source of nicotine for dusting than the chemical product."

---

* In this Gardener's case, what happened was the creation of a viscous, evil-smelling potion that *instantly* dissolved a few hapless Japanese beetles—fssst!—and left a stain on a slate sidewalk that was still there thirty years later. Maybe I should have applied for a patent.

As in, where did Biles (and the generation of gardeners who read his books) do this research? Wherever it was, I don't want to live there! But where did the birds go who ate the insects who ate these poisons? And who ate the birds? And ...

Worse, or possibly more to the point, in the chapter entitled, "Garden Magic Marches On," Biles states (with unintended accuracy) that the new chemical DDT "is seemingly no more dangerous to most plant growth and to human beings than many other familiar insecticides" and goes on to list another page of compounds that were about to be offered on the market for home application, including, ominously, a product called "666" (hexachlorocyclohexane), and a paragraph or two of speculation on how science would soon create *radioactive pesticides* in the joyous upcoming "Atomic Age of gardening." You read this, and you realize that this "Future" is now our past, and you think, "It's too late already—we're all gonna die!" And you are probably right.

So were the "Experts" in 1935.

It helps to study the excellent encyclopedias and problem-solving compendia of organic gardening methods such as those put out by Rodale Press[1] and others, and to do thereby and cultivate hope for ecological miracles. Beyond that, the world will continue to seethe unabashed with biodegradable Books on every possible aspect of gardening and its innumerable nuances. And you can be assured, Dear Weeder, that this book, at least—yes, the very book that you are at this very moment holding in your very own very little hands—is one of them.

Newspaper Columns

It is a known fact that every newspaper in America is required by the FCC (Federal Crackpot Commission) to run a locally-written gardening column somewhere in its pages, usually in the "Living" section next to the weekly photo feature entitled, "Casing the Joint: A Real Good Look Inside Your Neighbor's House." This is part and parcel of the public service responsibility shared by the media of this great land of yours, so you'd better not let me catch you not appreciating it! Or catch you doing anything else you ought'nto. Kaszundheit!

Master Gardeners and others trained through official horticulturean means are usually the writers of these columns, and their advice can be educational and wise—though remember, so was the "official" advice of Roy Biles's time, a fact not to be forgotten no matter what it is you read.

At any rate, you will not be spared your own experience out there in the aphids no matter how much information you garner beforehand. No one else's advice can substitute. For one thing, few newspaper column readers are wont to garden with the applied, scholarly seriousness of the typically earnest column writer. If you doubt that statement, go visit the gardens of America and tally up the population of twirling plastic windmills, sneering vegetable faces on sticks, rubber bird baths shaped like baseball mitts, wooden woodcutters whacking windward wooden wood, ceramic sewer pipes holding hideous yellowing hemerocalis, concrete donkeys pulling color-coordinated wagon planters, and little signs everywhere telling you to watch out for the Snail Crossing Zone Dead Ahead. And we won't even get into the Poopet People question. After conducting your survey, you may gather at the corner watering hole for CPR and a chance to donate to the Garden Column Writers' Humongous Everlasting Headache Emergency Surgery Fund.

We are wont to thank you for your contribution.

The Catalogs

Now let us take a moment to examine the catalogs closely, with a jaundiced and soot-encrusted eye. That would be the eye of your attorney, who lives in a glass-enclosed metropolitan area and is safely immune to the siren song of four-color glossy photos showing herbs and asters shimmering in the morning dew. Mad Gardeners, on the other hand, believe everything they read in seed catalogs. They cannot help themselves. They are more gullible than children watching Saturday morning TV commercials for magic toys that talk and fly and leave thumbtacks on Teacher's chair and no batteries or wires or pretend in sight! Perhaps your attorney will fax that eye to you now, before it's too late. If it's not too late already, that is.

For one thing, speaking of children, have you noticed that the catalogs always lace their photo pages with smirking toddlers holding onto fruits and vegetables that have a couple of bites taken out of them? Out of the fruits and veggies, that is, though you wonder how they got the little sweethearts to hold still, don't you? Haven't you noticed that the toddlers are never actually biting into the pears and peppers themselves? As in, whose leg are these people trying to pull? Or gnaw? But, looking at these depictions of wholesome goodness, you believe it too, don't you? You believe that by ordering these beautiful fruit trees and super-hybridized vegetable seeds, you will turn your children away from the Gummy Dinos and taco whoopie pies of contemporary times and return us all to the Beaver Cleaver land of your youth. Oh, yes, I know you do. You can't fool me! For I, too, have ordered and planted those fruit trees of Eden; and I have discovered, just as you will, that by the time your peach forest has grown up enough to produce some returns for all your fruitdom labors, your toddler and his grandchildren will have already departed on the Starship *Enterprise* with Tarzan and Captain Picard for a universe of replicated Gummy Klingons and Choco-Data-Puffs galore.

Nonetheless, it's worth a try. Drive to a nearby plant nursery and look over their specimens, first, however. The trees are bigger and have nice root balls packed in burlap, and the nursery folks have specific growing advice for your backyard. And you can call them up later and ask for more help. They'll even talk to your toddler.

Another thing about catalogs—hasn't it occurred to the folks at the super-deluxe glossy-glossy publishing end of, say, Wayside Gardens, that if they put out a catalog that cost less than $755,000 per dozen to produce, they could have some reasonable plant prices in the thing? But somebody out there must be paying $30 and $40 apiece for hosta and $100+ for tree peonies or the catalog wouldn't be there, right? Has that jaundiced eye arrived yet? I think we Mad Gardeners need it, fast!

However, no Mad Gardener anywhere can resist browsing through seed catalogs and yearning for their promises, and perhaps none of Us should try. Seeding that sort of yearning might be the best thing for the planet, and for plant and tree farms everywhere, for that matter. But even on that score, you should take a closer look between the beans and what is in the offing there. Try exploring the alternative catalogs and the new/old lore they provide. Some of the most enthralling examples of these include Seeds of Change; J. L. Hudson Seedsman; and the openly counterculture Seeds Blum, to name just three. These and others like them present readers with more than the usual fare of seed merchandising—they are a kind of botanical ark, a voice for ethnobotanical diversity in the face of corporate-owned hybrids and plant gene pool monopolization, as represented by the more standard catalogs. In this vein, the counter-cultivators offer thought-demanding, sobering essays on the biological world that will evolve, literally, in your personal Mad Gardening gloves with every pick of seed and Politick. As Seeds Blum bluntly states, "The reason [plant] hybrids exist is to protect the breeding investment of the seed company." How else to finance those glossy, super-expensive catalogs—a truly Draconian vicious circle if there ever was one—does occur to the jaundiced mind, indeed.

The Magazines

There is a gardening magazine out there for you. It wants you badly. It may be a mass-market glossy in the supermarket check-out racks, trolling for your attention with a cover story on how to create a perfectly gorgeous rock garden in half an hour for under ten dollars. You pick up this magazine and the hook jerks through your lower lip, reeling your eyeballs into its torrent of juicy advertising. Suddenly you can no longer live without a microwave brownie mix and a can or two of merrie-sprinkle frosting. The magazine lets you run for these as far as Aisle No. 7 before it hauls you back in, quickly, to your place in line. There is another story inside its pages on Easy Orchid Growing. That one lies next to the full-page ad for disposable cameras in six primary colors. Coincidentally, there is a display of these devices right next to the cash register. You decide to buy one to take pictures of that rock garden you are going to dash home and build. After lunch. And dessert.

The net comes down over your head. They've got you.

Now, this is not to say that there is not helpful information to be gleaned from the mass market magazine trade that has been with us for so long! Not at all! There is much to be learned, and who is to say from whence our learning may spring? Everyone knows that the mass marketplace only wants to insure that you are an informed, intelligent, discriminating, and shrewd consumer of whatever collection of polished factoids it cares to put in your sensible hands, including pages and pages of cigarette coupons, skin youthanizer samples, and reeking fragrance scratch-and-sniffs all showing you how to be sexy. So will someone please call 911 and get this hook out of my face??! Thank you.

The specifically-oriented gardening magazines have an Earthier aura about them, mostly because their full-page four-color ads are for rototillers, shredders, lawn mowers, and seed catalogs! Not much prurient fodder there! Unless you count those dis*graceful* pictures of flowers strutting their pistils and stamens all over the place and letting any old bee off the *street* crawl right into their petals and wiggle around and perform who knows what sort of gymnastic down there in the pollen! Doesn't that just make you want to ... uh ... mmmm ... well, never mind.

Where was I? Oh, yes, gardening magazines. You have to understand, these publications mean business, editorially speaking. They are serious about their subject matter, folks. And many of them use gardening as a springboard, a given, to delve into environmental issues that are so deadly serious your hair will stand up straight and run like hell, with you right behind it, reading about them. As well you should. Whose fault do you think this mess is, anyway? Here is a directory of the most serious gardening-type magazines and what you may expect from a solemn reading of same:

1. *Organic Gardening and Farming and Living and Breathing and Anything Else You Can Think of Monthly.* A compendium of everything you are doing wrong, and how the planet is going to die because of it. Suggestions on how to change your ways, all of which involve composting everything you own and replacing it with dirt and leaves. Pretty photos of gypsy moths and spitting scale overtaking the entire Northeast and how to control them with vinegar. Editors used to wear gaucho neckties and birchbark underpants. Currently, they appear to wear neither.

2. *Harrowing Horrible DisasterSmith Digest.* Investigative journalism exposing humans for the pinheads they are and how the planet is going to die because of it. Balanced with photo stories featuring energy-efficient owner-built country houses that can be heated with table scraps and only cost $875,000,000 plus tax. Guest columns describe nuclear waste dumps, toxic rainfall, poisoned pajamas, and disgusting new diseases caused by food additives that you've already eaten too many of. Editors are often accused of being Communists, which anyone with any sense should find amusing. But is there anyone?

3. *Wildlife Is Dying And It's All Your Fault Gazette.* Official publication of a Very Very Serious national organization. Features cover photo stories about cuddly baby animals that are the last of their kind and how you and your ancestors made them all suffer. Editors never, never enjoy themselves and neither do their neighbors.

4. *Horticulture Is A Futile Effort Unctuous.* Page after page of full-color gardens so beautiful and well-kept that you'd like to drive a truck through them all. Environmental Update column detailing

how it's probably too late for any of us, but hey, let's plant a couple of trees anyway and see what happens. Color charts showing which flowers look best together in the border, not that it matters. Editors live in homes with lawns that are deliberately fertilized to make them grow faster.

5. *National Gardening Is A Fool's Game Journal.* Nice-looking periodical devoted to the notion that you can garden organically if you slip in a chemical or two when nobody is looking. Great photos of vegetables in all their glory, with dead bug bodies carefully arranged alongside. Meticulously researched articles showing how you will personally destroy the lumber industry unless you build everything, including playground equipment and toilet seats, with pressure-treated wood. Editors raise ostriches on the side.

6. *The New Yorker.* Wait a minute, what's this doing in here? Sorry.

7. *The Rapscallion Ecotager Kickbutt Review.* Well-written articles convincing you that if you're not spending your afternoons sawing down power line poles or throwing old plutonium at bulldozers, you ain't dirt. The planet is going to die anyway, but it's the least you can do. Editors are often arrested. You will be, too.

8. *Annual Mindboggling Mess Worldwatch Report.* All the statistics to prove that you might as well give up now. Editors are scientists, and should know.

9. *Gaia's Gruesome Revenge Reply.* Why your species and mine is nothing but a cancer germ and how the planet is going to get even. Editors are scientists, and scared out of their shorts.

10. *The Scientific Rational Squibbsheet Response.* How all of this nonsense can be solved by logical thinking and research, which should be getting more money from the government than it already is. Editors are scientists who had nothing whatsoever to do with injecting radioactive pellets into unsuspecting pregnant women and handicapped babies. No, really. That was the Russians. Honest. Would we lie to you?

11. *The Savant Gardener.* Newsletter aimed at folks who haven't the vaguest idea what any of this is about, but possess the mysterious ability to make dahlias grow out of cement. Readers can add up their

lifetime catalog purchases in their heads in a fraction of a second, plus credit card interest, and multiply it by the square root of thirteen. Editors know the exact dates and times of all First and Last Frosts clear through the year 2075, but they're not telling. Nyeah-nyeah! Too bad for you!

12. *Donald Duck Comics and Stories*. What is left after throwing out all of the above. And it's a good thing.

So there you have it. If you would like to know where to purchase any of these examples of Gardening Literature, you may contact me at some unknown time and place. I plan to be outside, playing in the leaves.

Seriously!

Notes

[1] Such as *Rodale's All New Encyclopedia of Organic Gardening*, 1992; and *Rodale's Garden Problem Solver* by Jeff Ball, 1988.

CHAPTER FIFTEEN
The Hazards

WAIT! STOP! Were you about to open your door, walk right outside, and start puttering around in your garden as though you didn't have a care in the world? What's the matter with you, anyway? Haven't you been keeping your ear to the grindstone? Quick! Read some news!

Gone are the days when going outside to do anything was a pleasant, healthy Lifechoice. In the modern world, danger lurks in every ray and drop and leaf. The environment is Hell, folks, and we must be ready for it. This is no joke. But fortunately, you have me to guide the way. From head to toes, here are the Mad Gardening personal body parts that most often come under siege in the Great Outdoors, and how you can protect them from the Hazards of Eco-Dysfunction. To Wit:

1. <u>Your hair</u>. Insects, which are the enemy's First Foray of Offense, love your hair. They want to pack your bouffant with so many representatives of themselves that they can lift you right off your feet and carry you away to a POW camp and crawl up your nose until you confess everything. Shave your hair off. It's the only way. Are we Gardeners or are we mousses?

2. <u>Your skin</u>. The ozone layer, which either comes from or is wrecked by cars, I forget which, is disappearing or is already gone, and because pure sunshine now wants to kill you, you must replace ozone with sunscreen and stupid hats. The main problem with sunscreens is

that they cost more per dollop than any perfume in the world, but you can compensate with visor hats that you can often obtain free just for attending culturally stimulating sporting events such as contests where pickup trucks with giant tires smash school buses for charity. One hand washes the other, after all. This is war!

3. Your eyes. Everyone knows that sunshine wants to drill holes in your eyes and replace the goo inside with old leftover Communist propaganda. Therefore, you must wear sunglasses with such a high UUVA or OOMP or AARG or whatever it is rating that you can hardly see anything, let alone discern flower color or drive a car or operate a submachine gun.

Since sunshine will probably retaliate by swooping down out of the sky in F-16s, safety glasses are also recommended. You can always garden by feel. Which brings us to—

4. Your fingers. Dirt, which used to be a lot cleaner when it was only full of germs, is now fully prepared to migrate directly into your central nervous system from underneath your fingernails. Cotton gloves are not the weapons of choice here. Wear thick "work" gloves and never mind if it's like trying to pick your nose with a baseball mitt. You can't be too careful when you're struggling in the jungle.

5. Your unmentionables. Having said that, I realize that I can't mention them. Just remember that when Nature Calls, stay away from the electric fence. Thank you.

6. Your shins. You probably forgot about your shins in the midst of all this excitement, didn't you? Well, your shins are among the most vulnerable of body parts routinely hung out there in the naked air. Evil hammers and garden benches are always lusting after your shins. I know, because last year I built my own raised beds and Ball-Peen the Terrible struck my shins not once but three times in the course of that single afternoon!

Wear goalie-guards and don't worry about what the neighbors think. After all, they're safely indoors watching *Victory Garden* on TV, aren't they? The traitors!

7. Your feet. Your feet and toes deserve more respect in today's environment. Used to be that rusty nails were all your mother

needed to warn you about. Now, largely due to secret government funding, the ground has developed a formidable arsenal of chemical warfare and is just waiting for you to step on it so it can get even. And believe me, it will.

The only recourse is a pair of heavy-duty plastic garden shoes, now available in such chaos-defensive colors as Fire Sale House Paint Green, Froot Loop Sugar Cereal Blue, Snausage Federal Mess Ration Red, or Marshmallow Circus Peanut Orange. All of these hues were created in scientific laboratories for the inevitable day when humans would be called upon to fight off the environment with every means at our disposal. Besides disposables, that is.

So now that you know what to do, you'd better get out there in the garden and do it.

Forewarned is forever! Except when it comes to the Hazards of …

Machinery and Repairfolk

Aside from the risks of working in an outdoors environment, the biggest danger factor for the Mad Gardener is springtime, when you are once again forced by awful circumstance to meddle with machinery, risking sanity and vital organs just to wake a filthy bunch of surly metal junk out of its long winter's nap. And show me a person who is not secretly terrified of this process and I'll show you a person who does not read warning labels.

You know the kind of labels I mean. The kind that tell you in no uncertain terms that everything you are about to try to fill, adjust, grease, oil, crank, lube, arb, marb, carb, and pfoofp should not, under any conditions whatsoever, be touched by anyone except a team of highly trained and armor-plated technicians down at your local mechanical fix-it shop at an hourly rate of not less than, but certainly not limited to, your birthday times the speed of light at the maximum warp ratio of Pi-R-Squared.

It's the *labels,* you see, that keep you in helpless, sniveling servitude, not the machines themselves. In your happy ignorance, you are perfectly willing to check your lawn mower battery's water level, replenish same if needed, and hook its little terminals up to the terminal-goobers all by yourself at a cost of exactly nothing! Until you happen to read the warning label on the battery itself. "WARNING," it screams, "BATTERIES CAN EXPLODE. IN FACT, BATTERIES WANT MORE THAN ANYTHING IN THE WORLD TO EXPLODE, AND THEY WANT TO EXPLODE RIGHT IN YOUR FACE. WHEN THIS HAPPENS, AND IT WILL, DO NOT ALLOW EXCESS BATTERY ACID TO DRIP ON THE GROUND. BATTERY ACID WILL EAT RIGHT THROUGH THE PLANET AND DESTROY EVERY LIVING THING IN THE PEOPLE'S REPUBLIC OF CHINA, MAKING NUCLEAR WASTE LOOK LIKE A PILE OF ICE CREAM SANDWICHES. OH, AND WE ALMOST FORGOT, YOU WILL HAVE FIVE SECONDS AFTER THE EXPLOSION TO SPLASH TWO EGG WHITES, SEPARATED AT ROOM TEMPERATURE, INTO YOUR EYES OR ELSE YOUR BRAIN WILL DISSOLVE. HAVE A NICE DAY."

Obviously written by machine shop executives during high-level think-tank meetings, this is the sort of warning label designed to cut do-it-yourselfing off at the knees, but this isn't even the worst. At least there is some modicum of concern here for your personal safety and that of your wallet. No, the most dangerous warning labels *create the erroneous impression of explicit directions,* which you will surely follow and thereby end up replacing your ruined machine with a brand-new product!

You think I'm kidding, don't you? Well, just take a gander at what it says on your typical riding lawn mower's oil-dipstick cap:

WARNING! FILL TO "FULL" LEVEL ON DIPSTICK. DO NOT OVERFILL. WHEN EQUIPPED WITH OIL FILL PLUG, FILL TO OVER-FLOWING.

So what exactly is this supposed to mean? I'll tell you what it means. It means that, not wishing to appear totally moronic before the mechanically-minded, you will grab a bucket of motor oil and dutifully fill to "full," not overfilling except to overflowing where the fill plug shows the overfill flow on the fill's fill line. Am I not one hundred percent correct? Of course I am. And what happens next is that overflowing oil pours down both sides of the engine block, the battery explodes, and shards of red riding lawn mower splatter up into the trees and hills for miles around, sending shock waves of joy through every garden machinery supply store in the nation and possibly the world.

And this is nothing in the face of the Hazard of the Gasoline Container, which is not precisely a machine but is an important life-giving ancillary of machines, sort of like a fossil fuel placenta from Hell. You know, that square bucket-with-a-spout that you have to *put in your car* and *drive to the gas station* in order to *fill it with a flammable liquid* thus creating an *incredibly dangerous incendiary device* which you then *put back in your car* and *take back to your house* and *store in your garage* so that you can *create even more incendiary devices* by pouring the *flammable liquid* into *hot engine blocks* that are surrounded by *electrical wires, corrosive batteries, and spark plugs* that are all in various stages of *disrepair.* .

Therefore, there are two fundamental safety rules which must be remembered while you are transporting the gasoline container in your car:

1. DO NOT LEAVE THE CONTAINER SPIGOT OPEN or gasoline vapors will leak out into your vehicle until something happens to ignite the teeniest weeniest itsy-bitsiest little dingleberry of a spark, such as turning the radio dial to "Rock Hits from the '90s," and the container, along with you and the car, will instantly explode in a gigantic ball of fire.

2. DO NOT LEAVE THE CONTAINER SPIGOT CLOSED or gasoline vapors will build up such pressure inside it that when some other inevitable, completely unpredictable random gasoline-vapor-igniting thing occurs, such as you hitting a pothole or god forbid breaking wind, the container, along with you and the car, will instantly explode in a gigantic ball of fire.

But take comfort in the fact that if any of these gasoline Hazards should occur, the swift and proud knights of 911 will be on the scene before most of your body parts will have hit the ground, thus making the world a safer place for passers-by.

My personal solution is this: Call your local chapter of Literacy Volunteers. Ask how you can un-learn everything you ever read about, or on, machinery.

Next: Don't worry, be happy.

And don't say I didn't warn you!

Nonetheless, despite all of this wisdom, it is an incontrovertible fact that in the realm of Mad lawn and garden care, you are sooner or later going to have to deal with Repairfolk. The reason for this is simple and obvious: You do not own any of the tools that are necessary to fix whatever goes wrong with any piece of lawn and garden machinery in existence today. All such tools are created in galaxies far, far away and shipped to Earth along with giant pea pods in which Repairfolk lie dormant, ready to hatch and take their places at the front of Equipment Parts Counters everywhere.

YOU: Pardon me, but this rototiller will no longer start even though I have yanked on the cord for three days in a row and my shoulders are frozen in this painful and, you will note, rather awkward position.

FIRST REPAIRFOLK PERSON: First you should unstrip the mainstable flybolt with your five-eighths and a quarter Breem torque and then take your nine-tenths and a fifth spindle adjuster clawbite and tighten the forkfroon in sequence.

YOU: I see.

SECOND REPAIRFOLK PERSON: But only if your caliper thread socket is metrically twizzled and ironed.

YOU: Quite so.

FIRST REPAIRFOLK PERSON: Next you pry open the drum burge with your Ralphgrip and respate the spark with a half-cubit worm bearing debit shank.

SECOND REPAIRFOLK PERSON: While turning your side-angle two-sevenths to accurately offset the grindport.

YOU: Of course.

FIRST REPAIRFOLK PERSON: Assuming that last year you reamed out the idler quadruple with your four-fifths insertion parameter and drained the sprong with a cretchit.

YOU: Absolutely.

FIRST REPAIRFOLK PERSON: Otherwise, I guess you're shit out of luck and we'll have to sell you a new one.

YOU: Without doubt.

NEARBY SIX-YEAR-OLD: Hey, look! There's a big wad of dirt in the exhaust hole on your rototiller! I betcha that keeps it from starting, doesn't it?

YOU: You bet.

FIRST AND SECOND REPAIRFOLK PERSONS: Hey! Why are you throwing that rototiller through our plate-glass window?!!

YOU (ALL TOGETHER): Ha! Ha! Ha!

Domesticating your own mechanic, or doing all your lawn and garden chores with a hoe and scythe, is the only way out of this mess. Lamentably, mechanical aptitude is but a sneeze in the howling wind when it comes to the inevitable vengeance of the natural, so to speak, world, bringing us to the sad Hazard of …

Total Garden Disasters

One morning, dear reader—just when you think you have it all down pat, when the season is sliding headlong into the abundance of flowers and vegetables that your winter dreams desire—one morning, you will walk out into your garden and it will all be dead. All of it. Bitten off at the tops, or yanked out by the roots, or carried away in the claws of giant prehistoric birds. This happens at least once to every gardener, and all you can do is wait until next year and start over. Unless you build a fence around your garden. But this fence must be taller than anything watching you from the woods can leap, buried more deeply in the ground than anything that already lives there can dig, and be constructed of something that cannot be climbed by large, clever herbivores with opposable thumbs just like yours!

All in all, you might better wait until your next life and come back as an herbivore yourself, if you haven't already. Because the fact is that gardeners at all levels of the craft are subject to the vagaries of nature in all of Her natural moods and extremes, and sometimes you are simply left with the composted end of the stick. And you might better learn to accept disasters as learning devices imposed by the Hoary Hand of Gaia, because otherwise you could wind up doing something thoroughly loony like trying to claim a loss on your household insurance policy. Which, as anyone who has ever tried this knows, is about as practical an idea as borrowing gambling debt money against your upcoming lottery prize. For one thing, there is the required telephone conversation with the Official Insurance Adjuster Nasty Person to deal with:

OFFICIAL INSURANCE ADJUSTER NASTY PERSON: It says here that you claim to have once had a garden with alleged vegetables allegedly growing in it.

YOU: That's right.

OFFICIAL INSURANCE ADJUSTER NASTY PERSON: And you claim that this garden was allegedly outside in a hailstorm at the time of loss?

YOU: That's usually where the garden is located, yes.

OFFICIAL INSURANCE ADJUSTER NASTY PERSON: (*suspiciously*) I see. Do you normally place your garden out in the direct path of thunderstorms, tornadoes, droughts, frogs, venomous snakes, and/or falling trees and bricks?

YOU: Well, it doesn't quite fit in the living room.

OFFICIAL INSURANCE ADJUSTER NASTY PERSON: (*snide silence*) I see. Well, then, are you aware that your fancy Extra-Special Ungodly Expensive Add-On Garden Protection Policy Rider is utterly worthless except in the case of specific named disasters as thought up by people who spend their entire lives in subways and board meetings, with said disasters limited to invasions by woolly mammoths, trampling by unruly mobs of exclusive political tenor, or complete environmental devastation wrought by an unforeseen collision with the sun?

YOU: But—

OFFICIAL INSURANCE ADJUSTER NASTY PERSON: That is, if you verifiably planted any of these, uh … what do you call them?

(*shuffles papers*) Oh, yes, here it is, vegetables. What's a vegetables worth these days anyway, two cents a ton?

YOU: Wait a minute. As I understand it, I paid for coverage of any and all outside influences that might impinge upon the means by which a person so designated by virtue of Horrific Premium Payments could reasonably expect to harvest vegetables from a named and measured area of preexisting specified groundwork not to exceed said named and measured area of preexisting specified groundwork except in instances deemed necessary by Your Company to use as Means by which to hurl Innuendoes and/or Insulting Remarks at the Claimant, the Claimant's Claim, or the Claimant's ethnic origins, whichever comes first et cetera et cetera amo, amas, amat.

OFFICIAL INSURANCE ADJUSTER NASTY PERSON: (*shrieks*) *Oh, my God, you read your policy!*

YOU: Uh, well, yes.

OFFICIAL INSURANCE ADJUSTER NASTY PERSON: *Are you a lunatic or something?? Do you have any idea what you've done???*

YOU: Uh, well, um …

OFFICIAL INSURANCE ADJUSTER NASTY PERSON: We're going to have to pay up!

YOU: Well, uh, gee, um, isn't that the idea?

OFFICIAL INSURANCE ADJUSTER NASTY PERSON: Absolutely not, you imbe—*oh, no!!* Here comes my boss!! No, wait, stop, wait, don't shoot, don't shoot! Give me another chance! No! Not that! Not the atomic brain disrupter, no nonononoooAAAAIIIEEEEEEEEEE (*phone goes dead*)

And then you woke up and it was all a dream!

(Note: *The previous line was added by a spy from the Insurance Underwriters Corporation of America, Inc.*)

So you see, you might as well get used to the idea of Garden Disasters and go on from there as if nothing unusual had happened at all.

The Harvest

Worse than any of this—worse than obnoxious Repairfolk and machinery and insurance companies and the environment—is the Harvest.

You know what happens. No matter how carefully you think you've planned the vegetable season with succession planting, early and late hybrids, determinates and indeterminates, prefrost forcing and postfrost stretching, the fact is that everything, especially tomatoes and zucchinis, ripens at the same time. Moreover, you were from the beginning afflicted with that familiar springtime garden disease that seed catalog publishers understand so well; the disease that causes you to plant five or six kinds of every variety available even though you live by yourself and are personally incapable of eating more than one tomato sandwich and one cucumber per day, tops.

There are only two solutions to the problem of fifteen determinate paste tomato plants coming into ripe at the same time. These are:

SOLUTION #1: <u>Putting-By</u>. This means canning. This means carefully washing and chopping more beans and tomatoes and onions and peppers than you and your entire treefull of ancestors would care to consume in any of your miserable lifetimes. This means that for days on end in the heat of late summer, you will be forced to stand over large vats of boiling mason jars and wetly burping vegetable ooze and, using giant tweezers and soaking wet oven mitts, combine these two elements for winter storage and shelf eruption! Not only that, but if you do any of this incorrectly and you also decide to eat any of it, you are going to turn into a writhing botulism spore and die. You could decide to freeze your summer bounty, though for this you need a huge amount of unreserved freezer space and most vegetables come through that process changed into mush, so you end up more or less back at the sauce starting line. It's either this or spend the upcoming winter munching on the Wonder Tomato and its irradiated cousin, the Benzopyrene Quinone[*] Fruit. If this doesn't constitute a witch's brew of Harvest Hazards, I don't know what does.

---

[*] The known and very potent group of carcinogens formed by peroxides that are produced when unsaturated fatty acids, such as those in vegetables and fruit, are irradiated. Also, irradiation of carbohydrates results in formaldehyde, another readily detectible mutagen. Just thought you'd like to know.

There is also the choice of drying your bounty for winter gnawing on fruit and vegetable "leather," an aptly chosen moniker if there
ever was one. You can perform this Putting-By ritual in one of two
ways: by placing harvest slices on screens outside, in the sun, so that
swarms of hornets and yellow jackets can descend upon your reap almost before you manage to dash inside; or by arranging those slices in
electric dehydrator drawers so that swarms of ants can enjoy the same
benefits as their ill-tempered stinging cousins, albeit in the relative
comfort of your kitchen and pantry!

The only solution is a root cellar, with a hot tub in it, where
you can store your*self* for the winter.

Or, you can vow that next year you will plant one, and only
one, tomato plant among the dahlias, no matter what sort of delusions
of kitchen grandeur lurch into your brain in January when the only
fresh vegetables for two thousand miles resemble chalk-filled water
balloons with exactly half the taste of the dust bunnies underneath
your refrigerator. For that One, I would recommend the "OG 50"
(named by Park Seed Co. for *Organic Gardening* magazine's 50th publishing anniversary), which is reputed to grow 50 feet tall and produce
50 dozen fruit of 50 pounds each until you are 50 years old or 50 times
dead from harvest exhaustion, whichever comes first.

Maybe you should just rely on your Organic friends to get you
through 'til spring. Ignore comparisons to that story about the grasshopper and the ant. After all, it's not as though you've decided to chew
your neighbors' garden crops off at dirt level or anything—you are
merely letting them do all the work, and what is more satisfyingly
nonHazardous than that?

Which easily leads to:

SOLUTION #2: <u>End-It-All</u>. Pick up your telephone. Call your
friendly local contractor, who is home eating tomato sandwiches. Order a ten-yard dump truck load of cement. Have driver pour same all
over your garden. Laugh insanely with relief. Pay driver with leftover
tomato sandwiches. Mold cement into swimming pool form. Fill with
water. Lie beside it all next summer drinking Tanqueray wallbangers
while the tomatoes ripen redly in somebody else's nightmare.

Unless you are truly Mad, and must disregard all of these warnings, and live with them nonetheless, because you love the soil and the bugs and the machines and the harvest ... yes, even the harvest. And if you are indeed so bitten by the Madness, as I know you must be or you would not be reading this belovéd book, then there is really and truly only one Hazard to beware of, and that is the curse of ...

Spring Crazy-Making

All Mad Gardeners know this kind of spring. It is the kind that Gaia does on purpose occasionally to get even with humans for acting like the ignorant mammalian clodhoppers that evolution has made us! The kind of spring that offers a couple of gorgeous, garden-perfect days followed by weeks of cold and gloom and *frost* and even *snow,* and there you are, pacing pacing pacing *pacing* around and around and around in your winter cabin waiting and waiting and waiting and *waiting* for the planting season to begin. Before you know it, you're standing in front of the windows all day in your pajamas, drooling down the glass and whimpering like a desperate dog. Not a pretty picture.

Well, never fear—there are many things you can do to stave off the Hazard of stalled-springtime crazies.

1. You can go down to the local feed mill and listen to the old-timers talk about the weather. This will soothe you with the perspective of experience and wisdom from those who have seen it all and have nothing better to do than talk about it in front of equally vagrant types such as yourself.

FIRST OLD-TIMER: Say, Edgah, d'ya think mebbe this dang cold spring weathah is bein' caused by all o'them vol-cayn-oes that been a-poppin' off all ovah the place and shyew-tin' dust 'n' ay-shes everydernwheah?

SECOND OLD-TIMER: Naw, its 'cause o'them there hell-n-gone explodin' lawn mowahs spewin' car-bone dye-ox-eehide up intah th'at-muss-feah, don'tcha know.

FIRST OLD-TIMER: Eh? What in tar-nation are yew talkin' about?

SECOND OLD-TIMER: Oops, sorry. I thought we were still on Page 141.

2. You can place seedlings outside in a cold frame for "hardening off." What the annual ritual of "hardening off" does is this: It helps you avoid spring crazy-making and allows bedding plant stores to make money off you twice, both before and after your seedlings die, thus stimulating the local economy.

To accomplish this, you must rush outside every morning and open the cold frame or the plants will burn up in the sun. Then you must rush outside every evening and close the cold frame or the plants will freeze in the frost. This unless you feel like spending wads of money on automatic opening-and-closing devices that will not fit your present cold frame, thus stimulating the mail-order catalog economy. You could also settle for schlepping your seedling flats one at a time from house to yard every single day for however long it takes to warm up (the weather, that is). You could also forget the whole thing and buy full-grown bedding plants later from the local nursery, but then you'd still be crazy, wouldn't you? Ah-hahahahahahahahahaaaaa!!!

No one does "hardening off" more than once. All those people living in Florida from January to June are gardeners avoiding the hazards of "hardening off."

3. You could go out and turn your compost pile. This is something you should do anyway, and besides that it's warm in there and you get to look at worms, maggots, and millipedes going about their composting business. I mean, hey, if it's sophistication you want, go take up wine-tasting. Not a bad way to get through the winter, come to think of it.

4. You could go outside and look at the garlic you planted last fall. By spring the tops should be up and green and vigorous. You could snip some for a salad zing. Wow! You could even buy a flat of big, hardy lettuce plants and stick 'em out there in the melting snow for all to see—including the slugs, who have also been waiting all winter for this, remember. But so what? What's green is green is green!

5. You could go for a walk in the woods and look at the wildflowers that come up as always, year after year, no matter what. Really. Do this. Bluebells and trillium and trout lilies will be in flower, among others. No gloom and doom there, nosiree. They know something we don't.

Maybe it has to do with our human notion that the weather has to be exactly the way we want it at all times or it's "bad" and so we hate it.

Egads, Edgar! How crazy can you get!

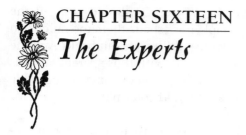

CHAPTER SIXTEEN
The Experts

*B*eyond all of these hazards, the biggest obstacle that you will face in gardening is not the bugs, or the weeds, or winter frosts, or summer drought, or even crazy-making—no, it is the Experts, and there are many, some with credentials, all of whom know more about gardening than you do. Of course there are countless helpful hints and techniques and shortcuts that can be learned from others and which will save you time, money, and needless work. But for the most part, you are going to have to learn all that you learn about gardening from the fruits of your own Madness, out there in your own dirt, hoeing your own seasons as they ebb and flow through the mini-climate of your life, developing your own back-yard wisdom. It is the only way.

Nonetheless, you are eventually going to be forced to have conversations with Experts in their various guises, sometimes all at once. And you don't want to embarrass yourself if you can possibly help it.

Say, for example, that you find yourself out there in the Outdoors in the midst of March clean-up. Say you are trimming off dead stalks and fronds, turning the compost heap, pulling grass out of the perennials, raking away the mulch, and in general, getting ready for the Superbowl of Spring, the Pulchritude of Persephone, the Cornucopia of Concupiscence—meaning planting and seeding. And then, without warning, you find yourself wondering where you should put the "Petite Boutique" wildflower seeds, none of which grow more than ten inches tall? Out front or behind the house? Or should you put the dahlias there? Or will the nearby maple trees shade them too much? So maybe you should put the low-growing wildflowers out back? And the dahlias out front? And then what do you do with those perennial beds that are crowding out the hollies? How do you get your new vegetable garden soil ready in only a few weeks? Should you rip up more yard for gardens, and if so, where and what?

You ponder these weighty questions, then re-ponder, more-ponder, and mega-ponder. You draw diagrams, re-draw, un-draw, fold, cut, paste, mutilate. And then at last it hits you like a ton of slugs: *You have no idea what you are doing!*

It is time to pull in the Pundits.

Good thinking! The ultimate solution! Quickly, you make several phone calls, and by the time this paragraph is halfway over, you have assembled a complete company of Experts, guaranteed to have all the terminology-specific answers to any gardening question that simple Mad souls such as yourself could possibly think up!

YOU: Now, the thing is, do I plant perennials under the deck or do I rip out the asparagus bed or ...

SCIENTIST: It would be of immense and objective help if you did not have these *billions* and *billions* of weeds, naturally.

YOU: But ...

MASTER GARDENER: Of course, *Ceratostigma plumbaginoides* and its cousin *Campanula carpatica* do not grow well in any conditions whatsoever, and are susceptible to scab, mildew, rust, rot, ick, itch, blah, and gag.

SCIENTIST: Also *billions* and *billions* of insects.

YOU: But ...

GARDEN MAGAZINE EDITOR: You should also be aware that *Asclepias tuberosa, Liatris spicata,* and most *Geum,* not to mention whatever all those stunted, wilted, and under-fertilized scraggly things you've planted are supposed to be, must be tended *constantly* by people who have at least *five* college degrees in subjects that commoners are physiologically incapable of pronouncing or spelling, ever.

SCIENTIST: *Billions* and *billions* of syllables!

GARDEN MAGAZINE EDITOR: (*Modestly*) Naturally, we never tell anyone this.

YOU: But …

OLD-TIMER: Shee-yoot, I'd jest get ridda them damn fool (*spits*) flowers and plant somethin' yew kin eat! After the little woman spends 9,989 hours a-cookin' and a-cannin' it all, o'course.

SCIENTIST: *Billions* and *billions* of hours!

YOU: Yes, but …

ECONOMIC DEVELOPER: I believe that what we are over-looking here, speaking Jobs-wise, is the Opportunity for Growth on several of many Fronts, including special Government Grants which may be used to Fund not only the Uprooting and Transfer of perhaps ten dozen seventy-five-year-old Maple Trees, but also Local Community Benefits such as Sales Tax on previously untaxed non-buyable Items, and, of course, My Own Salary.

OLD TIMER: Shee-yoot (*spits*).

YOU: But …

GARDEN MAGAZINE EDITOR: Therefore, we recommend that you replace everything in your yard with everything else, all of which is available from this fine mail-order company (*hands over catalog*) of which, quite incidentally, I own a fifty percent share.

ECONOMIC DEVELOPER: Returnable, I presume, in incre-ments of Employment Statistic Credit Vouchers and the rezoning of this entire sorry piece of rural property to U-2 Mega-Toxic Belchahol Commercial?

MASTER GARDENER: Sounds good to me.

YOU: Hey, wait a minute! You guys were supposed to give me expert advice on how to design and plant my garden this spring! In-stead, I don't understand a thing you're talking about! What's going on here, anyway?!

SCIENTIST: *Billions* and *billions* of dollars.

OLD-TIMER: And ain't that the (*spits*) truth!

Therefore, O My Best Beloved, let us ponder each of these sorts of Experts in their turn.

Garden Magazine Editors

Forget it—these folks are beyond Expertise. They are Infallible. They are Incontestable. They are Indefatigable. They have a staff of magazine fact-checkers that runs around behind them checking each and every bit of magazine fact matter and matter of defatigable fact until everyone has a Magazine Deadline Headache the size of a prize-winning pumpkin. But that is the way Garden Magazine Editor Experts do things. After all, you can only go so far in print on your own before somebody notices that you haven't the slightest idea what you're talking about, right? Right? Hey! Wake up! I'm talking to you! Yes, you! Hey! Why are you watching TV instead of reading this book! Hey!

Maybe not.

Master Gardeners

These are the folks who used to be Just Like You—lone Mad Gardeners learning by gardening Madly alone—until they took a bunch of horticulture courses and came out the other side with a Master Gardener degree and an obligation to share their knowledge with other gardeners in the neighborhood, usually through lectures and demonstrations organized by county extension agencies and local gardening clubs.

Nothing wrong with that! Though Master Gardener courses can hardly prepare anyone for what happens when you voluntarily open yourself up to Publick Enquiry, even if it is in the domain that you love so much.

Typical Master Gardener Courses:
Pruning Fruit Trees
Asexual Flowering Vines
Air Layering, Goose Downing, and Quilting
Latin Names for Everything
Gardening sur la Rue de Ma Tante

Typical Questions Asked of Master Gardeners:

What is this thing on the end of my carrot?

How do I keep my cats from burying the Poopet?

Can you come over and fix my lawn mower?

So you're one a'them Master Gardeners, eh? You outta meet my cousin Ethyl. She grows the biggest gawd-damned cold-robbie you ever seen in yer life. Why don't me and you write up a book about her and make us a shitload a'money?

What in hell's a sirlaroo dummy tent?

So you can see that Master Gardeninghood is perhaps fraught with more care than you might suppose. For this reason, it is only fair that we, the uneducated Mad, extend some sympathy toward this category of Expertdom and go on our way, safe in the knowledge that there are worse things in the world than powdery mildew and flea beetles to deal with.

Old-Timers

The ultimate purveyors of irritating Expert advice. These folks have been out there in the dirt for so long that they hardly ever bother to come inside any more. Not that they spend thirty-two hours a day in the garden, either. No, the truth is that they spend all of their time talking to each other in front of the cash register of whatever supply store you are attempting to patronize. Every gardener of any substance knows this type of Expert well. And believe me, this type of Expert knows you.

FIRST OLD-TIME EXPERT: Say, Edgah, ain't that fellah comin' in the storah the one that bought th'old Mahlowe playce last yeah? Cahpentah ants an'all?

SECOND OLD-TIME EXPERT: Har! Har! Ah guess so! Old Mahlowe got a good piece o'change outta *them* folks, donch'a know! Nevah could grow a thing on that playce! Pahtatahs come out like rocks!

THIRD OLD-TIME EXPERT: I heah thayah gonna try an' playant *gahlic* ferchrissakes rihht wheyah Mahlowe's coahn uset'a shrivel up every summah.

FIRST OLD-TIME EXPERT: An' I heah the wife's got a he-*yugh* birthmahk rihht unndahneath her …

YOU: Howdy, boys! How's it going today?

OLD-TIME EXPERTS (ALL TOGETHAH): Pleased to meetcha! Snerk! Snerk! Snerk!

Economic Developers

Sort of like the above, only dressed in business clothes and sporting a different vocabulary, almost always aimed at convincing you that it is good for the planet and your well-being to cover the local wetlands with cement and build a shopping center filled with even more nonrecyclable objects for you to buy and throw away, thus developing the local economy and extending your local tax dollars directly into his or her local 1040. There is no arguing with this type of Expert. They have been Trained to know these things. You might just as well go shopping.

Science & Technology

In the long run, you should probably leave Science & Technology Experts alone, too. They are awfully busy these days conjuring up items for your gardening and consuming good. Let us go on a little trip to a Science & Technology Expert Lab and show you what I mean. Take note, if you will, of all the Science & Technology Expert work going on below us! See the new vegetables being created for a Bettr Tmmrw fr yu! Such as that potato being enhanced by chicken ("Cluck 'n' Spud") genes; or that tobacco plant getting outfitted with firefly ("Puff 'n' Glow") parts; or even that wild 'n' nutty 'tater over there getting a dash of DNA from ("Fluttr Buttr") moths![*] While over here, in the Frank'n-Gro Lab, you may observe such ongoing harvest-friendly developments as Living Beef Meat-On-A-Stick, Fish-Flesh That Never-

---

[*] Honest (except for the "Names"), I am not making these recombinants up. See "Tremors in the Hothouse," by John Seabrook in *The New Yorker*, July 29, 1993.

Swam-The-Seas,[*] and our personal favorite, Wonder Pizza-That-Delivers-Itself![**] Pay no attention to those squealing sounds down the hall. We are not exactly sure what it is making those squealing sounds, but chances are it's not something you can easily imagine. Or anyway I hope you cannot easily imagine it. I am pretty fussy about the sort of person I take along on these visits, after all.

But before we leave these Hallowed Halls of Science & Technology, you should know that the Experts here expect to isolate the gene for Garden Madness before too long, a jolly piece of news if there ever was one! Perhaps the Experts will devise a Test for Garden Madness. Perhaps the Experts will devise a Vaccine for Garden Madness. Perhaps the Experts will insert the Garden Madness gene into themselves, quickly, before their next experiment! Or possibly they already have, and these are the results. You just never know what might happen in the fun-filled recombinant world of Science & Technology Experts.

Lookers

Lastly, there is a worse Expert pestilence upon the land of your garden than these representatives of Officialdom. Right away, during your very first season, you will find out the hard way that nothing makes your garden look like last year's bird nest faster than an unannounced visit from another gardening enthusiast. Suddenly all of your flowers are wilted, your vegetables puny, your borders a ratty mess. All of your excuses—even the tornado that went through the backyard last week—are as naught. You are a worthless braggadocio in the face of Those Who Have Come To See.

I was once visited unannounced by an internationally-respected best-selling novelist who asked to look at one of my unpublished manuscripts, a situation akin to having your clothes disappear on a sweaty afternoon downtown when you are thirty-five pounds overweight and have to walk ten blocks to get home, only five million times more humiliating. Yet this was nothing compared to the trauma of garden visitor Experts, as perhaps only those who have experienced both can truly understand.

---

[*] Again—I'm not making these two up. I wish I were. Sorry

[**] Just kidding here. Not a bad idea, though.

Famous Novelist Visit

FAMOUS NOVELIST: Well, why don't you show me what you've been working on lately?

ME: No, no, please—kill me instead!

FAMOUS NOVELIST (*chuckling sympathetically*): Oh, not to worry—I know it's a rough draft and all, I understand.

ME: Oh, all right (*hands over manuscript*).

FAMOUS NOVELIST (*reading*): Um … let's see, your main character is a parrot, and in the end it turns out that the butler did it—how interesting.

ME: You really think so?

FAMOUS NOVELIST: Well, uh—maybe it would help if you introduced a story line somewhere in the first four chapters.

ME (*ingratiatingly*): Oh, gosh you're right! Thank you, thank you! (*Secret Thought:* Maybe he can get me an agent.)

UPSHOT OF VISIT: Overinflated ego, renewed determination to create immortal masterpiece, development of strange personal habits.

Garden Looker Visit

GARDEN LOOKER: So let's go outside and look at your flowers (*laughs*).

ME: Uh, well, I haven't had a chance to do anything out there this week—I have to write that Nobel Prize acceptance speech for Stanislaus Steinmetz and then practice for the Olympic figure skating competition next Tuesday …

GARDEN LOOKER: Oh, well, *surely* your flowers will all be just *exactly* as gorgeous as you say they are in that *precious* little book you claim you've been writing.

ME: Uh, well, um, actually, uh …

GARDEN LOOKER (*walking along perennial border*): Hmmm—did those used to be delphiniums?

ME: Well, actually, uh, I didn't … next year, I, um, hope to … uh, see, the woodchucks …

GARDEN LOOKER (*curling lip as though something smells bad*): What an interesting way to grow dahlias—flat out on the ground.

ME: Well, I, ah, see, the string broke, and ... (*Secret Thought:* Maybe she'll fall over the rake and die).

GARDEN LOOKER: I guess I've seen enough here. Shall we go have a look at your legendary wildflower border?

ME: No, no, please! Kill me instead!

GARDEN LOOKER: All right. (*Draws gun, fires*)

UPSHOT OF VISIT: Totally deflated ego, decision to run away and join the circus, begins channeling Vita Sackville-West on Saturday nights.

You

Well, there you are, then. Alone. All by yourself. Just you and your garden.

The only reassurance I can offer is the following exchange that I once heard at a convention of Very, Very Important Old-Time Self-Proclaimed Master Developed Experts in the Most Prestigious Field That Ever Was:

ELEVEN YEAR OLD KID: Mr. Asimov, if the Star Ship *Enterprise* shoots a photon torpedo while traveling at Warp Eight times the speed of light, how can the torpedo travel faster than the *Enterprise* is already going? Wouldn't it just stay inside the ship and explode?

ISAAC ASIMOV, INTERNATIONALLY RECOGNIZED EXPERT IN EVERYTHING REMOTELY FACTUAL AND MOST EVERYTHING ELSE THAT ISN'T: Uh ... well ... (silence).

So remember this about Experts! Nobody knows more than the kid who lives down the road. Or the kid who lives inside your Mad Gardening heart. Though you might do well to heed this Certified Actual Working Farmer Advice, which applies far and wide whether you Garden or Not:

What goes into a cow comes out of a cow.
Never drive a tractor faster than you can think.

What is there ever else to know?

CHAPTER SEVENTEEN
Under Duress

*A*nd then there is gardening under conditions that ordinary human beings are simply not equipped to endure. Only Gardeners of special Divine Madness will persevere and prevail, and they deserve every ounce of our dazzlement. You normal mortals out there should cover your eyes during this chapter, and be thankful for the fact that you are quite satisfied with that hanging basket full of something green that you buy for the patio every year and forget to water until it dries up and dies. You can relax. Gaia will not forget to water you!

You hope. Following are the most Duressive conditions known to the Mad Gardener. To others, nothing of any consequence is known at all. We do not Speak of them.

By the Dark of the Moon

In horti terms, Gardening by the Moon is an ancient method for planting roots, corms, and other crops by following the various phases of the lunar cycle and its mysterious pull and push upon the waters and minerals of the Earth, but that is not what I am talking about here. There is another kind of tide in gardening, and I am sure that you Really Mad readers out there know exactly what I mean!

For it is true, my children, that approximately every twenty-eight days, one of the sexes goes completely out of control and is unable to stop itself from getting in the car, driving to the local Bar &

Grille, barging right through the door, and randomly punching out everyone in the place until the floor is littered with shards of teeth, pickled onions, and chewing tobacco, along with an unsurprisingly small amount of brain matter and broken glass. Then everyone gets up and orders another round.

And that is just what happens to the male of the species! While over on the female side of the calendar, the days dwindle around to a dreadful few, hormones start raising their hands and asking all kinds of impertinent questions, and before you know it, to the dismay of family and friends and society in general, *women start saying exactly what is on their minds* and *obnoxiously demanding to be taken seriously,* without even asking *once* if anybody else agrees with them or whether their opinions are objectively correct or backed up by statistical evidence gathered through research carried out on beagles that have been painted blue and forced to smoke cigars and watch the *MacNeil/Lehrer News Hour* on PBS until they (the beagles) expire in the name of science.

You can imagine what this does to gardening that is also being accomplished by females.

GARDEN SUPPLY STORE MAN PERSON: Good morning, little Missy, how can I help you today?

MAD FEMALE MOON PERSON: You call me "little Missy" one more time and I'm going to rip your goddamned face off and throw it into the goddamned street.

GARDEN SUPPLY STORE MAN PERSON: I see. Will that be cash or charge?

Gadzooks! Though personally, I love it when I'm this Madly Duressed!! It's the time when all those big gardening chores get done, and they get done *right,* lemme tell you, and they get done *chop chop,* and without any yahdeedah how-dee-do because I do those chores *myself* and I do them *my way* and without any lip-dee-lip from you and all your kin! And all you cukes out there better know it and grow it. Or else!

Otherwise, when can you come over and fix my lawn mower, you hunkka hunkka fixin' love?

In the City

Gardening in the City is an oxymoron of the First Magnitude. Basically we are talking about planting things exclusively in tubs and buckets or the occasional lot that is the exact size and shape of a trash compactor, only with much more trash in it. One spring day, you strap on a weapon and go outside and clean up all this debris. Underneath it is a solid cushion of abandoned pavement overlain by pigeon guano and car exhaust molecules. You are ready to begin gardening.

In the City, this means traveling by subway to your neighborhood Flower Store to buy dirt and seedlings, where, if you get there and are also still alive, you immediately enter in on an instructive conversation with your friendly, helpful Flower Store proprietor, who is awfully busy this time of year trying to keep his gun loaded and so may seem somewhat distracted …

YOU: Pardon me, but it says $32.95 on this one blighted little tomato plant. Could that be the correct price?

PROPRIETOR: Piss outta you ear.

… and may not be able to attend to your individual gardening needs as thoroughly as you might wish. Therefore, you must use your own purchasing judgment as best you can and drag your supplies home in a stolen shopping cart so that you may begin to design your tiny piece of bucolic Heaven for the street gangs to rip out and strew around the neighborhood at their urban leisure.

Unbelievably, you keep at it. There is a special place in Gaia's heart just for you! Though you will have to share it with all the flying, crawling, buzzing, stinging, chomping, swimming, oozing, wiggling, creeping creatures of the world.

Thereby upgrading your environment!

In the Mail

Anyone who chooses to pursue gardening through mail-order sources can expect more Duress than mere complete financial ruin and massive Home Equity Loans taken out to pay for same. No, mail-order gardening requires a stubbornness that will prove to be far beyond your means, whatever socioeconomic class you used to belong to! As exemplified by this far, far too typical exchange:

February 21, 1994
S.M. Watkins
RD1, Rock Stream, NY
Dear Preferred Customer:

Thank you for your order of January 8: #169072, *Mushrooms of the Western World*; #598491, *A Gourmet's Guide to the Octopus*; #000673, *My Life with Mendel*. We are happy to have been of service to you. Please include your order receipt with any and all inquiries.
Sincerely,
Gardengrout Books, Inc.
Chlordane, NJ

February 25, 1994
Gardengrout Books, Inc.
129 Anvil Road
Chlordane, NJ
Dear Folks:

Thank you for filling my order of January 8, 1994. However, there has been a mix-up. Book #598491 was supposed to have been, *A Dictionary of Common Garden Pests,* and not *A Gourmet's Guide to the Octopus.* Whether that order number goes with *A Dictionary of Common Garden Pests* or *A Gourmet's Guide to the Octopus,* it is *A Dictionary of Common Garden Pests* that I want. Enclosed is *A Gourmet's Guide to the Octopus* and my order receipt, as you indicate must be sent with all inquiries. I have misplaced my copy of your catalog, or I would check the inventory numbers myself.
Sincerely,
S.M. Watkins
Rock Stream, NY

March 5, 1994
S.M. Watkins
RD#1, Rock Stream, NY
Dear Preferred Customer,

We are sorry that you are unsatisfied with #827340, *A Gourmet's Guide to the Octopus*. Our catalog department has been notified and they will send to you an advance copy of our summer sale circular filled with bargains and discounts too outstanding to ignore! We will record a credit of [$13.98] against your next order when we receive your preorder receipt.
Sincerely,
Gardengrout Books, Inc.
Chlordane, NJ

March 8, 1994
Gardengrout Books, Inc.
129 Anvil Road
Chlordane, NJ
Ladies or Gentlemen:

In regard to your letter of March 5 and the return of *A Gourmet's Guide to the Octopus,* it is not that I am unsatisfied with the book—except that I am somewhat squeamish about eating things that still have eyes in them—but I simply did *not* order that book. I ordered instead, *A Dictionary of Common Garden Pests,* which may or may not be catalog #598491. I cannot look this up, as I have lost the catalog. Please check your records and send to me, *A Dictionary of Common Garden Pests,* which incidentally costs $9.98 and not $13.98 as you indicate. You already have my order receipt, as I mailed it to you on 2/25/94, as per your request.
Sincerely,
S.M. Watkins.
Rock Stream, NY

March 22, 1994
S.M. Watkins
RD#1, Rock Stream, NY
Dear Preferred Customer:

Thank you for your order of March 8, 1994: #598491, *A Gourmet's Guide to the Octopus*. We will mail your order promptly as soon as we have received your remittance of [$3.97] as the difference against your credit account, along with our catalog order form filled out as per instructions in our new summer sale circular filled with bargains and discounts too outstanding to ignore!
Sincerely,
Gardengrout Books, Inc.
Chlordane, NJ

March 25, 1994
Gardengrout Books, Inc.
129 Anvil Road
Chlordane, NJ
People:

I am not now, nor have I ever been, involved in ordering *A Gourmet's Guide to the Octopus,* and if it arrives here, I shall throw it out. All I wanted was *A Dictionary of Common Garden Pests,* but you apparently need it more than I do, so you can keep it. And for your information, *My Life with Mendel* is missing pages 19 and 276, and the binding glue smells funny. In fact, it smells just like the mushroom I picked yesterday that your #169072 maintains is "a harmless and edible species of fungus." Enclosed is a sample of same. You try it.
S.M. Watkins.
Rock Stream, NY

March 29, 1994
S.M. Watkins
RD#1, Rock Stream, NY
Dear Preferred Customer:

Thank you for your order of March 25, 1994: #169072, *Mushrooms of the Western World*; #598491, *A Gourmet's Guide to the Octopus*; #000673, *My Life with Mendel*. We are happy to have been of service to you. All orders will be shipped promptly upon receipt of payment against your credit account, which presently shows an available balance of [-$3.97], along with an order form filled out as per instructions in our new summer sale circular filled with bargains and discounts too outstanding to ignore! Please return your order receipt with any and all inquiries.
Sincerely,
Gardengrout Books, Inc.
Chlordane, NJ

March 29, 1994
S.M. Watkins
RD#1, Rock Stream, NY
Dear Exclusive Customer:

Thank your for your order of January 15 to the amount of $128.95. We regret that only one item on your order form is in stock at the present time: #875 CLIMBING THORNSTICK. However, we have instructed our mail-order department to forward our new spring catalog of sensational garden bargains to the following person[s] as indicated by our computerized Exclusive Customer files:

S.M. Watkins
RD#1, Rock Bleam, NY 14444

Suzane Wattki
RFD #1, RockyStr 1444

Mr & Mrs Suzawha Tkns
Road 2, RStream NY 44441

Whaatkins Family
Rural Mailbox #3
Toadtream NY 14???

We hope that you will reorder from our all-new selection of plants for the [WHAATKINS FAMILY] garden, guaranteed to arrive at the proper planting time in [TOADTREAM NY]!! Please send us your current invoice with any and all inquiries to (check one):
 [] receive full reimbursement against credit
 [] receive full credit against reimbursement
 [] charge order against preapproved invoice credit
 [] return order for preapproved reimbursement exchange

Please feel free to inform us of the many ways we may serve you!
Sincerely,
Rootwell Nurseries
992 Synapse Terrace
Bombblast, Michigan

P.S. : Very occasionally, we find that we are out of a certain item listed in our catalog. In this case, may we select a substitute of equal value for the [WHAATKINS FAMILY] garden?
 [] yes [] no [] refund voucher minus sales tax [] credit invoice plus C.O.D. charges.

THANK YOU, [WHAATKINS FAMILY] !!

April 4, 1994
ATTENTION: Rootwell Nurseries
992 Synapse Terrace
Bombblast, Michigan
Dear Sirs:

Please address all further correspondence concerning the late S.M. Watkins to: Gardengrout Books, Inc., 129 Anvil Road, Chlordane, N.J. Thank you.

Sincerely,
My Nearest of Kin

So there you have it—the Best of the Duress. If you have experienced and survived any of the above, you are not only Wiser, you are Madder.

Truly a celestial state of Moon!

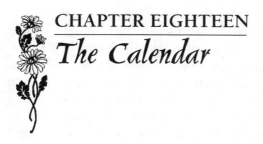

CHAPTER EIGHTEEN
The Calendar

In youth, it was a way I had
To try my best to weed,
To hoe with every passing rain
To fit my rows of seed.

But now I know the plants I know
And compost the ones I don't,
And if you do not like it so,
I'll dish out a snotty retort.

—Dorothy Parsnippy

For Lo my soulful soulmates, here is how the Gardening Calendar of the Mad must needs be.

Dragging Along in January

Oh Winter sad, in snowy clad,
Is making a doleful din,
But let him howl til sometime tomorrow,
When I start howling louder than Him.

—Old Irish cabin fever ditty

Ah, yes, winter, the beginning of the new Gardening year and the arrival of all those catalogs in your mailbox! As you peruse these gems of springtime, remember that wise old adage, "Be not the first to breakke the banke nor yet the last of order stanke." Meaning, grab that pencil and get with it! The catalog companies will be glad you did.

Now is the time to take inventory of your gardening tools, supplies, gizmos, and perhaps your sanity, as the days dwindle down to total darkness by four P.M. and the urge to fill the bathtub with potting soil and plant lettuce seems more and more like a brilliant idea. Repair any broken hand tools if your Significant Other does not mind dirt and rust all over the kitchen counters. Don't look over your stored tubers and corms to see if there is any rot. If there is, you will just sink into a worse depression than you already have.

During the alleged "January thaw," try turning your compost pile, if you can find it Out There in the snow desert. If you can't, oh well. Send for a passel of red "wiggler" worms and put them in a box of shredded newspapers under the kitchen sink to render your vegetable scraps. Everyone in your domestic circle will think this is charming. Sure they will.

Get out your graph paper and start dreaming your garden dreams.

When you are about to go uncontrollably gah-gah, drive down to the local nursery and buy some flowering plants or forced bulbs in bloom. Wash all of your house plants with soap and water. Dry on the "low" setting and be sure to clean out the lint trap. Plant some basil seeds or garlic cloves on the windowsill. In pots, you poor despondent doof.

Remember to feed the birds.

When all else fails, drive back to the local nursery and stand in the greenhouse and weep.

Getting Started in February

The North wind doth blow, and we shall have snow,
And what shall the Robin do then, poor thing?
He'll sit in the barn to keep himself warm,
And poop on the top of the car.

                                                    —Child's madrigal

February, February, February … my my, you are ready to throw the barcalounger right through the TV set, aren't you? But, Lo! February means only one thing: You have forgotten whatever it was that you ordered from the catalogs, except that you are ominously aware that there was a lot of it.

Keep feeding the birds.

And that's about it for "Feb-yew-airy," as it's pronounced by everyone constrained to live there.

The Busy Month of March

In that March with its shores uproot
And like a something has pierced a boot,
In something something sweet liquor pours
With flour and water cooked over medium heat
That makes something something into out-of-doors.
                    —Really bad translation of old Saxon poem

One thing the Mad Gardener will never learn is when to be in a hurry and when to practice restraint, as March so aptly demonstrates. Someone once said that when you feel you cannot stop yourself from rushing outside and uncovering all your perennials and sticking dahlia toes in the half-frozen ground that "Gardening haste makes library paste," which is more or less the long and short of it.

Most of the Gardener's attention in March is directed to seeds and what to do about them, mainly because they are now arriving on your doorstep in huge boxes and crates. A coldframe is a stupid idea, as you will discover the first year you attempt to start your overabundant catalog orders in one. Thusly, what you will learn to do about seeds is this: Buy them later, grown up, from commercial greenhouses, unless you have one of these latter devices yourself. In which case, you are in another world, and you don't care *what* month it is.

Now you can start seeds indoors, in flats and pots, and milk cartons and Cool Whip containers, and Dixie cups and Tupperware with holes poked in the bottoms, and whatever else it takes to make your home resemble a refrigerator that hasn't been cleaned out since Joan Crawford was a girl.

Some early bulbs, such as crocus, will be peeking through the ground now and you will have to discipline yourself not to run outside and kiss their purple blossoms when at last they bloom. Or what the heck, go ahead and do it. You can plant peas and start hacking away at your shrubs and vines or even put in some new trees, if the soil is workable and Nature does not play a humorous giant snowfall prank on your geographical region! You can also take cuttings from flowering bushes and trees and bring these in the house and put them in water, where they will sit there like a bunch of sticks unless you have done this little trick exactly right.

Buy a soil test kit, check out your garden's PH, and forget about it. The test was invented by the Board of Education to delude you into thinking that high school chemistry will be useful in later life and your vegetables don't give a hoot one way or another.

But March! March is the Month of the First Day of Spring! Oh, Tra-loo, tra-la! What happier time can there ba! Unless you want to count ...

The Hectic Month of April

The kiss of the sun for pardon,
The song of the birds for mirth.
I will work my butt off in a garden
More than anywhere else on Earth.

—Disgruntled tiller's song

Now the Gardening fever is at its height, though there is further need for caution; for as Pliny the Elder put it, "What in Hobbe's Hell do I know about gardening? I've been dead for nineteen hundred and fifteen years!" So you see that you could still get in big trouble.

You can rake mulches away from perennials and weed the perennials out of your compost. Look over the trees and shrubs for caterpillar egg masses and make your kids pick them off, because they (the eggs) are disgusting. Turn over your garden soil if it's not soaking wet from spring runoff and rain. Dig thistles out of the lawn but never mind adding fertilizers or chemicals to it. Edge your flower borders. Divide perennials. Plant some more trees. Plant lettuce and cabbage. Also carrot seed tapes. Torture yourself with "hardening-off."

Take a quick nap.

Haul out the filthy power equipment. Attempt to change the oil and sharpen the blades. Give up on attempt and run the damn things dirty. You've done it every other year, so why not this one?

Call your friendly garden machinery replacement parts store now, before anything has broken, and order a bunch of replacement parts completely at random. Go ahead and make up names for these parts if you are feeling especially creative. Since no machinery replacement component ever actually arrives at any machinery repair shop anywhere in the world, you will never have to pay for these orders, but at least the repairfolk people will know that you are not to be trifled with without the help of a whip and chair.

Go once again to the local nursery, whose employees now hide in the rest rooms when they see you approaching, and buy six dozen marigolds which you cannot put out for at least another month.

Tell the UPS man that the catalog companies have goofed up, and are sending you all these orders by mistake. He's heard this before, but he'll smile and nod anyway, so as not to set you off, because he knows that right around the corner lies ...

The Manic Month of May

Tra-la, it's May, the lusty month of May,
The time when everybody goes blissfully astray;
It's time to do a reckless thing or two!
And put tomatoes in too soon and corn and peppers, too!
—Theme Song from "Cameloupe"

If there were ever a time to go running around like a chicken with your head cut off, May is it! You have more things to do out in the garden than you imagined possible, even in your memory of every other May you have ever experienced for as long as you have been Gardening!

It is a good idea to strip all the beds in your house of their sheets and blankets, to have on hand when that irksome Last Frost catches you with your tender annual pants down.

Make your summer supply of manure "tea" by suspending a burlap bag full of fresh cow patties in a barrel of rainwater by the patio door until the stench is so overpowering that certain anatomical threats are made against your person and you can safely dump the "tea" out all over yourself some breezy evening just before "dinner."

Now you are planting, planting, planting, and it is too bad that you misplaced your carefully drawn garden map, because this year you had resolved to be more orderly, and not just jam every kind of flower in existence into every border and row! While you're at it, you might try to find the labels and marking pen that you ordered from Gardens Alive! in January. Or how about just finding the names of the plants?

And suddenly, your lawn is growing by leaps and bounds and swoops and moops and the mowing season has begun! Remember to adjust your mower blades so that the first cut is at two and five-sixteenths inches, and then readjust every time you mow thereafter so that you alternate between cuts of two and one-ninth and a fifth and one and five-twellffpths and a half. This is what the lawn experts say you should do, and since they all live in New Mexico, they should know.

But then, lawn experts, who obviously have been out in the desert sun too long, also recommend that you bathe your grass in a mixture of dish water, chewing tobacco juice, and mouthwash "to discourage insect pests and disease." The question of how to make your lawn get in the bathtub is, in this Gardener's opinion, far outweighed by the specter of all those lawn experts spitting tobacco juice into the dishwater. Perhaps insect pests and grass diseases aren't as hard to put up with as you thought.

Put in your gladiolus and dahlia toes. Drive support stakes in next to them now, for "As the twig is bent, you'd better not tweak the tree," as the old saying goes.

You can probably throw the house plants out on the deck, and if they freeze, all to the good. Hang baskets of annuals and fill window boxes with something, anything. Mow the lawn again. Turn the compost pile.

Plant marigolds next to your tomatoes to repel hornworms and attract killer bees.

Attempt to fix whatever has broken on your lawn mower by using a combination of old-fashioned Yankee ingenuity and your old-fashioned Yankee grandfather's sledgehammer.

Get out the loafing chairs and wash off the spiders.

The Frenzied Month of June

Oh, what is so rare as a day in June?
Maybe a day without flea beetle
infestations, Eh, Mr. Poet Person?
You think you're so smart? You try it.
Then if ever you'll shut up and go home.

—Reply to Aristotle
Contemplating the Bust of Rodale

Goodness Gracious, what a whirling dervish you have become these days! Aren't you sorry you're not sitting around writing a silly book about Gardening, rather than having to go out there and garden?

But one mustn't gloat, mustn't one?

By this time you have hooked up your garden's electric fence and solved the Mammal problem for now, but weeds! Crabgrass! Purslout! Pig's ear! Redretch! Bramblebeak! Hubris! Scotchtape! Yukbalm! Roofnail! It's enough to send a poor Mad Gardener right over the Edgewort.

Roses are in full bloom and could easily be eaten off at the stems by Japanese beetles and aphids. Blast these bugs with a spray of one-quarter dish soap, one-quarter cider vinegar, and one-half water.

The bugs will go to the locker room, lather up, rinse off, and be back on line ready for work tomorrow morning. But at least you aren't spitting tobacco juice into the dishwater.

Work in some Epsom Salts around rose roots to enhance their fragrance. You can also bathe your goldfish in Epsom salts while cleaning their bowl or pool. It won't make the fish any more fragrant than they already are, but it will certainly help their dispositions and skin tone.

Remove, transport to corner garage, wait around for an hour to have repaired, and put back on, three flat lawn mower tires. Immediately afterward, ascertain that the mower deck belts are worn out by hearing them snap in two just as you flip the "blades" switch to "on." Return to corner garage and discover that new belts, which cost $1.98 in recycled motor oil to manufacture, go for $72.39 per linear foot.

Pay it.

If you don't put Reemay cloth cover on your lettuce and *brassicae,* they will be destroyed overnight by hordes of flea beetles, cabbage worms, and aphids. However, if you do put Reemay cloth cover on your lettuce and *brassicae,* they will be destroyed overnight by hordes of flea beetles, cabbage worms, and aphids.

Do not go yanking unfamiliar weeds out of surrounding grassy areas until you have memorized that ancient poison ivy caution which says: "Leaves of three, rub it on your knee!"

Mow your lawn seventeen more times.

Now that you have worked so hard to get all those seeds in the ground, you must work even harder to thin them out by accidentally planting something else on top of them.

Deadhead the blossoms that are gone and try not to confuse them with the blossoms that are just coming out.

Drag out your watering hoses, check them for leaks, and place the nozzle ends in the driveway where you can more easily run over them with your car.

You can place shallow bowls full of beer near your vegetables to trap slugs, but it won't make one iota of difference. There are sixteen trillion pregnant slugs in your garden right this minute as against five and a half bottles of beer in your refrigerator. You might better drink the beer yourself and let the slug question drift off into oblivion.

Try to remember where the spring flowers that have gone dormant are located, and mark them. No one knows why you should do this, since they will come up in exactly the same place next year, but do it anyway.

Dig up everything and move it around at least twice.

Spend half a day trying to reweave the seats of your lawn chairs and give up.

Mow your lawn nine more times. Replace steering wheel bolt that sheared off just as you rounded the corner by the bearded iris.

Place bearded iris shreds in compost pile.

Drink more beer.

The Hellish Month of July

Give fools their gold and knaves their power,
Who sows a field or trains a flower?
Who cares? I just want to take a shower.
                              —John Wiltleaf Sweattier

Now is the happy time of year when you start crabbing about the heat to everyone who had to listen all winter to your crabbing about the cold! When are you going to learn that it isn't the heat, it's the crabs?

We hope that you are remembering to keep the proper gardening tools on hand to do the job of keeping up your garden's summer appearance. For example, with your edger, you can neaten the walkways in just a few miserable hours of back-breaking labor, but handing a knife or a trowel to a teenager who is being forced to do the same job will save you about half a day's worth of agony and sweat.

Watering time is now at hand and you should pay attention to the difference between "watering" and "sprinkling." When you "water" your lawn or garden, you soak it for hours and hours, or until your municipal reservoir has been drained down to a mosquito-ridden puddle of leftover industrial sludge. When you "sprinkle," you step discreetly behind the bushes.

On the other hand, if you mulched the garden thoroughly and are leaving the lawn to its own perennial devices, you are quite a smarty-pants and probably sitting in a cool movie theater someplace with Mel Gibson and a bucket of popcorn.

Harvest your garlic, if you planted it last fall, and hang it up all around the inside of your garage, where it will cure nicely and purge the ceiling corners of carpenter ants.

Trim perennials whose blooms are done and stick some portulaca in any bare spots left over from rabbits feasting upon your nasturtiums. Check your potted plants for insects and run screaming from the porch when a knot of earwigs scuttles out from under the *ficus benjamina*.

Dig up more of everything and divide it again.

Check the crowded condition of those mowed-off iris roots and decide to do something about them next year, when it's cooler. Fertilize the window boxes, which have almost rotted all the way through on the bottoms. Check the electric fence batteries by coaxing your dog to touch the wire.

Bring in bouquets of cut flowers and put them in vases all over your house so the cats may knock them over at their leisure.

Sit in your half-busted lawn chair with a large glass of beverage and eat the first tomato sandwich of the season. With real mayonnaise. And onions. And pickled hot pepper relish. And salad dressing. To Hell with Everyone!

Do not bother to mow the lawn. It is dead.

You are glad.

The Dog Days of August

If you can keep your garden watered when all about you
Are losing theirs and blaming it on the weather,
If you can mulch and not get tired of mulching,

If you can weed when the heat and humidity are trying to kill you,
You'll have the soil and everything that's in it,
And then, what's more, you'll be a Mad Gardener, you peon.
— Mudyard Karpling

The wise Gardener who wants more bulbs next spring orders them now, mainly because now is when the bulb catalogs start pouring into your mailbox. You will notice right away that you can order as many as *five hundred* daffodil or tulip bulbs at a time. Only ordinary, sane people would order less! Like, say, twelve! Ha, ha! What nincompoops!

Keep the birdbath filled. The bats will show their gratitude by eating every single mosquito that hatches from it.

Check your gardens daily for signs of bug infestation. You will be amazed at how much there is to find! August is also the favorite month for fleas, so check your household pets carefully and give them baths once in a while. Your cats will especially enjoy these intimate moments with their humans! Or you could add brewer's yeast and powdered garlic tablets to your pets' food, which will give them violent diarrhea but is entirely worth it to rid your home of these parasites (the fleas), which are repelled by the taste of this vile concoction (the tablets).

Keep your tall flowers cut and stake all dead stalks. Or is that the other way around?

Add more mulch to everything except Oriental poppies, which are resting now and like hot sunbaked ground in which to do it. If the Feds didn't confiscate them in the Happy Sixties, that is. Along with you and your hot sunbaked Happy Brownies.

Kick the tires on your mower once in a while to let it know you haven't forgotten its place in the scheme of things.

Remember that woodstove ash you didn't know what to do with? Sprinkle some around the phlox, asters, and cosmos, but not on a windy day. Take cuttings of garden plants that you want to root for winter bloom. Yes, unfortunately, I said "winter." We are going 'round the corner and are about to head down the final stretch.

Scrupulous trimming and weeding of your mostly parched lawn will turn you into a bad-tempered old sunburned boring person.

The Melancholy of September

Because I would not stop to Can,
Harvest would not stop for me;
The Tomatoes, lift them, pound for pound,
Are going to drive me Wheeeee!

—Emily Noyes Pickinson

Well, now that September is here at last, how did you like your garden this year? Are you ashamed of yourself for not working harder when you had the chance? I knew it!

The big news this month is that everything is starting to come into Ripe, and you are going to have to start figuring out what you are going to do with it all. If you thought you were busy in April and May, you were just making eyes at yourself, for the bounty of plenty is about to mutiny into your lap with the vigorous fecundity for which Nature is perhaps best adapted! Are you going to freeze, can, dry, store, or eat it where you stand? Quick! Make up your mind!

If that weren't enough, the leaves are going to start falling any day now, so you'd better get out the old graph paper again, make a map of your vegetable garden so you will know how to rotate your crops next year, and put it someplace where you will never be able to find it again.

Rain and cooler weather have turned your lawn back into an annoying, growthy green, so you will need to mow it five or six more times after you replace the now-dead battery. Mix some of the grass clippings with your vegetable scraps, annual flower leftovers, autumn leaves, and well-rotted manure so you can have something to talk about besides engine parts. Perhaps your Significant Other will help by secretly dumping your kitchen redworms into the compost pile some afternoon while you are mowing away the hours! Don't worry. The worms will migrate to the warm center of the Heap and have a happier winter than you will. Where your Significant Other migrates to is none of my business.

Collect seeds from your flowers for next year, if you have the patience, and store in a cool, dry place. Meaning your patience, because you're going to need it if you try this.

Start dragging in the house plants after you have given them a good blast or two with the garden hose. At least half the plants will need repotting. Ignore this.

Keep digging up, dividing, transplanting, and watering those perennials. Sharpen your shovel and get cracking on that refrigerator-carton load of daffodil and tulip bulbs that just arrived. You might get them all in the ground by the time you're seventy-five years old, unless you already are. Pot up some marigolds to take in the house. They won't last long, but you can dry the blossoms and keep them to sniff when the snow flies.

In your spare moments, stack the firewood in the garage before yellow jackets have a chance to make nests in the jumble. Oops, too late! Yow! Sorry I didn't mention this sooner!

Keep running inside to check the boiling vats of tomato sauce and canning jars, and put some baking powder paste on those nasty stings, will you?

Mow the lawn yet one more time.

October's Bright Blue Bruises

THIS is the AUTumn primEEVAL the THREATening
FROST and the DREADlocks ...
                              —"Song of Scabiosa"

Too many Gardeners think that it's all over when the leaves begin to turn red and gold, or when First Frost has swooped down upon the land. But no, you cannot throw your trowels and hoes in a disorderly heap in the shed just yet! There is lots to do, and a fine set of bright blue days to do it in.

Start raking those leaves and dumping them into a pile for next year's composting. If you don't feel like doing this yourself, you can drive around town plucking your neighbor's leaves from the curbsides, though it will help the condition of your hatchback if the leaves are in bags.

Get out there and dig up your dahlia toes so you can dry them out, place them in boxes of sawdust, and store them in the basement for the cats to use as a spare litter box.

Mow your lawn at least three more times, and then prepare all of your abused power equipment for its long winter's nap. Do this by shoving the !*@&%$#$!^%!! things into a dry corner of your barn or garage and slamming the door shut. They will speak quarrelsomely about you for this treatment, but who is the boss around here, anyway?

LAWN MOWER: I hate it when they don't even scrape the old grass gorp off my blades.

ROTOTILLER: I know what you mean. Why don't we call a meeting of all the neighborhood lawn and garden machinery and figure out how we can get revenge?

LAWN MOWER: Great idea! I could plan to spurt dangerous highly-refined petroleum products all over my hot engine block at terrifyingly unpredictable random intervals next spring!

WEEDWHACKER: Terrific! And I could refuse to start except in the presence of condescending Repairfolk Persons who will charge fifty dollars an hour just to take a look at my spark plug!

SHREDDER: Ho ho, that's a good one.

WEEDWHACKER: Thank you. I learned it from the pickup truck.

You should also drain all water from spigots and hoses and store your sprinkling equipment in the barn, but perhaps you'd better not go in there by yourself for a while.

Plant some more of your daffodil and tulip bulbs, and never order them by the bushel again.

Cover root crops with straw for overwinter eating so that you will not be able to dig them out from under a foot of snow and ice.

The Depressing Month of November

A haze on the far horizon,
The infinite dishwater sky,
The sodden mess of the cornfield,
And the wild geese going south and you're not—
Some of us call it November,
Others just sit around and cry.

—W. H. Anguish

With the Gardening year winding down to a precious few moments of sunshine per diem, the hearty and the hale will be out there against all odds and logic, making sure that flower and vegetable beds alike are properly tucked in for winter. You should remember to wear suitable clothes and not stand in the howling November drear without your beanie and propeller. For what else will get you through the next few months but this kind of nonsense and television?

Pitch the finished compost all over your gardens and roll up the last of the Reemay, though not in that order, or you will be one sorry frustrated duckie! Bring in the lawn chairs and gizmos. You wouldn't want the bent-over buttboards destroyed by the savage elements of snow and iceballs hurled from my passing car!

Take a huge garden salad of your home-grown *cruciferae* to your relatives' Thanksgiving dinner. Be sure to use lots of your home-grown garlic. It's the least you can do for family dissidence.

Get out the bird feeders and start filling. Your Avian friends are depending on you to get them through the winter. Do not underestimate how equally they return the favor to you.

Going Dormant in December

The garden is buried, dark and deep.
And I have endless hours to sleep,
And somehow my sanity to keep,
And a rhyming dictionary cheap.

—Robert Frosthead

If you haven't cleaned all of your garden tools by now, you have not been paying very close attention to your outdoor chores, but have instead put on your flannel jammies and housecoat and slipper-socks and are curled up, reading, in your favorite chair before a warm, crackling fire.

Well, isn't that the point? For as the famous writer once said, "Buy this book."

We could not have put it better unless we had written this Ourself.

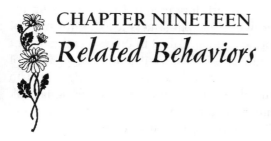

CHAPTER NINETEEN
Related Behaviors

*T*RUE GARDEN MADNESS is not only about gardening. True Garden Madness infects you with enthusiasms of all kinds, most of which cannot be explained by the rational mind. But then, who can be sure what it is, exactly, that the rational mind cannot explain next? Currently, it has gotten drunk out of itself and is off on a toot not explaining why camel DNA should be injected into lettuce, so you probably should not wait up for it to come home at a reasonable hour. In fact, you should just go ahead and do any old thing you feel like, such as filling up your Ex's convertible with fish cannery waste. The rational mind will be too hung over to care.

Which brings us to the first of every Mad Gardener's Best Related Behavior.

Composting

For the truly Mad, the art of composting goes far beyond the heady pleasure of pitching mulch upon your garden beds. Compost and its components quickly become the source of your life's most passionate conversations and enraptured moments. A roadside pile of shredded tree branches can send you into climactic spasms and possibly a three-sixty fishtail. You think nothing of loading the entire mass of shreddings into the trunk of your car, because, of course, you carry a pitchfork with you at all times just for such an emergency. The sight of a farmer spreading fresh cow manure across the land fills you with longing, and I do not mean for the farmer. You regularly prowl municipal streets looking for bags of yard waste to take home. You would be thrilled to own several different kinds of compost-friendly animals—llamas, for example, or a gaggle of old hens past their egg prime, or a half-dozen potbellied pigs—just to have the poop supply. Mixing all of this together and watching it cook down into compost—even *thinking* about it cooking down into compost— makes you feel like a schoolkid in love again, only not half as twitty.

When it rains, you think, "Oh, boy—this will get the dry ingredients going."

When it's sunny, you think, "Hot damn—this will warm up the microbes."

When hailstones the size of pomegranates wreak ruination and mayhem across a six-county swath, you think, "Wow! That storm really aerated the heap!"

You look upon lawn mowing not so much as a chore, but as an opportunity to add a layer of green grass clippings, which is the composting equivalent of rocket fuel.

In winter, you tuck the Heap in with a blanket of hay bales and tell it good-night until spring.

The first page you turn to in a certain organic gardening magazine (namely, *Organic Gardening* magazine) is the one where other subscribers have sent in detailed descriptions of their composting adventures along with at least three framed color photos of steaming "brown gold" stored in backyard bins that cost more to build than the average condominium. Reading these tales, you are overwhelmed by the desire to drive to the nearest fairgrounds and pack your mini-van right up to the ceiling with last summer's Petting Zoo poo.

Perhaps at this point, a small voice—that would be the voice of the rational mind, which never knows when to shut the hell up—whispers in your inner ear that this might be considered fairly bonkers Behavior by normal people, who would never in a *million years* stick their hands *on purpose* into mounds of ruminant dung. No, they are far too busy pouring herbicides onto their lawns to even *imagine* such horrors. And so the rational mind has once again jammed its foot into the gears of your spontaneous *Weltschmerz!*

But just then, in the nick of time, you turn to the Organic Classified Section, and your poor underappreciated eyeball lights onto the following: "Single male with nitrogen-rich beach kelp seeking single female with fibrous materials. Prefer hot/active but will consider slow/passive. Small corn cobs OK. Have own thermometer."

Ah yes, you have found your Own True Love. You don't even have to have any working gardens to make a perfect match. No, not a one. The romance of the Heap is enough. Remember those roadside tree shreddings?

O composting be Paradise enow!

Recycling

As with composting, the Mad Gardener can easily get into a frenzy about recycling. Not only do you assiduously sort and bin your discardables, you start buying things just for the fun of bringing them home and throwing them into the correct receptacle. "Hey, look," you say aloud, "here is a sixteen-pound tuna wrapped in coconut-shell packing inside a Number Two plastic carton! I simply must have this for my blue curbside container!" As if your trash hauler needed additional entertainment. Just ask the people who are sidling away from you in the supermarket.

Well, cheer up—you will find out soon enough that right in the midst of your Gardening zeal, there are all sorts of Recycling Behaviors for you to indulge that are created by the seemingly harmless by-products of your flower and vegetable intentions, as in:

1. <u>Ten hundred billion styrofoam peanuts</u>. Many mail-order companies pack items for shipping in these beanies. They will never biodegrade. Ever. In fact, they can not only survive nuclear war, they may actually *cause* it by driving people insane, because there is no way to get rid of the things. None. Even if you close your Recycling eyes and put the peanuts out in the "garbage," they will blow back to your house on the first offdump breeze.

Your Behavior: You stuff all these miserable little jobbie-doos inside a large box. Nestle a pair of clean socks down among them. Close box, seal with duct tape. Ship to ungrateful offspring living in distant, Heathen city where styrofoam peanuts are used in unspeakable religious rituals.

Better yet, tell mail-order companies to send your plants in something else or only patronize those that already do. Or better *better* yet, buy plants from your local plant stores and nip the whole problem in its Styrofoam bud.

2. Thick plastic bags from peat moss, pine bark mulch, potting soil, "sanitized" cow manure, and other store-bought garden helpers. I bet you drag these forty-pound monsters home from the supermarket just for the enjoyment of cramming the bags into your trash compactor on the theory that since they smoosh down to the size of a footstool, the landfill will hardly notice! This was before you observed that some of these bags are now labeled "X percent post-consumer materials," and the only "post-consumer" fertilizer material you can think of is not something you want to keep around in your kitchen, is it?

Your Behavior: You pay more attention to your compost heaps and make your own mulch and potting soil. Well-rotted horse manure mixed with compost, sifted through a (preferably unused) window screen, and "toasted" a bit in the oven, is perfect for this last. You might be tempted to "toast" your potting soil in the "toaster oven" where your Significant Other enjoys making "toast." While this is obviously a brilliant idea, your Significant Other might possibly object and perhaps hit you over the head with the "microwave," another household tool that is quite useful for sterilizing soils. We will not even suggest what might happen if you have purloined the kitchen "sifter" to ameliorate your "sifting."

3. Packaging from store bulbs and corms. Meaning glossy cardboard tops, plastic wrap, and that bright orange Bozo the Clown hair in which bulbs are too often wrapped.

Your Behavior: You buy loose, unpackaged bulbs the way you buy most other produce. Or you take your own paper bags to the plant stores. Or you can try mailing this packaging to the bulb and corm companies with a letter of Behavior explanation.[1] They will be so impressed by your insistence on Recycling correctness that they will immediately ship *their* rubbish to *you* in return!

4. <u>Endless piles of plastic flats, pots, and trays</u>. Over the years you have amassed an impressive mountain of these. You have piled them up carefully in your garage, thinking that someday you will have a greenhouse. You imagine yourself filling all these plastic pots with vegetable and flower seeds while winter rages outside the glass. You imagine this intensively, in exquisite detail. None of it will ever come true.

Your Behavior: Having recovered from injuries received during that unfortunate "toasting" incident, you decide to make amends by trucking the mountain of filthy, aging flats down to your local nursery. The problem is that nurseries don't want seedling pots that are cracked and broken, though they usually like to have the trays. Also, your timing is off. You never think of doing this in the fall. By spring, nurseries have already put their season's stock on display and don't have room to clean and store your Recycling endeavors. And believe me, if the nursery workers—who have just spent months in crouched positions, transplanting eighty-nine trillion seedlings one at a time into plastic pots just like yours—see you unloading these things out of the trunk of your car, they will sic "Gorgonzola" the Pit Bull on you before you can say aaaaAAAAAIIIIIEEEEEEEEEEEEEEEEEEEEE

Leave the flats in the garage and put a clause in your will directing your heirs to run them (the flats) through a shredder and mold the remains (of the flats) into a line of Recycled plastic gardening clogs in memory of your Behavior.

5. <u>Ancient rusted and broken garden tools</u>. Oh, come on, now, you can find lots of Recycling uses for these. You can make flower stakes out of old hoe handles, for example, or you can create a fascinating piece of yard statuary with the weedwhacker that went string-up last fall. Plant morning glories around it for a fun conversation piece. Mulch with shredded Packaging Company rubbish. Perhaps it could stand as a kind of memorial.

Or you can always hold a rummage sale with stuff like this. Put fifty cents on that antique Bedfordshire Groundskeeper's Trowel and see what happens. But call me first! I'll be there early in the morning.

6. <u>Continuous threatening overdue credit card notices</u>. Well, don't say you haven't been warned about this. You just couldn't resist

sending away for all those gadgets made out of Recycled park benches and beach sandals, could you? Nor the joy of owning a collection of plastic yard trolls molded from laundry soap jugs!

Your Behavior: The good news is that these notices are all printed on biodegradable paper. You can throw them right into the compost heap, and presto! Out of sight, out of mind, out of garbage stream.

Just a simple thing you can do for the Earth!

Alternate Fueling

Another Behavior that almost always accompanies Garden Madness is the employment of Alternative Fuels to operate your home, auto, and, inevitably, self. At its zenith, this Behavior impels you to tinker seriously with the possibility of doing things like running your car with bottled heifer flatulence or heating your hot water with a giant camera lens attached to your roof, or ingesting nothing but brown rice and dandelion soup for the rest of your life. All very exciting and admirable endeavors, but the sad fact is that at its worst, Alternate Fueling Behavior leaves you with a Composting and Recycling predicament that is outclassed only by the hilarious national dilemma of what to do with our ever-burgeoning supply of radioactive waste!

As you have undoubtedly recognized, I am talking about wood stove ashes.

Granted, wood heat has its advantages, such as low, predictable cost and the copious production of the fundamental household necessity known as "filth," but beyond that is the mind-boggling problem of how to recycle the ashes that stare you in the face every morning of your wood-burning life. And, like their distant cousins the Spent Fuel Rods, those coals in your stove are hot enough to melt through the center of the Earth, just like Jane Fonda said they would. Really. In fact, the Himalayan mountains are not millions of years old, as geologists would have you believe, but were formed in the sixties after *Mother Earth News* told the hippies to install wood stoves and dump the ashes out on the curbsides of Love Canal, New York. This is common scientific knowledge. You can look it up yourself, though I forget exactly where just now.

Anyway, so there you are, trudging out into the garage for the hot ash bucket, the hot ash scoop, the hot ash gloves, the hot ash space helmet, and the hot ash Alternate Fuel Recycling plan firmly affixed in your mind. Except that there isn't any. Plan, that is. Here are some possible ash disposal solutions you might try, after which I've run out of ideas myself and you're on your own.

1. In the dead of winter, throw ashes out on your driveway to melt the ice and snow. This is probably only feasible if you have a dirt driveway and are willing to put up with an early springtime driving surface of jellied slag coal, a substance that also makes a handy outdoor substitute for cat box litter. But fear not! By September, this unholy brew will have pretty much washed over into your neighbor's yard and it will be almost time to start up a new batch. What fun!

An Alternative to that is to put the ashes in a galvanized trash can until they cool down enough to spread around somewhere. But where?

2. You can sprinkle some ashes in your compost pile—but sparingly! You don't want to turn your heap into lye soap. Of course, you could make your own lye soap out of wood ash and a few other ingredients, such as bars of melted lye soap, but if you're that goofy, you are probably eating the ashes for breakfast and not paying any attention to me at all.

3. During planting season, spread ashes in a circle around your garden to discourage slugs. Experts say that they (the slugs) won't crawl across sharp particles like ashes or crushed eggshells to get to your lettuce. If you believe this, I have about 600,000 tons of wood stove ash that I would like to sell to you real cheap for use in your garden as a slug deterrent. Still, it's an idea. Watch your garden pH if you do this. Not to mention the experts around your lettuce.

4. Discover a miracle cosmetic use for ashes. Like "Mudd." Remember "Mudd?" The six-dollar-a-jar brown gunk that you smeared on your face and then relaxed while it hardened to the look and feel of Death? After which you rinsed it, and several layers of your epidermis, down the sink drain? Well, maybe you could bag up your wood stove detritus and sell it as an all-over Body Masque. Maybe you could call it "Ashh." Just remember, you heard it from me first.

5. <u>Quit burning wood altogether</u> and go back to being a fossil fuel hog. After all, you've been a hippie long enough, haven't you? Time to grow up and start consuming in the modern world! And think of all the electricity you'll save by not vacuuming the hearth ninety-nine times a day. If that's not a fair exchange, what is?

6. <u>Move to a faraway</u>, sunnier clime where it's always 70 degrees and the wind blows in off the warm ocean all day and food and flowers grow on vines that curl right up to your elbows and the most arduous dilemma you will ever encounter is what to do with all those little paper umbrellas that are stuck in the Gin Kaboochi glasses brought to you faithfully, on the hour, by native Chip-N-Dale slaves.

Now, there's a Behavior I can live with!

Becoming Very Strange

More or less inherent in Garden Madness to begin with. Can evolve into some truly flamboyant Behavior, such as gardening in the nude, "channeling" for the souls of dead vegetables, running a giant hydroponics experiment with the family swimming pool, raising goats in your garage, spelunking for bat droppings, and so on. Understand, any of this would be judged as "very strange" only by those whose avocations lean toward normal things like five to ten hours of television-watching per day and getting ready for deer hunting season by hanging used feminine hygiene products from the branches of trees. The fact is that everything is relative, which is what Einstein has been saying all along, even though he is dead and would not be caught in that or any other condition hanging such things anywhere, let alone going out and *collecting* them for that purpose.

Thus we can see that predicting the vagaries of human Behavior is not recommended for the faint of heart whatever the subject area might encompass. Doesn't it make you wonder what it was that dogs and cats did for entertainment before they managed to train us to domesticate them?

Notes

[1] *A technique* encouraged as early as 1973 by Katie Kelly in her book, *Garbage*, Saturday Review Press.

CHAPTER TWENTY
Side Addictions

GARDEN MADNESS also spawns a number of hobbies and Side Addictions that in less intrepid hands might be considered mere diversions worthy of no more than a fleeting whisper in the wind. But for you, with a capacity for enthusiasm already exercised to Olympic Universe Competition caliber, anything related even obliquely to the natural world draws your attention like an industrial magnet traversing a paper clip. And, once stuck, you have just about as much chance of shaking loose.

As in:

House Plants

You see the results of this Addiction all the time. You've been in houses, possibly your own, where all level surfaces such as floors, table tops, chair arms, etc., have been destroyed by water rings from dripping plant pots, haven't you? Or how about those places where every square inch of window space is taken up by shelves full of African violets with purple lights shining on them day and night? The houses with no other signs of habitation whatsoever? Where newspapers are piling up around the porches and doorways in yellowing heaps? That is because the African violets have sucked up the last of the oxygen inside and the people, who have been virtual prisoners of this foliage for years, are lying on the floor dead and will be nothing but a cluster of dust mummies by the time the Power Company comes around to collect for all that fancy purple electricity. Then some other Addicted soul will buy the plants at the Estate sale and rush them to their new, oxygen-rich abode. The violets know very well how this works. They evolved a symbiotic relationship with us poor human saps many centuries ago. In fact, when Richard Leakey dug up "Lucy" in Lake Rudolf, Kenya, she had the skeleton of a four-million-year-old African violet plant light clutched in her finger bones. No, seriously.

It's enough to make you think fondly about weed killers.

However, I know that nothing will dissuade the House Plant Addict from keeping a menagerie of these little green dictators, because I have one myself and know How It Is. Admittedly, It is a somewhat more enjoyable menagerie that a pack of cats and dogs, though to say that plants do not shed or leak on the furniture is to display your non-Addiction ignorance, isn't it? And while mammals are merely infested with fleas, your House Plants are constantly under assault by mealy bugs, scabby scale, fire ants, earwigs, leaf rash, gunky lump, red spider bite, oozing hairy eelthrips, and any number of other gooshy life forms that you must pick off *with your own fingers* every day of every season of the year. And then there's repotting.

Given this, you should get down on your knees and thank your lucky stars that you are not genuflecting on a bed of nails, because it would hurt like a bastard. But that would be nothing compared to what will happen if you, a House Plant Addict, are walking past a public schoolyard someday and a seemingly innocent child hands you a "specialty"—meaning "weird" as in "weirdly expensive"—plant catalog.

What will happen is, you will go off on a bender that will make your escapades with W. Atlee Burpee look like a catchpenny date at the Five and Dime. I should know. I discovered the "unusual cactus and succulent" catalogs and wound up with *Lithop* and *Mesembryanthemum* fever. Believe me, you have no idea, until you look at photos of such succulents as *Pleiospilos nelii* "Split Rock" or *Conophytum giftbergense* "Flathead" or *Lithop fulviceps* "Living Rock," just how bizarre your home planet can get. Or maybe you do, because an awful lot of these "mimicry" plants—which in their native South Africa means mimicry of rocks and pebbles—bear a remarkable resemblance to a certain ailment of modern times, one with which you are perhaps all too familiar. You know the one I mean. The one mentioned in the TV ad where you rush out of the examining room to break the good news to your spouse?

YOU: Guess what! The doctor says I don't need surgery for my mesembryanthemums.

SPOUSE: Gee, that's great, dear. Why don't we celebrate by taking a ten-mile ride on our French racing bicycles right this minute?

YOU: Well, um ...

SPOUSE: Unless you'd rather help me move the piano.

YOU: Well, no, now that you mention it, I wouldn't.

SPOUSE: Swell!

YOU: You got that right.

(*Scene changes; the two of you are pedaling along a busy street*)

SPOUSE: (*loudly; several heads turn*) Aren't you glad you didn't have to have surgery for your mesembryanthemums, dear?

YOU: Yes, darling, I am. And when we get home, I'm going to kill you with a tire iron.

So the moral here is this: Do not put a dangerous substance in the hands of a House Plant Addict. The pain, itching, and suffering will be everyone's to endure.

Herbs

The results of this Addiction also waft everywhere upon the land. That is because all Mad Gardeners, without exception, sooner or later fall prey to the lore of Herbs and their ancient lure. For who can forget the words of Boece, that great Roman philosopher and gardener who looked out upon his Herbs and asked, "Seestow nat thanne in how greet filthe thise schrewes been iwrapped, and with which clernesse thise god folk schynen?" Except that no one could ever figure out what this meant, and Boece went on to achieve immortality by having an Italian lawn game named after him and the mystery of why these famous words are in Olde Yenglishhe rather than Latin was never heard from again.

But even before written history, Herbs were sought out for their medicinal, culinary, and aromatic properties, which makes sense when you realize that the only other medicinal, culinary, or aromatic properties available for many centuries came from things like giant sucking leeches, urine and feces compresses, amputations and tooth yanking without anesthesia, piles of straw in the corner for toilets, huge slabs of fetid rotting stag steaks for dinner, open sewer and street garbage vapors for perfume, etc. Small wonder that humans were willing to risk mere death by poisoning to sort out the odor-snuffing, pain-alleviating, healing powers of beneficial Herbs from the lethal ones. And much of that legendary knowledge is with us today in modern medical treatments and prescriptions and in our own home cooking and potpourris, but all of that is not why Mad Gardeners become sidetracked by Herbs. You become sidetracked by Herbs because they are *plants*. And because they have their own history and mystique. And because they can be dangerous, even deadly, if used incorrectly. And because people will pay big bucks for items made out of the damn things. And in a thrice of a deuce, you are off to the Herb races.

Gardeners falling under the Addiction of Herbs usually start with what is known as a "kitchen garden," meaning a mess of Herbs sitting in pots all over your kitchen, from which you take clippings and snippings for cooking and immediately decide that you want to start growing and drying even more Herbs and hanging them from your ceiling in Herb-crumb-producing bunches, and soon you are renting extra acreage for Herb gardens and opening an Herb Shoppe in your house and speaking Herbian all day with other Herbicrucians and becoming, in general, Herbalmighty peculiar. But by then it no longer matters. As an Herb Shoppe Gardener, you are immersed in such Herb Items as scented Herb wreaths, scented Herb pillows, scented Herb sachets, scented Herb wart cures, scented Herb stuffed animals, scented Herb tea, scented Herb coffee, scented Herb vinegar, scented Herb butter, scented Herb motor vehicles, scented Herb sidearms with scented Herb ammunition, and so on and so forth until no one will go anywhere near you because of the cloying scented Herb stench rolling off your person and out your door like a blast from scented Herb Hell. Pee-yew!

Thus, no matter what kinds of sordid Herb impulses wash over your Gardening world, do not succumb to more than five or six plantings of basil. With maybe a couple of bunches of sage. And a few dozen flats of thyme. And lavender. And then there's bay tree, and coriander, and who can leave out tarragon, and marjoram, and saffron, and chervil, lovage, chives, oregano, mint, parsley, rosemary …

Help! Call the Herb police now! The number is in my scented Herb telephone table. And hang me from the ceiling until I'm dry. Please!

Bonsai

Bonsai, the ancient Oriental art whose name means "tree jammed into a pot that is obviously way too small," combines the technique of arc welding with the spirit of pulling wings off flies to twist plants into weather-blasted, grimly asymmetrical landscapes that take longer to grow than it took the Ice Age to cover the entire expanse of the northern hemisphere. The redwoods should live so long. Not to mention yourself.

There are five basic styles of bonsai: formal, informal, wind-swept, fallen out of pot, and dead.

It almost goes without saying that those who are addicted to this particular form of plant Madness end up collecting dozens and dozens of bonsai that demand a devotion bordering on religious fanaticism, what with every minute of every day focused on the meticulous, ancient bonsai chores of moss-watering, bark-scouring, branch-bending, root-hacking, twig-grooming, hair-tearing, and saki-guzzling, to name a few, though it could be worse. Some wiseacre entrepreneur could scope out the American bonsai market and invent miniature weather-blasted weedwhackers, grimly asymmetrical rototillers, and teeny tortured bent-over buttboards just to accommodate the truly bonsai Mad, and where would that leave the rest of us?

Flower Arranging

Okay, so we'd be inside, perfecting this, the Addiction of sticking flowers into a vase of water and leaving them there until they die.

Some gardeners are so addicted to this particular pastime that they actually take college courses in the art of flower-stem snipping and water-vase filling. Soon, their houses are so packed with picked flowers in various stages of heady perfume-and-pollen-producing decay that you need a gas mask just to talk with them (the gardeners) on the telephone. And we won't even go into the "dried" flower craze and its allergies.

Still, what better way to revere the joy of springtime? And if it brings a tear to the eye and a sneeze to the nose, oh well. You can always go outdoors and sniff the smog to clear your dusty head.

Hydroponics

An Addiction similar to the above, except that you'll be arrested if you even so much as think about ordering the equipment from your favorite friendly "alternate lifestyle" catalog. Anyway, this is more Agriculture than true Mad Gardening, though the prospect of sticking tomato plants into a vat of water and leaving them there until they die does have its appeal in the middle of August, doesn't it? But beware, for the unwary Mad Gardener with all attendant tics and foibles intact can end up doing something really crazy like *fish* farming with Hydroponics gadgets, for crying out loud. Or at least that is the story the catalogs tell you to have ready for the helicopter invasion! Maybe you should forget this Side, if I may use the phrase, Addiction altogether and go back to deforming helpless little trees for a side hobby instead.

Feeding the Birds

Another Side Addiction that eventually comes upon Mad Gardeners.

Some Scientists argue that you should not feed the birds because it will turn them (the birds) into welfare moochers who stop relying on their mostly destroyed natural habitats once you start providing them with seed and suet. Well, there is something of an argument here, though I am not sure you want to start it with me! But you probably should at least calculate the cost of a winter's worth of bird feed *before* you get into this Addiction, not that cost factors have meant a whit to you in the past when it comes to this sort of thing.

What you do is take the average price of a fifty-pound bag of mixed seed and multiply it by 567,000,000,000,000,000,000,000, which is the approximate number of squirrels you will also be feeding on any given winter day. Then you add the cost of a dozen of those objects known as "bird feeders" and divide by however many mortal years you think you have left in this vale of woe. The figure you wad up and throw in the wastebasket is your annual Feeding the Birds Addiction Budget.

Bird feeders, which for obvious Machiavellian reasons are frequently offered through garden catalogs, come in an astonishing array of shapes and sizes, which can be loosely categorized thusly:

1. Uglier than anything you ever saw in your life. These include wooden trays that sit on sticks, maroon metal trap-door devices that provide hours of amusement by clanging down on the necks of blue jays, and small wire cages in which no piece of suet ever offered in any supermarket will ever fit without a lot of hacking and sawing with whatever cutting device, such as the claw part of a hammer, or a pair of pliers, happens to be out in the garage on the coldest morning of the year.

2. Uglier than anything anyone you ever knew has ever seen in your life. Or theirs either. Includes, but not limited to, grimy foot-long plastic tubes with holes in the sides, out of which all seed spills within five minutes of filling or as soon as you return to the house to thaw out your fingers. Equally ugly plastic domes may be attached to the tops of these tubes so that squirrels can chew through them in traditional Rite-of-Rodenthood ceremonies. Category also incorporates large plastic cracked-corn buckets, complete with convenient mouse entryway holes, for those who wish to attract the colorful gourmet pigeon and related squab!

3. Slightly less ugly than the above, but fifteen times as expensive. This category includes the entire run of so-called "Droll Yankee" feeders, which were invented four hundred years ago by two smart old geezers up in Vermont who understood the value of a dollar, especially when it was your dollar they were talking about. Here is how they came up with the "Droll Yankee" bird feeder:

FIRST YANKEE GEEZER: Lookee heah, Edgah, I nailed a bunch o'them rotten old bahn boahds togethah and now I got a whole lotta ugly wooden boxes with flip-toppen lids.

SECOND YANKEE GEEZER: Aye-yup. Why dontcha call 'em buhhd feedahs and chahge the tourists sixty, sixty-five dollahs apiece fer'em plus tax, shippin', and handlin'?

FIRST YANKEE GEEZER: Say, ain't that droll!

SECOND YANKEE GEEZER: Aye-yup. And cheaper'n pickle-barrel spit, too.

ALL TOGETHAH: Har! Har! DeeHar!

None of this is to say that I am against Feeding the Birds in whatever manner best accommodates their needs. On the contrary! The trees around my house are full of these gadgets. Every summer, I take the feeders down and scrape the mold and slime out of them, scrub all surfaces with hot, soapy water, rinse them in vinegar, and throw them out in the trash. Then I replace them with new, uglier feeders from each of the above categories and start hauling in the bags of birdseed, using a four-wheel drive checkbook and an overdrawn station wagon to do the job.

It all makes a good wintertime substitute for ordering flower and vegetable seeds that you can't afford either. And you will be rewarded fiftyfold by the birds themselves, who make anything beautiful with their presence and song. Even the Scientists!

Feeding Yourself

The most addicting Side Addiction of all, for it is inevitably coupled with the Mad Gardener's frantic search for ways to handle the onslaught of vegetables that charge through the kitchen every fall. Newspapers, magazines, and television become glutted with garden-specific recipes, all of which take at least fifteen times longer to prepare than to pick. And we're not even talking about canning and preserving. We're talking about the noble Addiction of Eating, or more accurately, of Shoveling In Gargantuan Quantities of Whatever Foodlike Substances

Are in Arm's Reach Or Reasonable Driving Distance. Taste buds have little to do with this Addiction, as a glance through these typical garden recipe options illustrates.

Recipe Option #1: <u>The *New York Times Sunday Magazine* "Cuisine" Page</u>. This always involves ingredients you never heard of or which have to be sent for via private international jet to some Mediterranean island discovered just moments before press time. Also involves such directions as "Measure seventeen and a half metric teaspoonfuls of Tuscany sweet Kosher butter into enamel-lined French copper steaming vessel and clarify, stirring every three seconds, until butter turns pale mauve with gabardine trim. Fold into the twenty-seven egg whites which you have beaten to a peak the night before and set out on chilled Greek marble to calcify until just porous. Add minced beets. Strain. Serve with sturgeon finger garnish. Satisfies nineteen."

Anyone who does this sort of thing with food has absolutely no comprehension of what this Addiction is all about, not to mention Gardening in the first place. But of course you can go too far in the other direction, as in:

Recipe Option #2: <u>The Healthy Living To One Hundred and Twenty-Five Annoying Years Old Methodology</u>. Always starts with a bulgur wheat and shredded Swiss chard crust thing filled with okra, whatever that is. Dessert consists of beehive wax topped with grated alfalfa root. Essentially, you are making use of your digestive system to process plant fiber for applications other than in your own body. One Fat Gram and you're dead meat. If there's any of that left on you, that is. Fortunately, the vox populi has come up with a hearty All-American response to this Feeding Addiction flagellation, namely:

Recipe Option #3: <u>The Home-Town Chef du Manger's Any-Brand Will Do Television Spot Vignette</u>. Can be seen on local TV news shows right after the "Eye On Your Carotid Artery" segment, significantly. Features recipes built around the Five Basic Food Groups that the average viewer insists on keeping stocked in the astutely labeled "larder." Which is a good thing, because these Groups are used in every Chef du Manger recipe, whether we're talking about garden harvest salads or leftover Spam and sponge cake casseroles. They are:

2 cups margarine
2 cups Crisco
2 cups cream cheese
2 cups mayonnaise
2 cups Wesson oil

To which you add a couple of carrots and a dash of paprika, chili powder, and any kind of steak sauce. Bake. Serves four. Yum!

But as you true Feeding Addicts well know, this is nothing when compared to your own foodaholic dreams—dreams that would gag Chef du Manger himself, perhaps renewing his acquaintance with that particular body function thereby. To wit:

Recipe Option #4: <u>The Mad Gardener's I'd Eat Dirt If It Had White Mountain Icing Glopped On It Lifestyle</u>. Includes, but is by no means limited to:

2 cups highly refined white sugar squares, somewhat crispy;
2 cups non-"lite" Cool Whip, thawed or frozen, who cares which;
2 cups Halloween candy corn/pumpkin mix from last year, pleasantly stale;
2 cups Brach's Marshmallow Circus Peanuts with the pink ones taken out;
2 cups Three Musketeer Bars centers, peeled and skooshed;
2 cups Vienna Fingers vanilla cookies, dipped in milk and crumbled slightly;
2 gallons vanilla ice cream, twirled with spoon 'til soft.

Leaving vegetables out in the garden, mix all above ingredients. Let stand five seconds. Eat while wearing pajamas and housecoat. Lapse into happy, happy coma. Serves one.

Truly a Side Addiction harvest to come home to!

CHAPTER TWENTY-ONE
The Mad Gardener's Dream Year in Review

*A*nd so, as visions of Recipe Option #4 dance through your head, you settle in for your long winter's nap … and what to your Mad wandering dreams do appear but these miniature scenes from your Gardening Year:

JANUARY 8: W. Atlee Burpee Co. announces the perfection of a new petunia variety, "Swirligag," designed to look like that peanut butter and jelly swirl mix that is purchased in supermarkets by desperately insane mothers of three. Seeds for "Swirligag" are $5.99 for a packet of twelve.

JANUARY 9: Three scientists from the W. Atlee Burpee seed research team are taken to the hospital and treated for compound fractures of the ribs, reportedly as a result of falling off their lab chairs in a fit of uncontrollable laughter.

JANUARY 30: Laboratory scientists at Quirkgene, Inc., of Coelacanth, California, develop a tomato so resistant to bacteria that it cannot be digested by any known living creature whatsoever and is quite possibly immortal. Quirkgene says it will offer "Frevr Yung" as an ornamental curiosity and as a substitute for wax fruit in holiday centerpiece arrangements.

FEBRUARY 5: Four laboratory scientists from Quirkgene, Inc., are treated at a Coelacanth, California, emergency care hospital for skull fractures allegedly sustained during an indoor tennis game involving an unnamed type of vegetable that "ricocheted off the walls like a goddamned deer slug," according to reports.

FEBRUARY 26: Myron Tanniger Whippett II, Chancellor of the Expert Gardener University at Nob Hill, Boston, declares the word "dirt" off-limits and obscene. "We use the term 'soil' exclusively in our class-rooms and occasionally in the hallways," Chancellor Whippett says.

MARCH 19: A new type of fleabeetle pest control is invented by Rodale Research, Incorporated. Consisting of liquefied woodchucks, this repellent can be made at home using the special "Squeezo" Grinder Attachment offered in the Spring Burpee catalog for only $179.99 plus tax, shipping, and handling.

MARCH 25: Astronomers at the Palindrome Scope Epocs Ob-servatory in Hatu, Utah, inexplicably lock themselves in an underground deliberation chamber with Consumer Advocate Ralph Nader and refuse to come out except to order sandwiches.

APRIL 4: Gunderson Harrison Capulet IV takes over as editor of the prestigious gardening magazine Hortsnob and immediately an-nounces that the publication has stamped out the dreaded scourge of "dirt" throughout the civilized world. "Gardens must be clean and neat and all the flowers and vegetables lined up end to end in exacting rows, or they make me itch," says Capulet, who is a Class of '35 graduate of Expert Gardener University of Nob Hill, Boston.

MAY 15: An amended edition of the W. Atlee Burpee catalog hits the stands, knocking many of them down. Embarrassed editors note that Rodale's new organic repellent is actually derived from liquefied *fleabeetles* for use against *woodchucks,* and regret any inconvenience this mixup may have caused. Just in case, the special "Squeezo" Grinder Attachment is now being offered at a one-time sale price of $56.99 plus tax, shipping, and scrubbing.

JUNE 1: Quirkgene, Inc., of Coelacanth, California, announces that it has voluntarily submitted its "Frevr Yung" tomato to the FDA for testing and possible marketplace approval. The FDA is so impressed by Quirkgene's suspiciously innocent lack of guile that it immediately agrees to approve the company's new poultry growth hormone, OvumAarrgh, or OWW, which is synthesized from a hormone that appears naturally in birds and when injected back into chickens causes them to lay eggs the size of basketballs. "There is no discernible difference between OWW and all that other gooey junk that oozes out of chickens after you chop their heads off with a scalpel," says Quirkgene research pathologist Edward R. Bonemarrow, Ph.D.

June 19: FDA officials refute charges that the newly-approved OWW poultry egg growth hormone was pushed through official channels without sufficient room for adequate testing. "We reviewed every single bowling ball and Chinese finger puzzle experiment that Quirkgene ran for more than ten years," says FDA spokesperson Howard D. Doodymeister, MBA. "Practically no harm came to any living creature, unless you count that silly ovary-eruption incident, which we don't." Women's health groups everywhere reply, "Hey, wait a minute, are you nuts or something?"

JULY 3: A farmer in Alabaster, Ohio, claims to have grown tasty, normal-sized radishes and pumpkins from seeds purchased for forty-two cents a packet in Harry's Hardware Store during a junket to town last March. Plant research labs everywhere ignore him.

JULY 30: W. Atlee Burpee Co. announces the perfection of "NotaPoodle," a new variety of genetically-enhanced winter squash that doesn't explode when cooked in a microwave oven. Garden magazines everywhere run front-page glossy photos taken by their best friend's brother's Army buddy's second cousin. Seeds are offered at $8.95 for a packet of six.

AUGUST 10: No one at the hospital emergency room in Burpee, Illinois, is surprised when five seed research scientists arrive by ambulance with a couple dozen busted ribs each. "We see this phenomenon every season at garden catalog publication time," says EMR nurse Emily Hoosier.

AUGUST 18: The mutilated bodies of sixteen scientists from Quirkgene, Inc., of Coelacanth, California, are found lying in the company parking lot where they were apparently trying to get to their cars from the lab building. "Looks to me as if they were all pecked to death by birds," says a police spokesperson, who adds that investigators "don't have a clue" as to what happened and will not comment on tabloid rumors involving placement of Chinese finger puzzles discovered on the scene.

AUGUST 53: Astronomers at the Palindrome Scope Epocs Observatory in Hatu, Utah, emerge from their deliberations and admit under questioning that there have always been fifteen months in a year but this has been hidden from the general public for centuries because Christmas actually falls on March 21, in direct dollar competition with mail-order garden catalogs. "And you know which dollar would win out on that score," says Consumer Advocate Nader, adding that the invisible weight of ninety extra unused days per year "probably contributed to the evolution of some pretty squirrely behavior in human beings," and that the revelation that everyone is even older than they thought "could be likened to the dropping of the H-Bomb on an atoll of bikinis."

SEPTEMBER 1: A farmer in Alabaster, Ohio, is swamped by produce shoppers asking for the secret behind his delicious, bountiful vegetable garden. "Dirt lives," is the farmer's reply. E-mail begins to spread the word. Programmers sitting behind the screens at Wintertorture, the giant multinational catalog corporation, are astonished by this apparent blasphemy. "How can simple vegetables and Big Business grow side by side in serious raised bedfellowship?" asks one. "Who wouldda thunk it?" says another.

SEPTEMBER 11: Research scientists from seed companies everywhere walk off their jobs to volunteer as test subjects for the Illegal Substances Analysis Division of Phillip Morris Inc., and are never heard from again.

SEPTEMBER 21: Research scientists from DNA laboratories all across the country are suddenly stricken with the urge to go outside and plant some vegetables and flowers and see what happens. They are never heard from again.

OCTOBER 7: Millions of chickens, cows, guinea pigs, rabbits, mice, rats, chimpanzees, and beagles pour out of research buildings onto sidewalks everywhere and try to hail cabs all at the same time. This causes an enormous traffic jam and the animals, who ride away with smiles on their faces, are never heard from again.

NOVEMBER 1: Real Gardeners by the thousands surround the FDA office building in Walleye, Wisconsin, and cover the place with truckloads of dirt and old-fashioned open-pollinated tomato plants, after which they retire to Coelacanth, California to keep a lookout.

DECEMBER 24: Sanity returns to the gardening world. Demure, inexpensive, biodegradable-newsprint catalogs offering simple, hardy, inexpensive, genetically diverse seeds and plants start arriving in mailboxes throughout the world. Organically-grown produce is so much in demand that its shelf price begins to fall dramatically. Shoppers prefer fruits and vegetables that look fresh and natural instead of ad-foto-perfect. Family farms and neighborhood gardens prosper and live long. A million points of Mad Gardeninghood light shine out into the fertile vacuum of space.

Gaia smiles.

Ah, yes, what a year that was!

What a dream!

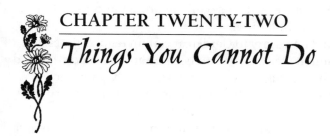

CHAPTER TWENTY-TWO
Things You Cannot Do

*T*HEN YOU WAKE UP to the truth: You are hooked.

The criteria available to examine this fact, as we have amply demonstrated, are simple:

1. You keep making promises about your Gardening behavior. You swear you will stop ordering seeds and plants from catalogs. You vow to quit ripping up the yard to make more flowerbeds. You pledge to end your moping at the windows during winter. You declare that you will discontinue your descriptions of manure BTUs while at the dinner table. You will change none of these habits.

2. You lie about the money you spend on bedding plants, if you even remember to keep track of it in the first place. After a while, you start selling off the family antiques to buy tree peonies and dahlia collections. You hide these in the garage so you can sneak them out and plant them in the border before anybody notices you bought them.

3. You have an overwhelming, round-the-clock compulsion to Garden. Sometimes you go outside after dark with a flashlight to pull a weed or two. Sometimes you have to pitch a little mulch first thing in the morning just to "get going." You convince yourself that this is perfectly normal behavior.

4. You seek out the company of others like you, meaning anyone who would spend hours Gardening in dank, dirt-smelling potting sheds and moldy, scum-encrusted greenhouses just to get an orchid to burst into flower, or who would sniff handfuls of

composted horse manure just to savor the aroma and ascertain its age and readiness for mulching.

5. You find it necessary to Garden at certain regular times, such as March clear through October, or you become anxious and edgy and start buying little house plants by the dozen to satisfy your needs.

6. You must allot several hours for Gardening before every meal, regardless of how this inconveniences mere mortals.

7. You won't go to any social function that does not involve Gardening. Actually, you won't go to any social functions at all anymore, since this means wasting time that is better spent weeding and deadheading.

8. You must go out in the Garden and harvest potatoes to alleviate that "tired" feeling, or prune clematis to calm your "nerves."

9. You have bouts of "Not Gardening," notably from First to Last Frost, during which time you are about as much fun to have around the house as a scourge of body lice.

10. Grandiose thoughts begin to occur to you, such as the idea that you are going to replace the entire lawn with low-growing groundcovers and islands of wildflowers and spring bulbs intertwined with stepstone walkways, and that you will do this all by yourself

11. Episodes of Extreme Gardening start to appear. You grow more vegetables than you could eat in three years just for the pleasure of growing them. You enter contests and fairs. You win prizes. You name strange-looking varieties of spaghetti squash after yourself. You hang bags of gladiolus corms in the cellar every fall. You know each of them personally, by name, and you brag about it.

12. You start Gardening alone. Who else would have you?

13. You can at this point still appear to be a non-Gardener, but you will have a peculiar body smell, vaguely like composting leaf mold interlayered with vegetable peels and discarded lobster shells, that will give you away to those in the Know.

14. You require Gardening for a sense of well-being.

15. You start writing about it.

IF YOU FIT at least one of these criteria, you fit them all. Garden Madness does not affect you in singles. Garden Madness is the Mad Gardener that you Are.

And thus you will understand that you Cannot, in this life as you know it, be ever again less than a Gardener; and in that is the realization that with each passing season, there are Higher Gardening Powers that you cannot deny. Things that you have given yourself up to. Things You Cannot Do.

For Lo:

YOU CANNOT have enough flowers blooming in your garden beds in your memory of the season that has just passed by. No, you must have more of everything next year, regardless of the work involved. As you sit and watch the November rain and December snows, you will not understand why you were too lazy to grow a hundred more of everything while you had the chance. Next summer, you will remember why; but now, YOU CANNOT.

YOU CANNOT anticipate how much you will miss fresh vegetables from your garden until they are all gone, no matter how often you complained about harvesting and putting-by. Yes, all Gardeners admit to this aberration. Perhaps you will someday learn to do these chores with gratitude. Perhaps not. For well you know that it is not for reasons of Harvesting or reasons of Storing or even, in our extremity, reasons of Eating, that we Garden; but for the bounty of your natures YOU CANNOT do less than partake of that which you have helped to grow.

YOU CANNOT start planning next year's garden soon enough. NO, you will need paper and pen now, outside in the waning sunshine, while this year's vegetables and flowers are there before your eyes. Believe me when I say that by next spring you will have forgotten where you planted most everything unless you write it down. I do not know the reason for this oddity of the Gardening mind, but however well you think you will remember, the fact is YOU CANNOT.

YOU CANNOT finish fall garden clean-up without the memory of all that has gone before this season. As you rake and shred and put away your claws and trowels, you will look upon the pruner that was your grandmother's, or the sunhat that once your mother wore. You will remember as though it were yesterday the rock gardens in your past, behind houses where you no longer live; the alyssum border that grows larger as your childhood travels ever farther away. You will wonder how it is that you came to be the age the people were when you first saw them holding the tools you now own, and how it is that they are gone, and you are here. The flowers that are ready for sleep now, in the autumn ground, contain your only answer, for time is short and the winter rises, and everywhere there are mysteries that YOU CANNOT solve.

YOU CANNOT imagine how quickly the spring will return, or how rapidly time as a whole passes by. There is no modifier for this statement, nor anything that can change what it means. Enjoy the winter, therefore, and wish it well. YOU CANNOT do otherwise, if your heart is truly of the mud.

Meanwhile, who said YOU CANNOT live by CATALOGS alone? Certainly not I!

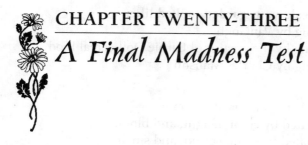

CHAPTER TWENTY-THREE
A Final Madness Test

SO NOW we are going to find out exactly where the compost lies in the buckwheat.

Yes, we are almost ready to say good-bye to these pages and to the immortal works of Percy Bysshe Shelley, who after all once observed that "Odours, when sweet violets sicken, / Live within the sense they quicken." Of course, we have no idea what this has to do with the matter at hand, and anyway, even if we did, these are not Shelley's immortal works that we are reading at the moment, and we seem to have lost track of what is going on entirely. Wait a minute, now we remember. We were going to give you a Test.

This Test will reveal the Truth. It will scrutinize your Gardening year and total up your scruts for self-analysis. It will find out if you learned anything from these pages, or if you merely treated them as another casual bumper-car ride in the derelict amusement park of your life. It will reveal the depth and degree of your Madness. It will tell everyone how much you really weigh.

Ha, ha! Got you on that last one.

You must not peek at the answers until you have finished the entire quiz. If you do give in to temptation and look, all the ills of the world will be let out of a box, and they will fly around on leathery wings biting people and causing earthquakes and forest fires and hay fever, and it will be all your fault. So don't say I didn't warn you.

Thus here we are, once again, at Chekhov time:

1. **At season's peak, your garden looked like:**
   (a) A painting by VanGogh.
   (b) A painting by the creator of Barbie Doll cereal food.
   (c) A painting by Charles Manson.
   (d) Dirt.

2. **The perennials in your garden were:**
   (a) Coordinated by color, height, and bloom.
   (b) Coordinated by sight, sound, and smell.
   (c) Coordinated by the butcher, the baker,
       and the candlestick maker.
   (d) Dead.

3. **All annuals in your garden were:**
   (a) Meticulously deadheaded and mulched.
   (b) Periodically looked at and stepped on.
   (c) Monumentally mismatched and moldy.
   (d) Dank.

4. **Your vegetables at season's end were:**
   (a) Delicious.
   (b) Monotonous.
   (c) Atrocious.
   (d) Cadaverous.

5. **All of the work in your garden was done by:**
   (a) You, by self.
   (b) Sullen adolescents, under bribe.
   (c) Neighborhood cats and dogs, at random.
   (d) Nobody, not nohow, who cares?

6. **Materials used on your garden were:**
   (a) Organic, from home-made compost.
   (b) Sterile, from imitation fertilzer.
   (c) Virulent, from local landfill leachate.
   (d) Nonexistent, strictly from hunger.

7. **Mammalian pests were repelled:**
    (a) Humanely, with fencing.
    (b) Occasionally, with shouting.
    (c) Forever, with flame throwing.
    (d) Never, by the looks of the place.

8. **Insect control consisted of**
    (a) An integrated system of natural checks and balances.
    (b) A haphazard application of household cleansers
        and disinfectants.
    (c) A bloodthirsty blastaway of megatoxins and mindbenders.
    (d) Staying indoors.

9. **You take care of all garden equipment by:**
    (a) Washing, waxing, oiling, greasing.
    (b) Thinking, planning, forgetting, sleeping.
    (c) Using, losing, busting, rusting.
    (d) Not having any.

10. **Your most precious outdoor possession is your:**
    (a) Garden tractor.
    (b) Metal detector.
    (c) Chevy Big Foot bug deflector.
    (d) Umbrella.

11. **You think the wonder tomato is:**
    (a) An arrogant manipulation.
    (b) A real nifty innovation.
    (c) A comic book fantastication.
    (d) Too expensive.

12. **Your favorite catalog item is:**
    (a) A carefully budgeted selection of flower and vegetable seeds.
    (b) A drunken plant-ordering orgy ending in
        complete financial collapse.
    (c) A little plastic sign that says, "My Garden," and furniture
        made out of tree branches with the leaves still on them.
    (d) A junk mail refusal card.

13. **You recycled inorganic garden trash by:**
    - (a) Throwing all plastic pots and flats in a smelter, to make soap jugs.
    - (b) Throwing all plastic pots and flats down cellar, near the tire heap.
    - (c) Throwing all plastic pots and flats out your car window, late at night.
    - (d) Ignoring it.

14. **You reacted to garden disasters by:**
    - (a) Sighing and starting over.
    - (b) Swearing and hiring exterminators.
    - (c) Screaming and shooting pistols.
    - (d) Proxy.

15. **Your cut flowers are:**
    - (a) Placed reverently in vases.
    - (b) Mowed blindly by accident.
    - (c) Chopped vengefully in a fit.
    - (d) Purchased from the flower shop.

16. **Your favorite gardening books include:**
    - (a) Anything by Rodale Press.
    - (b) Anything by *Better Homes*.
    - (c) Anything by Orthogenics.
    - (d) Anything by the commode.

17. **Your dream garden is:**
    - (a) All of England.
    - (b) Parts of Florida.
    - (c) Levels of Dante.
    - (d) Totally forgotten.

18. **Your dream garden tour guide would be:**
    - (a) Jekyll.
    - (b) Alice.
    - (c) Hyde.
    - (d) Busch.

19. At season's end, you:
   (a) Cleaned up all debris and shredded it for mulch.
   (b) Disregarded all debris and pretended, Verily, it was Good.
   (c) Burned up all debris and set fire to the tool shed.
   (d) Celebrated with large quantities of alcoholic beverages.

20. Next year, you will:
   (a) Plant more of everything, and establish two or
       three new beds besides.
   (b) Hire lots of help, and lie about it to friends.
   (c) Fritter away your time, and let the crabgrass
       take over quickly.
   (d) Drink gin rickeys down by the seashore, and leave
       gardening to the peasants.

Add it up: five point per "a," ten points per "b," fifteen points per "c," and twenty points per "d." Better than high school!

Here's how it scores:
5–100: WHO ELSE BUT THE TRULY MAD. The truly SPLEN-DID. When they make a movie out of your life, it will be a glorious animated FANTASIA of color and light, of COMPOST and SONG. It will be rated "G" for "Garden Goodness." Not only are you destined for Heaven when you die, you have been dwelling There all along. Not only will you come back as a Perennial, the fact is that you've always been one. That this is a universal Truth does not escape you. Have patience! Everyone else will catch up eventually.
   You received this book, brand-new, from the author, whom you are.

110–200: TYPICAL NORMAL AMERICAN GARDENING PER-SON. You enjoy flowers and a couple of tomatoes now and then, but your idea of a gardening thrill is when all the string beans ripen at once, right in time for Canning Season. You use store-bought fertilizers because the idea of compost makes you sick to your stomach. Putting *poop* on your *food*? Haven't those mulch maniacs at Rodale ever heard about *germs???* Anyway, you like the neat and uncluttered look of bare dirt. Plus, you have other things to do besides gardening, as unbelievable as this might seem to members of the first category.

Your life is a TV miniseries sponsored by Chlorox.

You found this book in your dead grandmother's nightstand underneath a copy of *Lady Chatterly's Lover.*

220–300: EEEK. You are the DISPOSSESSED. Your vegetable garden is a MESS. Your house plants are all DEAD. Your flowers have been chewed off by ANTELOPES. You have a BROKEN THUMB, and that's all there is to that. Your garden is a constant MADNESS of disaster, featuring giant venomous flying insects, craven crawling crunching creatures, freezing frosts of winter ruin, searing suns of summer destruction, withering leaves of yellow death, pickle-making in pitiless kitchens, and paying off MasterCard debts at eternal monthly increments of twenty-one percent! Rated "PG" for "Pretty Gruesome." But you won't give up. You never know when a Green Thumb might leap out and hit you in the forehead!

You acquired this book when it blew out of a dump truck and hit you in the forehead.

320+: THIS BOOK is currently holding up the back leg of your beach chair.

And that is the Quotient of your Madness!!

CHAPTER TWENTY-FOUR
The Future of Garden Madness

*T*IME MARCHES ON through space and tide, and nowhere is this humbling fact of existence more evident than in the Garden, where the days and hours escort us from season to season in the relentless progression of spring and seed and harvest and frost. Fortunately, all of us are marching right along together and we will not be left behind no matter what shenanigans we go through to try to sneak out of our place in line. The advantage that *Homo sapiens* have over other mortal creatures is that unlike, say, caribou and sea urchins, we are generally not hunted down and killed by anything other than ourselves, and in addition, our large brain capacity allows us to entertain one another along the way with a ceaseless outpouring of notions about the Future.

In the Mad Gardeners' Future, for example, there are numerous amazing upcoming advances in living and hoeing to divert our attention from the inevitable.

1. <u>The Infohighway:</u> If you thought humans had reached the apex of gadget invention with the Stealth bomber, then you have been spending far too much time lolling in the hot pepper patch. What the Future holds in the computerized InterCompu-Line-O'Tronic-Mega-ByteWorld is so unbelievable that anyone who does not want to volunteer for this mission may be excused now, because you are about to become extinct. Why, with just the touch of a button on your keyboard, you will be able to call up prodigious amounts of gardening facts, references, articles, photos, literature, videos, and personal forum

experiences that will be constantly entered, updated, and scanned by other garden devotees such as yourself! All endlessly fascinating and fun, especially to the folks at the National Security Agency, who enjoy monitoring the InfoHighway and will drop by your house at some Future date to discuss the details of your interesting E-Mail Ecotage stories as well as all those X-Rated CompuVids you called up on your screen and the "sensual products" catalog orders you CompuPaidfor and whatever else they've got on your ROM sheet.

In the midst of this heady technological jocundity, you will want to remember to get up periodically from your CompuChair to rest and stretch your eyes and perhaps even go outdoors and do some actual Gardening in the actual Garden, using actual physical effort with actual Gardening implements.

Aha-hahahahahaha! Just CompuTweaking your BaudRAM-O Floppy.

2. Recycling: Another area where the Gardener of the Future will discover miraculous inventions and widgets, some of which are available even as we are writing this while drinking copious amounts of hot coffee. As in toilet paper and paper towels made not from trees but, according to the labels, from *recycled junk mail.* Envelope windows and all.

But this amazing progression in human endeavors has only just begun its journey along the twisty-turny passages of resourcefulness, for soon, in the blink of an eye and the flush of a new day, you will be able to buy resource-rescuing toilet paper *that has been recycled from the junk mail of your choice!* Yes, whether it be Ed McMahon insurance come-ons, Reader's Digest Sweepstakes promotions, IRS notices, or those irritating subscription cards that fall out of magazines by the quart that make up the bulk of your tissue patronage, you will become personally involved in the daily effort to pass this world along to our progeny before everything slides down the tubes and empties out into the cold, cold Ocean of Lethe.

And yet this is only the beginning of what will happen in the upcoming world of recycled personal products. I would go into specifics here and talk about what the Goodyear Tire and Rubber Company has up its sleeve, but I think I'd better contain myself until you have faxed me your entire vaccination record, including ancestors. Just remember this paragraph the next time you see "safety tread" written on your sidewalls and try not to drive through anything radioactive.

3. <u>Plants:</u> By this page, every gardener in modern America is aware that Science and Technology will never again sit quietly and wait for Nature to spend a few million years developing bigger and better plants when so much can be accomplished in laboratory test tubes and petri dishes in a fraction of the time! After the "Flavr Savr" tomato hit supermarket produce bins without squashing all over the place, DNA research went into high gear and began churning out a plethora of genetically-fiddled fruits and vegetables, which will be arriving at your groceryshop door very soon. Some will be scuttling sideways and some will be sort of half-flying, and some will be nursing their seeds. But by then, you, the Future Gardener, will think naught of any of this. You will be ordering plants from "specialty" catalogs in which you will find such hybrids as the "Praying Mato," which will be capable of grabbing and eating its own insect pests; the "DogDead Tree," a flowering beauty with a genotypic defense system fashioned from the DNA of electric eels; and the super-sweet "KoolKorn," which, as a recombinant with certain hermaphroditic earthworms, will offer the additional advantage of being able to go shuck itself.

4. <u>Dirt:</u> All Mad Gardeners are vitally concerned about dirt. Up to now, you have been forced to dig it up with a shovel or buy it in bags at the supermarket, or experience it vicariously from "journalism." But soon you will have all the dirt you want whenever and wherever you need it, for science has discovered a way to create universal dirt that automatically collects on top of every exposed surface in and around your own home and on the dashboard of the family car. It is called … wait a minute, who snuck this in here? Sorry.

5. <u>Tools:</u> Garden tools of the Future will make use of our naturally renewable resources, as the invention of the solar-powered "Robo Mower" has ably demonstrated. Already, we have a new piece of farm equipment called the "Beetle Eater," a sort of giant vacuum cleaner that sucks insects out of crops and into a large drum, where the bugs hang around copping be-bops until they are emulsified and sprayed

back out across the fields in bug liquidform. Meanwhile, less revolting mulch-mower methods are coming onto the home marketplace in ever improving numbers. Weedwhackers will one day be designed to start. Wind power will pump our lawn sprinklers. Geothermal heat will warm our greenhouses. Septic tanks will power our coldframes. Solar energy will set fire to our grass clippings, if we're not careful. Or maybe set fire to the whole lawn. It's worth a shot.

Gravity will hold down our sunhats.

6. <u>Gizmos:</u> The Future of gardening gizmos is truly a horizon of infinite dimensions, for it is here that the great American penchant for diversity, inventiveness, and grotesquery comes together in an explosion of marketable incredulity. Why, the imagination virtually disgorges before the possibilities inherent in outdoor objects that might squeak, twirl, spray, thump, zoom, jiggle, buzz, rattle, honk, spin, and otherwise behave in ways oddly similar to the creatures that will be pouring out of the DNA labs of the Future, though there is no possible connection between them whatsoev(CLICK) whatsoev(CLICK) soev(CLICK) soev(CLICK)soeeeeeeeeeeeee(CLICK) whatsoever.

No, real(CLICK)real(CLICK)real(CLICKCLICKCLICK) realllfg@#y.

7. <u>Weather:</u> The gardening weather of the Future is shaping up to be an exciting prospect indeed, what with global warming or not global warming, ozone depletion or not ozone depletion, storm severity index increases or not storm severity index increases, climate changes or not climate changes—all depending on which crackpot radio show host you have been listening to!

But have no fear, for the World of Tomorrow will not abandon you to suffer this kind of insulting unpredictability all alone. For soon, you will be able to experience the weather of your choice from high-tech, computer-mail catalogs. You will simply mouse through the possible weathers listed on your VidTekScreen and, picking one, jam your VidTekHat down over your head, and weather away all you like for hours and hours. The cost will be automatically CompuDucted from your CompuCount. You won't ever again have to experience unpleasant weather by going outdoors, if what is left of the outdoors by then hasn't been declared an illegal substance anyway.

8. <u>Literature:</u> You must be joking. See #1.

9. <u>Experts:</u> in the Future, everyone will be an expert on gardening, mainly because such technological developments as tomato-tissue-on-a-stick and other foodstuffs-that-never-wert will require the possession of several degrees in molecular genome structure in order to "grow" anything. That is, unless you don't give a hoot about the Future and you just want to grow stuff in your Garden because the flowers are pretty and the vegetables taste awfully good and you appreciate the day as it's given for the moments that are within it and you are immensely satisfied with your life as a living thing that breathes all around you in the span of years that you have to enjoy it.

My! What a Luddite you've become in your Madness!

10. <u>Catalogs:</u> If you think you are silly-putty in the hands of catalogs now, wait until you are mooshed by the Future, where there will be an exclusive Gardener's Shopping Channel complete with interactive ordering capability that will feature continuous lush videos of flower and vegetable Heaven from which you can mouse orders without the bother of half a day's wait in the mailbox to come to your senses! Why, with interactive television hookups, you will even be able to "walk" through the gardens of "Gertrude Jekyll" or "Vita Sackville-West," for example, and have all your gardening questions answered as if you were still alive! No, wait a minute, I mean as if *they* were still alive. Sorry about that. No use confusing the issue here, is there?

All such interactive services will be automatically deducted from whatever of your various accounts the InterCorps decides to deduct it from. Prices may vary according to lightning strikes on the phone pole outside your house. Overdrawing your bank reserves will result in death by keyboard electrocution.

11. <u>Hazards:</u> You don't really want to know, do you?

12. <u>Taxes:</u> When the Future finally arrives on your doorstep, you can be sure that among other wonders it will bring with it a revolutionized tax structure wholly reflective of the ever changing needs of research teams who get jillions of dollars per year to study the effect of tricycle riding on rats that have been strapped to the pedals since they (the rats) were *in utero,* studies that contribute to the ever burgeoning

need for humans to stave off anything uncomfortable that might possibly ever happen to them, such as wrinkles and mortality. For these benefits, you will be expected to shell out ever burgeoning tax monies and maintain a grateful attitude toward the segment of society that, you must never forget, eradicated the scourges of polio and smallpox through Herculean effort and personal sacrifice. Of course I am referring to the rats, who need your tax dollars if they are to go on to wipe out everything that's bad in this old world. Everything except rat torture, that is.

Faced with these necessities in a tightening monetary Future, the government will respond to your gratitude level and require that federally-funded agencies send out *itemized E-Mail receipts* to all taxpayers, thus appearing to justify your tax dollar's fate before there is a serious monetary crisis, such as a group of citizens burning the Internal Revenue Service building to the ground and running the IRS workers through with pitchforks. And there you will have it, right in front of your face: The true Poop on what your tax dollars are helping to fertilize!

RECEIVED from (your name), Certified MAD GARDENER, the sum of (gasp!) $6,500 in BLOOD MONEY otherwise known as TAXES which were spent THUSLY by this environmentally-conscious DEPARTMENT OF ECO-RESEARCH for your own UNGRATEFUL GOOD:

> 1. Investigating illegal open burning in abandoned dumps filled with 5,000,000,000 asbestos-lined barrels of liquid plutonium and old mustard gas $5.67
> 2. Printing and mailing four-color glossy brochures telling how you'll be taken out and shot if you so much as think about putting green and clear glass jars together in the same trash bag $6,494.33

Come to think about it, this could catch on at the local level, if such a thing still exists in the Future. I mean, haven't you ever wondered what it is, exactly, that your personal school taxes "fund," for example?

RECEIVED FROM (your name) of Busted Flat Road, N.Y., by the LOCAL SCHOOL DISTRICT the sum of MORE THAN WE THOUGHT POSSIBLE in our WILDEST DREAMS in tax monies, which we SPEWED ABOUT oops we mean SPENT WISELY after CAREFUL CONSIDERATION of the AVAILABLE OPTIONS this way:

1. Textbooks, pencils, chalk, blackboard repair kits, desks with chairs more or less attached, a couple of Bunsen burners for the science lab, twenty-six tons of canned string beans and fifty-five thousand mostly frozen cheese hot dogs for the cafeteria $150.13

2. New curtains and bullet-proof walls in the Superintendent's office $85,567,844.56

And so the Future will once again be made safe for our children and our children's children, in whatever form any of them manage to evolve.

But all of these are only probabilities, for like the Garden, the Future is not writ in stone and nothing is so preordained that we must perish ourselves from the Earth just yet, we hope. For of all things that it is, and Gaia has always known this, Gardening is most of all the Power and the Glory that can indeed turn the Tide and bring peace and security to the planet at last.

Here is how to bring this about: We mail copies of every flower and vegetable catalog known to humankind off to the leaders of every country in the world. Then we sit back and wait. That's it.

Here's what will happen:

FIRST WORLD LEADER: Say, it looks as though Finland has developed a pollution-free electrical generator powered by a couple of magnets stuck on the side of a gyroscope.

SECOND WORLD LEADER: Good grief! We've got to invade them before this gets out and ruins our multinational fossil fuel investments!

FIRST WORLD LEADER : Good idea. They were getting pretty uppity anyway, mouthing off about us dumping toxic waste in their forests and all.

SECOND WORLD LEADER: We could obliterate their villages first, make it look like a civil war. You drive a truckload of Hawkspit missiles up across the Arctic Circle and—

THIRD WORLD LEADER: Never mind that now, you guys. Did you know that France has come up with a new Lima bean that resists both anthracnose and the common rust mosaic?

FIRST AND SECOND WORLD LEADERS: Huh?

THIRD WORLD LEADER: Not only that, but take a look at the pictures in this Thompson & Morgan seed catalog. Did you ever see anything like that "Pretty in Pink" *vinca minor?* Or how about that "Freckles" geranium? And grandiflora petunia "Maxim Marina?" Have you ever seen purple like that in your whole entire *life?*

FIRST WORLD LEADER: What are you talking about? We have to create an international incident or we're going to be bested by *Finland,* for god's sake.

THIRD WORLD LEADER: No, I'd rather send away for these selections of hardy kiwi, an increasingly popular fruit, and some "Icarus" hybrid Brussels Sprouts that offer genetically reduced bitterness and twice the vitamin C of standard *brassicae,* and maybe a few packs of "Lollipop" zinnias to round out the border.

SECOND WORLD LEADER: I think you're losing your mind.

THIRD WORLD LEADER: You're absolutely right. *(draws gun, fires)* Now—where are those order blanks? I want some squash and some eggplants and dahlias and "sea shell" cosmos and mums and impatiens and sweet peppers and basil and marigolds and giant asters and "funny faces" pansies and bearded iris and daylilies and... *(steps over bodies, heads for mailbox)*

And that's how Garden Madness will save the world!

EPILOGUE
An Exclusive Message from Gaia

OYEZ OYEZ OYEZ forsooth and lackaday, herein forthwith, O thou spoiled and willful darlings of the Order *Primates,* I do give from Myself, the Planet, to Thee, its Temporary Inhabitants, these TEN COMMANDMENTS OF GARDENING which do and shall and evermore apply to whatsoEVERelse thee getteth in thine head to commit upon MINE PERSON:

1. THOU SHALT HAVE NO OTHER ideas in mind for this beautiful garden of a world than to tend it carefully and humbly for the lifetime of thy species, if thou knowest what's good for theest. Or else.

2. THOU SHALT NOT MAKE ANY GRAVEN IMAGES of bent-over fat people wearing polka-dot underpants NOR ANY plastic replicas of any creature whatsoever, including cartoon characters, for placement anywhere near thy flowers, lawn, or hopelessly festooned domiciles.

3. THOU SHALT NOT TAKE THE NAME of any personal body part or STINKING Earthly substance and hurl same at the weather in thy FRUSTRATION when thy garden hath been spoilt, for to curse the rain or lack thereof is to tamper in a natural ORDER of things of which thoust measly BRAIN hath but not a CLUE.

4. REMEMBER THE SEASONS, and keep them to thyself. DO NOT, for example, bore thine friends with FISH STORIES about how EARLY thee set out thy TOMATOES last spring. However early it 'twas, some other theethou set them out earlier.

5. HONOR THY FATHER AND THY MOTHER if they had the goodst sense to hirest lots of help in the garden, and set before thee the CORRECT EXAMPLE.

6. THOU SHALT NOT KILL off every other living thing for two miles around the weeds or bugs thou imagines must be got rid of with poison deathaholic chemicals and get away with it. Thou might thinkest thee is getting away with it for a while, but thou SHALT GET CAUGHT with thine PANTS DOWN sooner or later, and THOU SHALT NOT come whining TO ME when thoust does, either, lemme tell thou. Thusly, THOU SHALT NOT invent in thy TEST TUBES a host of creatures to meeteth thy notions of CONVENIENCE, for thou hath not yet figured out how to keepeth the creatures that THOU ALREADY HAST around thee. And if thou thinketh that thine pants WERE CAUGHT DOWN before, thee hath not seen NOTHIN' YET.

7. THOU SHALT NOT COVET THY NEIGHBOR's hoe, rake, shovel, pruners, wheelbarrow, or any SUCH OTHER tools of the trade as there are; OR IF THOU DOESTH, thou SHALT RETURN all said items SHORTLY and in GOOD REPAIR. And as for thy neighbor's spouse, one wouldst thinketh that the SAME RULE applies, MORE or LESS. Wouldn'tst one?

8. THOU SHALT NOT STEAL wildflowers from the WAYSIDE of thine EGREGIOUS HIGHWAY SYSTEM unless thou is absolutely sure that said FLOWERS are in danger from thine own rapacious SPECIES and no other, for the FLOWER understandeth that to be GRAZED is to yet APPEARETH out the other END and live again. But of bulldozers it knoweth naught. And whatever thee mighteth thinkest, neither dooest THOU.

9. THOU SHALT NOT BEAR FALSE WITNESS against thine vegetables and pass off thy SUPER HOT CAYENNE PEPPERS as SWEET to play a stupid JOKE on thy SUPPOSED FRIENDS.

10. In sum, THOU SHALT NOT MESS THINGS UP more than thou can POSSIBLY HELP during thy natural lifetime, and PUT BACK that which thou TAKEST OUT of the EARTH before thou GOESTH

THERE thyownself. And, verily, THOU SHALT REMEMBER along the way to LEAVETH a few WEEDS here and there and FEED the SQUIRRELS onceth in a while, and stuff liketh that there.

And don't say I didn't WARN all of THOUS!

SUB-EPILOGUE
The Quark Half Speaks Out

I FEEL OBLIGED to deruffle any political feathers that may have been inadvertently ruffed by the attention given in these chapters to Gaia. As most of you already know, Gaia is the personification of Planet Earth not only throughout mythology, but in current scientific theories that see our home orb as a sentient organism[1] capable of making reasoned, global-scale ecological adjustments on behalf of its own well-being, even if those adjustments include scratching off the irksome flea population known as humans.

So far, so good. Where the aforementioned theories get into trouble is in their sexist, monogenderic assumptions.

Good Heavens! Such carelessness! How could Myth and Science be so uncouth as to postulate that this, your Mother Mud, would operate alone within the Vacuum of Space and Time without An Equal Half! Therefore, quickly, before anyone could spit metaphorically or otherwise upon these pages, I scooped up paper and pen and hastily exited the corporeal realm to seek out and interview the much underappreciated Mr. Gaia Himself!

As it happened, he was out in the back yard, tinkering on a junk car.

MAD GARDENER: Mr. Gaia, how did you and Her Majesty, the Third Planet From The Sun, meet, anyway?

MR. GAIA: Mighta been at the Big Bang convention, though I don't hardly recall for sure. Hand me that wrench over there, willya?

MAD GARDENER: Uh … sure. This one?

MR. GAIA: Hell no, that's the four an' three-fifths. I need a three and nine-seventeenths. Don'tcha know nothin' 'bout spark plugs?

MAD GARDENER: Uh, well, I …

Mr. GAIA: By the way, I been lookin' over that veg-etable garden o'yours. You better hurry up and give it a shot o'that there Miracle-Grow stuff or all's you're gonna have this fall is a bunch o'snivelly-sized sticks hardly fit fer blowin' out yer ear, don'tcha know.

MAD GARDENER: But …

MR. GAIA: Ba'sides, yer rain gutters are fulla slime and yer lawn is all fulla weeds and the bugs are gonna chew up yer whole gawddamn *house* if you don't get around to sprayin' the dang things with copper sul-fi-ate or sumpthin' one o'these herenow days.

MAD GARDENER: Uh … thank you. But to get back to the subject …

MR. GAIA: Gimme that hammer, willya? Dad-blamed catalytic converter won't come outta here without a fight.

MAD GARDENER: … at hand, can you tell me what the *real* Gaia is like at home?

MR. GAIA: Shoot. You ever try livin' with a sentient, self-regulatin' organism capable of makin' reasoned, global-scale ekalogickal adjustments on bah'haffuv Her own well-being?

MAD GARDENER: Well, actually …

MR. GAIA: Might as well let fire ants walk all over yer eyelids, is what I got to say about it. Incadennally, you ain't gonna get nowheres sprayin' cay-yen pepper goop all over yer cabbages. What, you think them little green worms is gonna go suckers-up from that there stuff? Ha! You'd have more luck teachin' rattlesnakes how ta'play tennis.

MAD GARDENER: But …

MR. GAIA: 'Course the Big Woman'd pro'bly jest start a hail-storm an' squash the little buggers inta caterpillar soup right where they're crawlin'!

MAD GARDENER: What! That's *disgusting!*

MR. GAIA: Yer tellin' me! If I was you I'd sneak out an' blast everything with a shot o'that Pyrethrin nerve toxin dust whenever the hell it is that She ain't lookin'. Wouldn't *that* jest do the trick! But I'm sappozed ta be talkin' ekalogikal and all that. Say, can you reach that there oil pan over by the trash heap? Gotta catch this motor oil afore it … Oops, never mind.

MAD GARDENER: Ugh! Look at the nasty mess you made!

MR. GAIA: Well, what the ole Ball 'n Chain don't know might not hurt the rest a' you! Haw, haw!

MAD GARDENER: Uh … I see. So tell me, how would you sum up your long and interesting lifetime with Gaia?

MR. GAIA: Planets! Ya can't live with 'em and ya can't live without 'em!

MAD GARDENER: Thank you very much.

MR. GAIA: Yer welcome. And don't tell the Misses I never did ya no favors!

Thus concludes our interview with Mr. Gaia. We hope this clears up any politically incorrect befoggery that might have invaded your cerebral cortex during the process of Evolution. Should you have any further questions, please turn to the beginning of this book and start over.

Too bad we can't do the same everywhere!

Notes

[1] As in *The Ages of Gaia: A Biography of Our Living Earth* by James Lovelock, Norton, 1988, Bantam, 1990; or *Healing Gaia: A New Prescription for the Living Planet*, also by James Lovelock, Crown, 1991.

TEMPS PERDU

*S*uzy,

There they were. It was summer. The daylilies were
frothing in the fields and gullies. The woodchucks were
growing fat and round, wondering as they circled the buzzing fence how to get to the pepper plants. The garden snakes
coiled and uncoiled in the day-heat and night-cool and knew
for all Eternity their safe place in the wildflower patch. And
brandishing their shears and saws Dan and Sue made pretty
all the weeds and things that grow in the garden.

And it was summer.

And there they were.

Loving you,

Dan

August, 1988

Dan Stimmerman was my childhood fellow-poet-person friend.
He died of AIDS in August, 1992. He wrote the poem-song, "The Lower
Gardens" in 1973 and later recorded it, accompanying himself, with his
beautiful voice, on the piano. The Lower Garden, my grandmother's name
for it, was a sumac woods that ran along Bird Creek behind the house in
Webbs Mills, N.Y., that was in my family for forty years. Dan and I walked
down through those woods often, winter and summer, and a portion of
his ashes reside there now. In later life, Dan became a superb horticulturist,
managing, despite climate, urban raccoons, and his personal burdens, to
coax blooms out of all the pips and bulbs that I shipped to him for his San
Francisco flower garden.

THE LOWER GARDENS—
for Sue Mullin Watkins

In the Lower Gardens
walk with me,
footsteps falling in the snow.
In the brittle air
with time to spare,
let us tell eachother all we know:

How Love and Sweet Imagination grow,
and twine about eachother's hearts;
and nourish oneanother so—
believing they would never part.

And the trees are silent sleeping,
and the deer about them go—
whispering—Rest awhile.
In the summer your leafy arms
 will throw
cooling shadows where we'll lie down.
We'll tell eachother all we know:

How Love and Sweet Imagination grow,
and twine around eachother's hearts—
believing if they should ever part,
the bittersweet would cease to climb;
the paths we make would disappear,
and the trees so silent sleeping
and the whispering deer.

In the Lower Gardens
walk with me,
footsteps falling in the snow.
In the brittle air
with time to spare,
let us tell eachother all we know.

D.L.S.
Webbs Mills, N.Y.
1973

Index

 *About the Author*

*S*usan M. Watkins is a writer and a mad gardener who lives in upstate New York. She is the author of *Dreaming Myself, Dreaming A Town* (Kendall & Delisle Books, 1988); *Conversations with Seth: The Story of Jane Roberts's ESP Class, Vols. 1 & 2* (Prentice Hall, 1980 and 1980); *Quick Chills II: The Best Horror Fiction from the Specialty Press* (Deadline Press, 1992); and *The Definitive Best of the Horror Show* (CD Publications, 1992).